RUST BELT CHICAGO:
AN ANTHOLOGY

Similar titles by Belt Publishing:

The Akron Anthology

Car Bombs to Cookie Tables: The Youngstown Anthology

The Cincinnati Anthology

A Detroit Anthology

Happy Anyway: A Flint Anthology

The Pittsburgh Anthology

Right Here, Right Now: The Buffalo Anthology

Rust Belt Chic: The Cleveland Anthology

Rust Belt Chicago: An Anthology

RUST BELT CHICAGO: AN ANTHOLOGY

Edited by Martha Bayne

First edition 2017
ISBN: 978-0-9977743-7-5

Belt Publishing
1667 E. 40th Street #1G1
Cleveland, Ohio 44120
www.beltmag.com

Cover art by Tony Fitzpatrick
Book design by Sheila Sachs

TABLE OF CONTENTS

Beyond the Belt

MARTHA BAYNE

Chicago is built on a foundation of meat and railroads and steel, on opportunity and exploitation. But while its identity long ago expanded beyond manufacturing, the city continues to lure new residents from around the world, and from across a region rocked by recession and deindustrialization — and the patterns and problems of the Rust Belt don't disappear once you hit the Skyway headed west. In fact, they're often amplified, as the scale of the third-largest city in the country would demand.

A city defined by movement that's the anchor of the Midwest, Chicago is bound to its neighbors by a shared ecosystem and history. A city of migrants and a city of strivers, at once part of the glittering global economy and resolutely tied to its geography, Chicago's complicated — both of the Belt and beyond it; the buckle, as it were. At Belt Publishing, we thought that the question of what Chicago's relationship is to the region at large deserved a book of its own.

It's not an easy question to answer, though, as I learned editing this anthology. This is the ninth in a series of city anthologies published by Belt, but where the other books have sought to tell the stories of often overlooked (and underwritten) communities like Flint or Youngstown, Chicago is neither. Rather, twenty-first-century Chicago is defined by a (justly) intimidating literary legacy that stretches from the Midland realism of Dreiser and Sinclair through Richard Wright, Gwendolyn Brooks, and Saul Bellow, past Nelson Algren, and on to Studs Terkel, Stuart Dybek, and Sandra Cisneros. Chicago has been the subject of novelists, poets, journalists, and scholars for more than a century — and they're not letting up anytime soon. Who could hope to compete with that? Who would want to?

The initial call for submissions for this book went out in early 2016, and the response was overwhelming. By October I'd whittled down the candidates to a manageable forty or so stories, poems, and essays — and then Donald Trump was elected president. In the aftermath of the election, I reassessed, and sought out additional work that spoke to one of three themes: deindustrialization, and the economic space Chicago shares with Flint, Detroit, and, Gary, just around the bend in the lake; the shared landscape and ecosystem of the Great Lakes states; and movement, always movement.

Chicago's famously a city of immigrants, from the historically Irish enclaves of the South Side to the Mexican neighborhoods of Pilsen and Little Village and the Devon Avenue corridor that's one of the largest South Asian neighborhoods in North America. And across the twentieth century, Chicago famously was the destination of choice for the millions of African Americans who left the South as part of the Great Migration, and came to indelibly shape the city's culture and politics.

But with the Rust Belt thrust into the post-election spotlight, Chicago's function as a big — and at least relatively thriving — blue city in the middle of the Midwest itself seemed worth recognizing as well.

Thus, this book is bookended by migration and its effects: whether it's Britt Julious migrating from the West Side to Oak Park, Gretchen Kalwinski leaving her inner Region Rat behind in northwest Indiana, Rayshauna Gray tracing her family's path from the South through Chicago and on to points unknown, or Rob Miller remembering the waves of Detroiters who made the journey down I-94 in the 1990s and on into the twenty-first century. Journalists Kari Lydersen and Mark Guarino go deep into Pilsen's Mexican bars and Uptown's Appalachian music. And we're honored that Aleksandar Hemon, who landed in Chicago from Bosnia in 1992 and never left, is letting us reprint his "Reasons Why I Do Not Wish to Leave Chicago," an ode to the city originally published in 2006.

But it's not all about movement; some stories are fixed firmly in place, like Michael Van Kerckhove's remembrance of a north-side food pantry, and Sharon Bloyd-Peshkin's chronicle of the last days of River North's Clark & Barlow Hardware. Meanwhile, Kathleen Rooney walks the streets of downtown, on the move, sure, but with her feet squarely grounded in the city's strict geography.

Much of the work in these pages overlaps, defying easy categorization. Linda Garcia Merchant's "The Urban Rural" is as much about division and dislocation as it is about place. Wyl Villacres's "Sorry Shit Sucks" uses fiction to create an intimate articulation of Chicago's crisis of police violence — something the city shares with Cleveland, Detroit, and other Rust Belt neighbors, and a subject addressed with journalistic clarity and precision by Sarah Macaraeg and Yana Kunichoff, in their award-winning article "How to Win Reparations."

As an editor, I hear the writers collected here singing to each other like the bird on the cover — an Arctic Bunting that artist Tony Fitzpatrick notes has no business being in Chicago, yet first popped up in his birder's eye perched on a mailbox downtown in the early nineties. At times the song soars in harmony (just count how many times that lake comes up) and at others sounds in notes of strategic dissonance. What truths about Chicago sports can be teased out from the conjunction of Kevin Coval's "Disco Demolition" and David Isaacson's "Hard Hat, Lunch Pail"? What can be extrapolated about Chicago's industrial past and future from the multiple views offered here of the flaming factories of East Chicago, Hammond, and Calumet, and the beauties of the natural world that persist in such toxic turf?

There are gaps, to be sure — multiple books can (and have) been written about Chicago's endemic segregation, only touched on here, and a condition common to Rust Belt cities region-wide. And Chicago politics, rich and mythic though they are, barely get a nod! It's one book, one song, responding to one cacophonous city. I hope the gaps speak as much to the poems, stories, and reporting still to be created as the work here testifies to what's been done.

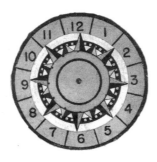

CITY of MOVEMENT

Chicagoland

SONYA HUBER

Chicago is a dark jewel on the lake, an implacable garnet, a bristle of quartz towering next to a turquoise expanse. These stones are set in a bezel of grey highway. A rough backdrop highlights their sparkle as further rings of grey asphalt reach outward, framing a semi-industrial backdrop called Chicagoland.

To an outsider, the word "Chicagoland" might evoke a theme park where you can ride the Capone-a-con or the Checker-Club Blues Experience, where you'd line up to buy eight dollar hot dogs on a poppyseed roll with relish and a pickle and then hug a plush-costumed figure dressed like Jane Addams. If Chicagoland were a theme park, I would pay to visit, and then I would feel empty, wanting the ineffable that would be absent.

I grew up in New Lenox, Illinois — twenty-four miles from the nearest edge of the city limits. To explain and locate New Lenox, I say, "It's far southwest of the city, right next to Joliet. You know: *Blues Brothers*, the prison," and people all around the world nod and say, "I've driven through there on I-80."

Am I a suburban kid claiming affiliation with a city I only drove into for grade-school museum trips and supervised parental expeditions to buy Christmas chocolate at the old evergreen-colored Marshall Field's? Yes. Kind of. I am also someone who took high-school drives to see bands at the Cabaret Metro on Clark Street, who drove up to play indoor soccer and drove home on the cold highways alone, listening to Paul Butterfield on the radio and absorbing the blues, taking for granted that the night in every city would be soaked in such wailing and ache. My friends and I drove downtown aimlessly, not having money to actually do anything and not knowing what to do, then driving home. I am someone who later took the train in to work, then still later moved into the city, crossing a divide and falling in love with the neighborhoods knit together by the L.

I am not from Chicago, but I am from Chicagoland.

At first, I couldn't explain what I meant — I just *knew*.

Back when my husband was my boyfriend, he overheard me tell a stranger I was from Chicago. He scoffed at me in that gentle mocking I seem to invite from the world at large. "You're from corn, not Chicago," he might have said.

"No," I replied, insistent, maybe rising from my seat to express something with a finger upheld, putting something into words that up until now might never have needed to be uttered: "No, I am actually from a place that is called...Chicagoland."

He joked with me: "I'm from about two hours west of Pittsburgh. Is that Far East Chicago?"

"No!" I said. There is no East Chicago in Chicago. It's just the lake. Though just across the border is East Chicago, Indiana — which is somehow, inchoate in my mind, also Chicagoland. He drew a rough map on a scrap piece of paper. I tried to sketch the boundaries and he reached in with a pen to circle the entire Midwest.

It turns out we were both right.

The friendly round-faced man with glasses and a work shirt who appeared on our Zenith television told me as a child that Empire Carpet served greater Chicagoland. Invisible ladies' voices sang a number — "588-2300: EMPIRE!" — that I remember even when I cannot remember the phone number of either of the homes where I grew up.

Chicagoland was built by advertising, tentacles of transit, and waves of immigration lapping on the prairie's shore. Colonel Robert R. McCormick, *Chicago Tribune* editor and publisher, is said to have put the term "Chicagoland" into common usage in 1926 on the paper's front page: "Chicagoland's Shrines: A Tour of Discoveries." He gave this gritty kingdom a name and claimed that his land reached out 200 miles in every direction to include parts of Wisconsin, Indiana, Michigan, and Iowa.

Today the *Tribune* defines Chicagoland as the city itself plus all of Cook County, eight Illinois counties including Will, and two counties across the line in Indiana. The Illinois Department of Tourism plucks Chicago out and describes Chicagoland as the remaining portion of Cook County plus Lake, DuPage, Kane, and Will. The Chicagoland Chamber of Commerce is inclusive: the city plus its ring of six counties.

Today in Chicago, the term "Chicagoland" is a practical and unselfconscious term of internal reference. Businesses use it to denote their locations, phone companies and government agencies and transit authorities use it to describe their coverage and service areas.

I don't know whether the north suburbs call themselves Chicagoland, or whether they need to. I know they have distinct and glowing identities all on their own. You can say "Evanston" and people know well enough: Northwestern University and a "beautiful town."

New Lenox, while beautiful in its own humble way, is not "beautiful." It is a former farm town in Will County that has aged in mildly horrific ways like a cheap facelift. We are an affordable bedroom community, and our face has frozen lumps of botox McMansions studded in between the wrinkles of vinyl-sided older neighborhoods that used to be the only places to live. We are the intersection of I-80 and the third beltway of I-375, the economical alternative.

To me, Chicagoland is the unclaimed and unnotable spaces like these, where waves of immigrants settle as they move out of downtown but somehow never escape the city's grasp. Chicago is not present without the liminal space you must cross to get to Chicago, and Chicago is not one of those snooty places that cares whether you are "in" or "out" of a dividing line. Chicago is a bristling dominion that looks out across the corn and goofily, cheekily wants it all.

Chicagoland is a ruined beauty, the roadside that glitters with grit that edges the corn. It is the kingdom bounded by highways that have names instead of numbers: the Edens, Kingery, Lake Shore Drive, the Dan Ryan, the Stevenson. We are the ends to all those roads. Chicagoland is Chicago's garage. We are the long, low, rusted warehouses where Chicago parks its snowplows and stores its extra couches. When Chicago takes off its coat, we hold it. We park its car.

Sometimes I say I am "from Illinois," but that feels as disingenuous as saying I am from "Chicago." I am not a rural kid by nature, nor am I urban. Nor am I suburban, with its connotations of safe, contained experience. Chicagoland anchors the city like a rivet on the Rust Belt. Joliet East High School's mascot was the Steelman. When Chicago turns fitfully in its sleep and remembers steel and the stockyards, Chicagoland nods its head and holds those stories in its contaminated chain-link squares of earth.

Chicagoland is Svengoolie, the weird zombie-clown host on 1980s local Chicago network television who introduced old horror movies and whose signature joke was to simply intone, "Berwyn!" Berwyn is a non-remarkable town due west of the city: take Cermak out past Cicero between the spokes of I-290 to the north and I-55 to the south. If you are from Chicagoland, you know that the drive out will be a stretch of strip malls and a mix of Mexican and Polish delis, Irish bars, fast food joints, nail salons, and auto parts stores. Berwyn once featured a strange tall sculpture called "Spindle" by Dustin Shuler, which was a tall spike on which eight cars were impaled like bugs.

"Spindle" was featured in a drive-by scene in the Mike Myers and Dana Carvey vehicle *Wayne's World*, which was itself set in Aurora, another Chicagoland town still farther west in the same pie-slice of highway. Chicagoland is Wayne and Garth, two metalheads in a shitty imaginary basement in Aurora, wanting to party but crying instead, "We're not worthy!"

Chicagoland is worthy in its secret ways and will take itself down a notch before you get the chance to. It is in the gleam in Wayne's eye and the pointed edge of the Spindle that was torn down to make way for a Walgreens. Chicagoland either is or is not Chicago itself, and Chicagoland doesn't need to know the answer to that question, because it loves Chicago like nobody else loves Chicago.

LaSalle Wrote It Down Wrong, 1687
KEVIN COVAL

gringoed the whole place after/word.
every street and building some flat
mispronunciation, some misshaped
mouth   some murder.

Chicagua wild
garlic in Miami
Illinois indigenous
utterance.   some funk
music.   some rampant weed
returning. indefatigable
perennial and persistent
some dark malignancy.

Chicago is a mass
of machinery built upon mass graves
the beginning of a long death march
an inadequate water
down. an erasure, an eraser
pink as the whiteman's tongue

PREVIOUSLY PUBLISHED IN *A PEOPLE'S HISTORY OF CHICAGO*
(HAYMARKET BOOKS, 2017).

poetry

A Skillet of Suns and Oceans
IRIS ORPI

I came to Chicago at the end of summer
I was there when the first leaves changed colors
and each day was a feast of so much beauty
I didn't really mind the cold
I got pregnant in December
and my first trimester was in step
with my first winter
I didn't know if it was the one
or the other
but that's when I started craving
for the tastes and smells of home
and this tantalizingly complex, cultured city
felt like a brutal abomination
in its foreignness
as my husband and I drove
past different restaurants
in the snow
looking for a place to buy
Philippine tuyo,
stopping every so often
so I could vomit
on the salt-covered pavement
amid the smells of steaks
and hotdogs and burgers
and gyros and tacos
and fried chicken with secret herbs and spices
and signature popcorn and
the famous deep dish pizza

feeling so alienated and alone
and when we finally brought home
the prized fish that is,
in all actuality, a poor man's dish
in my native country,
I had to cook it
with all the windows open
in our eighth floor South Side apartment,
out of consideration for our neighbors
who might be offended
by the aroma of sun-dried herring
sizzling in corn oil
breaths of ice from the lake
and its glacial banks
accepting the begrudging invitation,
filling the place in gusts,
coating the walls with
frigid non-forgiveness
like the inside of sickly lungs
and there I was,
wearing a two-hundred-dollar wool coat
in my own kitchen,
defiant, ashamed,
homesick and hungry
and fretful for the tiny life
humming inside me,
looking out at a world
of too-early nights and frozen roads
and seeing but suns and oceans
in that skillet,
standing in two places at once,
nine thousand miles apart.

Notes on Summer
(Or, Black Girlhood Is a Thing)
BRITT JULIOUS

I.

Summer is fleeting and so am I. The me of a good summer is as temporary as the leaves on the trees, the thick viscosity that glides across our limbs we call "humid air." It is as temporary as a gelato cone, the remnants of which I'll lick off my fingers and down my hand and even across the tattoo on my arm some time later today and tomorrow and for the rest of the days when the heat feels equally brutal and rejuvenating.

When the me of a good summer arrives, I try best not to acknowledge it. To see the fulfillment of hot days and cold drinks pouring down my throat is like spotting an animal in the wild. This momentary thing is lovely and great until it is gone. In reality, I am trying to recapture the me of my youth.

II.

I say I grew up in two places, and that is somewhat true. Oak Park, a suburb of Chicago, is where I spent the majority of my time. We first lived in an apartment before purchasing our own home on the southwest side of the town. But, maybe through the lens of nostalgia, I recognize Austin as my home too.

My grandparents live in the Austin neighborhood in a beautiful and traditional American four square house. There, the sidewalks are wide and easy to maneuver. Sometimes I pounce across the concrete of my current hood, crimping my limbs against storefronts and light poles so as not to take up space as others — young mothers with rowdy children and strollers, packs of girlfriends out for a night on the town, aggressive young men looking not for a hand, but a pair of breasts and an ass to grab — pass me by.

But in Austin, I remember how wide the block seemed. Sometimes I sat down on the sidewalk and from my line of vision, the houses reached far beyond where the eye could see. Even now, when I visit as an adult, I can see the history there. When we moved to Oak Park, my sister and I tried to play outdoors, but we largely played inside. This was different than in Austin, where the freedom and joy of girlhood played out on sidewalks and in backyards.

When I say there is history there, I mean there is a history of childhood, of innocence, of the power of play. Our Oak Park block was quiet, but in Austin there was there there. There was the energy born out of time enjoyed. It was something I didn't know I needed until it was not there.

Strongest in my memory is a young girl named Nicole. She lived down the street from my grandmother. She had long, dark, curly hair and a pinched face that I thought was lovely at the time, but makes me wince now. I'm not sure why.

She was older than me, but didn't seem that way. I followed my older sister Kourtney around like a shadow and Nicole in turn did that to me. A part of me was secretly thrilled by this. No longer was I reliant on the whims of someone else. Instead, my ideas of fun, my actions, my words held precedence in the mind of another person. I was a leader who knew it but never got the chance to show it. It was not lost on me too that her name was my sister's middle name. There was a lineage in our girlhood, from the second name of my kin to the first name of my friend.

We played together in summertime, mostly. I was out of school and my parents needed our time to be spent. I remember this not because of the weather, but the amount of play. School is a blur, but summers stand firm in my mind. Play happened when the sun was heaviest. Friendships formed heaviest during this time too.

She followed me around to the corner store where we purchased cheap candies. She followed me a half a block down to the woman who sold sno-cones from her front porch. She followed me as I got into inappropriate arguments with my grandparents' next door neighbor, Mr. Underwood, about things he said that I found dumb. She followed me even as we ran up and down the block. I was a chubby kid, so I think she slowed down to follow me when we did that in particular.

I don't know when we met, but it's difficult to discern most things from one's early childhood. The way memories form during that time is that suddenly something or someone is a part of your life and that is that. So, suddenly Nicole was a part of my life. Suddenly she was there and I didn't question it.

Right now, I am thinking about my grandparents' large backyard. There is a rose bush square in the middle, surrounded by lush grass. My grandparents would inflate a kiddie pool and fill it with cold water running through a hose and we'd jump around and play. Nicole never really said much. Instead, she let me do the talking and talk I did: about how I knew mosquitos had it out for us, about how much better orange slices were than chocolate, about why my grandmother made the best macaroni and cheese in the world and no one could say differently to me.

Most importantly though, Nicole was an actual friend. She was there and she listened and she didn't question one's intentions. She was present. She laughed harder than anyone I knew and stomped her feet when she was stressed. She was human and viable.

"I hate when you are not here," she used to say and I felt the same way.

When you are a child, you need people like that in your life, and when you are an adult, or even just on the cusp of becoming one, you realize how difficult it is to find that in others. Suddenly, the realities of the world strike hard and fast and don't let go. Suddenly, there are responsibilities and sadness and men, hovering over your mind and your limbs, eager to take and take and take until they don't need you anymore. If you find a friend like that and you are not seven, you must hold on to them as much and for as long as possible. The world doesn't spin for young women with sturdy ground to walk on and grow.

The more my family settled into our life in our house in Oak Park, the less the Austin neighborhood felt like a home. It was a quick, five-minute drive to my grandparents' house, but even that seemed too far away. Houses create homes and homes create new narratives. My family was building a new narrative for ourselves. There was a fork in the road and we took a different path, one that allowed us to fulfill lifelong dreams but also separated us, however slowly, from the things we once knew.

"You know, Nicole always asks about you," my grandmother would say to me when I visited as I got older.

"So?" I would respond.

"Don't you want to say hi?" she asked me.

"Why would I do that?" I would respond and then curl up on the couch with my heavy head placed solidly on my grandmother's lap. I was there to visit my family. I was not there to see other people. My grandparents' home and in turn, the Austin neighborhood, became a place I went to and not a place I came from. It was not me anymore.

But I did see her one day. My grandmother was particularly convincing and so I walked down the street, but I couldn't remember where she lived. The houses hadn't changed, but they all blended in with each other at that point. An American four square was an American four square was an American four square. The only thing I recognized on that block was my grandparents' home, shining like a light against the blurred structures surrounding it.

There were people on the porch of one home, an older woman and a young man, and they looked at me as if they knew me, and not from a pleasant experience. They looked hard and long and I tried to keep their gaze until I looked down, exhausted by the weight of their stares. I walked back and when my grandmother asked if I said hello, I said yes. She never truly asked me about it again.

I am not sure when girlhood is lost, but I am sure of all of the ways I tried to recapture it. I began to dance as a young girl and the more I danced, the more in control I felt. These are my legs that bend and curve, my arms that flex. Freedom stemmed from the control I gained and to dance was to be free. I didn't recognize it then, but I pushed through the grueling rehearsals with the knowledge that once I learned a routine, it would become something I could call on at a moment's notice. At any moment after, I could become this powerful being in control of my movements and myself, unhurried or torn apart. My movements were choreographed and not choreographed. When I had a moment to move about the floor on my own terms, that is when I felt most alive. It was a moment without judgment, just sadness and anxiety and excitement manifest through a pirouette, a switch leap, a flick of the wrist. As I got older, I leaned in to this activity. Each performance was a temporary girlhood high, a me reclaimed, a sense of self and empowerment found.

Black girlhood is summer. It arrives quick and dies just as fast. Suddenly we are young women, even if we don't feel it, even if we know intrinsically there is life left to live. In childhood, we are given the freedom to firmly be ourselves. There is nothing too high or too far or too great for us. No, instead, everything is within reach. It's not just innocence. It is, I think, a true sense of self. It is ourselves at our most actualized. As adults we will do whatever is necessary to recapture that feeling. I still feel it now, that desire to recapture the me of my girlhood. It is also why our friendships feel truer in that time than maybe any other time in our lives. Unburdened by the weight of the world, we are free to be ourselves.

That is why summer feels so precious and why Chicago summers especially feel so critical. When people say Chicago summers are better than anywhere else, they are not lying. I feel that deeply in my bones. It is Chicago summers that shaped me, made me confident, made me into a strong and capable woman before I ever really knew it.

How to Buy Bread on Devon

KELLY O'CONNOR MCNEES

It's best, of course, to go in the morning.

Take the Red Line, if you need to, and the westbound 155 bus, and get off on California. Don't buy a sari, though they are very beautiful and come in every color and you will want one. Don't buy gold bangles or cardamom by the ounce or Indian mangoes or tea or coconut juice. You are saving your money for bread — remember?

If you aren't sure where to begin, go see Alex at the Argo Bakery. Ask for *puri*, a long, toothy loaf with a beautiful charred crust. Compliment the unusual circular clay oven in the middle of the room so that Alex will tell you it is called a *toné*, and that he built it himself when he first opened the bakery. If you get there at the right time, you might see the baker stick the dough against the superheated inside wall by slapping it on, then plucking it out when it's finished with a tool that looks like a garden spade. Notice too the tray of steaming *hachapuri penovani*, the national dish of Georgia, so important that the cost to make it is used to measure the country's inflation. The "penovani" means layered, so rather than traditional leavened bread, this version uses puff pastry to enfold a mixture of farmer's, feta, and mozzarella cheeses. Eat it as soon as you can without making a scene. Buttery flakes will spray all over you when you take a bite, as if you're being showered with confetti. Maybe buy an extra for the person you're trying to get to fall in love with you.

Before you leave you might see *lavash* on his menu and ask for it too, and Alex will give you a look like you're not very bright.

"*Lavash* is *not* Georgian," Alex will say.

Don't say, puzzled, ". . . but you have it on your menu . . ." because the bread of Devon is nothing if not mysterious, and you don't want to stop Alex from saying next, "You want *lavash*? Come on, I show you."

Follow him next door to Somer Foods, a Middle Eastern grocery store, where he will wave to the owner and thread you through the long line of genial shoppers to shelves along the wall containing many kinds of bread. "*Lavash*," he will say, and pull out a bag containing four placemat-sized ovals, stippled brown from the tandoor. Alex might make *lavash* too, but Somer's, it seems, is better. Bread is serious, and the baker's code requires credit where credit is due and the proper humility in the face of something marvelous. In Armenian tradition, a mother-in-law drapes *lavash* on the shoulders of a new bride to ensure fertility. Bread can feed you; bread can bless you.

Remember with a surge of joy that you have a freezer, and press on. On the same block, find Levinson's, where every day but Saturday you can buy a fresh loaf of *challah*, soft and sweet and golden from its egg wash. Holding it in your hands, you will understand why this loaf is used each Sabbath to commemorate the manna that fell from heaven in the desert. Why it is braided to look like the arms of friends embracing.

Keep walking west on Devon — is the sun setting yet? — past the Croatian Cultural Center, past the Russian Jewish Community Center, to Taza, and if it is any day but Sunday, buy a bag of diamond-shaped loaves of Iraqi *samoon*, baked in a nine-hundred-degree tandoor oven. As you hand your two dollars to the smiling woman behind the counter, you might wonder what brought her here: did she plan to come to Chicago, or did circumstances in her country force her to seek refuge? But you probably do not speak her language and cannot ask, and anyway why should she share this most personal story with you, a stranger from up the road? She has already been so generous in sharing her bread.

Other places sell Persian wands dotted with sesame, called *barbari*, and blistered Indian *naan*, but it's getting late now and you're running out of time. Plan to come back next week.

How do you buy bread on Devon? You say there are a thousand things about water, flour, yeast, and salt that I do not know. Countries and histories and stories I want to learn. You buy bread on Devon by being hungry.

ELSEWHERE IN A FLASH

KELLY HOGAN

I'm the last one awake, sitting alone at 5:30 a.m. in the front lounge of a rattling tour bus with outdated funeral parlor wallpaper and 110 percent shot shocks as we hurtle way too fast through another mountain pass with our lives entrusted to a bus driver we met just four days ago. My ten fellow band and crew members are snoring in their coffin-sized bunks behind the closed door just past the galley. Yellow rectangles of twenty-four-hour Waffle Houses flash by, blurred like melting sticks of butter. The baby blue light of dawn is beginning to silhouette the leafless trees along the highway and I feel alright — a little exhausted, a little drunk, a little lonely. I live in Chicago, but it's this bus that feels like home.

I moved to Chicago twenty years ago from my hometown of Atlanta. I was thirty-two years old and I was in the middle of horrible times. The sudden deaths of some family and friends and band members left me broken and restless and I really needed to be somewhere else — some place where I could feel clean and awake again. I'd never lived anywhere else, but I'd traveled all over the place with my rock bands and experienced a lot of cities. I ultimately decided to move to Chicago because, even though the climate and feel and tempo of the city were vastly different than my hometown, something about it reminded me of the South. The Chicagoans I'd met were straight-shooting, blue-collar square-dealers. Sausage-eaters. Secret hillbillies.

So I moved to Chicago and I loved it. I ended up living all over the city, moving nine times in eleven years — Roscoe Village, Logan Square, West Town, Ukrainian Village, Humboldt Park — but never anywhere swanky. I endured car break-ins, stolen grills and lawnmowers, one runaway chicken, and the neighbors' domestic disputes. I got used to the empty crack bags on the sidewalks and the crumpled Doritos bags blowing down the streets — a lot like my beloved Cabbagetown in Atlanta.

The last place I rented in Chicago was a third of a shitty coach house behind a two-flat in a gun-happy section of Pilsen. It was only the second time in my life that I'd been able to afford to live alone and I initially thought I was lucky to find this tiny place, but it ended up being by far the grittiest of my nine Chicago addresses. My neighbors on either side loomed ridiculously close and were unapologetically loud and aggressively unfriendly, with their barking dogs, booming music, and revving engines.

A lot of crazy shit went down in that neighborhood — yelling, screaming, fist fights, gun shots, muggings, an attempted rape just outside my kitchen window — and then there was the time I was blasted awake at dawn by the horrifyingly visceral sounds of someone being run over by a police car in the alley outside my bedroom window, just fifteen feet from my head. When I'd come home between tours to recharge, the stress was too much. I couldn't rest. I was done with the city, I said. I needed to live closer to a creek.

In 2008 I moved 139 miles north to a little town in Wisconsin called Evansville, about twenty-five miles south of Madison. It wasn't a fancy picture-postcard place — just some quaint old houses, lilac trees, dairy farms, corn and soybean fields, plus a windmill factory, a Family Dollar, a Piggly Wiggly, and a few taverns that featured fried cheese curds, Friday fish dinners, and the occasional meat raffle. It felt like I'd moved from Gotham City to Mayberry, and rural Wisconsin did begin to remind me of the rural South. Sometimes I'd even be lulled into thinking I was back home in my mom's small Georgia town amongst "my people" — until some guy in a Green Bay Packers hoodie would open his mouth and squawk out some of that pointy and squashed-down upper midwestern accent: "Oh ya! Don'tcha know!" Ever since I first heard that accent from a Beloit gas pump jockey in 1990, it has never ceased to blow my mind.

I worked out of Chicago the whole time I lived there, though — driving back and forth for rehearsals and shows and flying in and out of O'Hare. But damn if I didn't end up living in Evansville for *eight and a half years.* That's almost twice as long as I'd lived anywhere at any time in my life. Even as a kid we'd bounced from apartment to apartment, so to live at one address for that long was strange for me.

But even though I planted flowers and mowed the grass and shoveled snow and filled the bird feeders, I guess I wasn't really there. Most of my life happened in transit, and as an agnostic without a family or children, I didn't have much in common with the local folks, who were primarily connected to each other through church and school. No matter how many times I said hello and initiated conversation at the local pharmacy, or tipped large at the corner bar, people always seemed to look at me a little funny. The cumulative disconnect — not to mention the many hours of constant driving back and forth to Chicago in all kinds of weather in less-than-dependable vehicles — finally made me decide to move back to the city. When I did, I found myself moving boxes that I'd never even unpacked.

Somehow those small town years became a blink. A flashbulb pop and sizzle. A blur. Almost nothing.

I moved back to Chicago in 2016, to Humboldt Park, the same neighborhood where I'd lived for about four years total in two different rentals back in the early 2000s. In a strange coincidence, I moved into a basement apartment owned by my former Atlanta landlords from twenty years ago — a married couple who moved to Chicago a few years after I did. It had been pretty violent when I lived there before, and I'd had some scary gunfire near-misses, but my landlords assured me that a lot had changed in the past twelve years since I'd left, and that things had gotten better.

There was definitely a lot of gentrification happening all over town. Huge condos were going up and blacking out the sun for the little houses next door. Produce markets were turning into fancy grocery stores, complete with wine bars and tuxedoed fellas playing grand pianos next to the grass-fed beef. Hell, I probably couldn't even afford to live in my old Pilsen crudhole nowadays.

But my new place offered pretty much the same as before. Gang dudes were still pacing on the street corners and they were still so, so young. Little thuglets who couldn't even grow a mustache yet — too young to feel the heft of mortality or to have any real idea about the consequences of their actions. But there they were, visibly twitching, eyes darting sideways, their hands under their t-shirts, fingers resting on the heavy guns in their waistbands.

It unnerved me for the first few weeks, but I wasn't afraid, exactly, just sad and pissed off at the hubris of those fuckers who were acting a fool outside the houses of the Borinqueño families with kids and grandparents, families who'd lived in this neighborhood for generations — and all the rest of us who were just trying to go about our business without getting shot.

But, quicker than I even thought I would, I was able to reverse eight years of screen doors, quiet nights, and chimney smoke, and get back into a cautious, city-savvy routine — not walking my dogs on certain streets, not walking them after dark, not parking my car in certain places, and carrying around pepper spray and six keys on my key ring for one small apartment, with all its iron gates and security locks. It soon became a kind of reflexive shrug — a weary acceptance of my curtailed freedom, heavy like the weight of an x ray apron, but familiar.

Now I'm right back into the swing of things in the city. The action never stops. My phone is always ringing. There's always something going on — something new, interesting, challenging, inspiring — but it doesn't feel like it did the first time. And I'm a little surprised and hollowed out by that, because at this point I've lived over two-thirds of my adult life as a Midwesterner, and I really do love Chicago — and I think it loves me back.

There's always been an incredibly supportive and open, cross-pollinating arts community here — vital and tight-knit, but not exclusive. My artistic home base was a scrappy little bar called the Hideout where I bartended for over nine years, and I've played literally hundreds of shows. The month I moved back to town, the Hideout held a block party with live music to celebrate the twenty years since the current owners bought the place. I sang songs in three different bands that day, and all former bartenders, myself included, were invited to work a shift. One of my first customers was a kid I used to babysit when I first got to town. I changed his diaper for crying out loud. "Here's your beer . . . sir."

But while it still feels like my city, somehow it doesn't feel like home this time. All of a sudden, "place" doesn't seem to matter to how I feel.

I've been touring as a musician since I was twenty-three years old, but in the last eleven years it's been my only employment, and I've been on a tour bus almost constantly — or on a plane, in a cab, in a shuttle, on a train. It's almost never my own hands on the steering wheel, but I'm always being moved forward, pushed along by the tour itinerary. These days I immediately nest in airport terminal gates, bus bunks, hotel rooms, backstage dressing rooms — but after nine months in my new place in Chicago, I'm still surrounded by boxes and I haven't even fried an egg.

Back when I first moved to Chicago in 1997, I suffered waves of longing for people and places in Atlanta, but after going home for a few visits, I slowly realized that I wasn't homesick for a place, but for an era in my life. I was homesick for a time — not the city itself. This was a sad realization at first — that I was longing for something that wasn't there anymore and would never exist again. Then I thought...maybe this could be turned into a survival skill. The ability to move anywhere, to be anywhere, and make it your home. Infinite do-overs. A reset button. Instant anonymity. As many times as you wanted. As often as you had to. A superpower. It's kind of a lonely superpower, but a superpower all the same. Maybe I've gotten too good at this.

RUST NEVER KEEPS: NOTES FROM THE DETROIT DIASPORA
ROB MILLER

As an intra-national migration, it lacks the breezy pizazz of a dapper, Nat King Cole Route 66 travelogue. Watervliet and Ypsilanti don't roll off the tongue like San Bernardino and Gallup, New Mex-i-co. Interstate 94 fails to conjure the epic Western scope, pioneer determination, raging rivers, and hostile Indians of the Oregon Trail — it's more Escalantes than Conestogas. The trip from Detroit to Chicago is four hours and change by car, with six-lane bridges over any trickle of water, and the only Indians to worry about own the casinos. Before there was a craft brewery or a farm to table enterprise in every town between the two cities, there were just party store/gas station combos stocked with Stroh's and Slim Jims. The only wastelands you cross are the industrial phantoms of northeast Indiana and the bland beating heart of southwest Michigan's Gerald Ford country club Republicanism. Driving past Bob Evans, Meijer Thrifty Acres, and Win Schuler's (tubs of bar cheese!); past Paw Paw, Dowagiac, and Climax, it hardly feels like a Mother Road.

The Detroit to Chicago migration lacks the seismic cultural impact that came when the dust of the Delta was shaken off and the mythologies of Highways 41, 51, and 61 were born, electrifying the blues, setting the template for rock and roll, and, generations later, inspiring European music geeks by the Aircon busload to seek out der authentik Bluesmusik. Instead of a sell-your-soul crossroads, there's an off-ramp massage parlor called the Velvet Touch. Instead of the cotton fields of Yazoo City, there are the cereal factories of Battle Creek. Think Tony the Tiger and Toucan Sam, not Robert Johnson and Muddy Waters.

But it did happen, from the mid eighties to the late nineties, the traffic between Detroit and Chicago headed in one direction. And as with all human passages, some things were left behind, but a lot of things came along, connecting the cities by more than just another dreary stretch of unremarkable highway.

For those, like me, born and raised in and around Detroit, coming of age in the oil embargo hangover of the seventies and Reagan eighties, Detroit was fast becoming a shell. It was not yet the cause célèbre of tourists fascinated by large-scale industrial decay, or a magnet for urban apiarists, craft distillers, and custom bike fabricators. Before the rest of the world knew it as Ruin Porn, we just knew it as ruin. Before there were glorious set pieces of postmodern beauty, there was the memory of a bank where you opened your first account with paper route money, the restaurant you went to with your grandma, the union hall where your uncle bought you Faygo while he drank icy beer and smoked, a car company where all your neighbors worked.

It was bleak, in other words. Creative opportunities were in short supply. There were dead-end jobs at the whim of the car economy and not much else. The bottom hadn't been reached, it wasn't even in sight. Detroit's was a decades-long Hurricane Katrina, the shock blunted and numbed because it took a generation (or two) to bring a city to its knees, rather than a long weekend. It was a hollowed out core surrounded by suburbs of man-sard–roofed professional plazas, car dealerships, and strip malls spilling to the horizon.

Many of us chafed to achieve escape velocity. We knew there was more somewhere else. But where and what? Cities like Denver, Phoenix, and Atlanta are all fine places (well, not really Phoenix); they have their histories and civic contributions (again, Phoenix not so much), but Chicago and Detroit built the modern world. Everywhere you go, something you see, something you travel in or on, points back to these places.

As for the coasts, most of what I knew of New York City was gleaned from illicit viewings of *Kojak* on the black and white portable TV upstairs while the folks were downstairs getting gassed on SoCo Manhattans. It was dark and dirty and full of pimps, hustlers, junkies, and "turkeys." No way, man. And LA, let's just say I'm not inclined to disagree with William Faulkner's assessment that "everything in Los Angeles is too large, too loud and usually banal in concept. The plastic asshole of the world." Plus, all that sun and good weather just seems wrong.

Indianapolis, Cleveland, Pittsburgh, Cincinnati, even Toronto, as well as thriving university towns like Ann Arbor, Lansing, and Columbus, are closer. But still — we went to Chicago.

It started as a trickle. Somebody's sister moved there, or a buddy went for a job or a concert. Then another would go. After a while, it seemed everyone knew somebody there or on the way there. We heard stories of a city of neighborhoods. In their voices you could hear excitement, amazement even. We sensed possibilities and opportunities that for us, in our time and in our place, did not exist in great quantities. So we went, carrying with us our memories of what a city was and hopes for what a city could be.

In Chicago, we promptly found kindred spirits in a place where you go to work. We shared industrial skylines, histories of industry, immigration, boom and bust. But we Detroiters carried with us the appreciation, first hand, that it could all disappear. We came and we stayed, and we fit right in.

Growing up in Detroit, there was an inborn awareness that we made shit. Big shit.

World-changing shit, and a lot of it. Cars, trucks, tanks, and everything that went in them. In grade school, men like Ford, Olds, Dodge, Chrysler, and Reuther were civic giants, their names spoken with reverence. In high school, we learned about the rise of unions and the middle class, V8s, forty-hour work weeks, paved roads (the first stretch of paved roadway in the world was a ten-minute walk from my grandparents' house), interstates, and suburban sprawl (often referred to as "progress"). Math class had lots of "If Car A goes 0 to 60 in a quarter mile in 6.5 seconds, how long will take to go a mile" type problems. For school field trips, we didn't go to art museums: we went to Dodge Main, the noise filling our chests with fear and pride. Everyone's dad was a Car Guy. A GM guy, a Ford guy, or a Chrysler guy. If you weren't making cars, you were selling them, designing them, selling parts for them, or fixing them.

Chicago, too, is inextricably tied to building, rebuilding, and remaking the world; a city on the make, full of big dreamers and big ideas. It burned to the ground in the Great Fire, then thrust itself onto the world stage with a brashness and audacity that's shocking to look back at. Big Shoulders, stacker of wheat, World's Fair, Ferris Wheel, stockyards, McDonald's, Bubbly Creek, reverse the river, make no small plans. McCormick, Mies, Ward, Burnham, Armour, Swift, and Field remolded the city, and the world, in ways both awesome and awful.

When we got to Chicago, we found open stores, a culture not wary of walking or mass transportation, and a lakefront that hadn't been ignored and abandoned. Every neighborhood had a butcher, bar (or three), diner, thrift shop, bookstore, bakery, and place to get a really good Polish. Our experience of a city as a place of blight and emptiness was upended by the hustle all around us. There were so many people doing so many things, all day, every week. It was gritty and dangerous at times, yes, but there was the thrill of discovery and a pervasive feeling of possibility.

My first week in Chicago, I walked to Cardena's, the long-gone local grocery store in my not-yet-at-all-fashionable Roscoe Village neighborhood. They had tapped a keg and people were blithely doing their shopping with plastic cups of beer in hand. Free beer! In the market! Just...because.

I went to the Maxwell Street market and bought six-packs of blank Maxell cassette tapes, a dozen pairs of socks, a used Eddie "Cleanhead" Vinson LP, and ate hot links and ribs out of a homemade smoker. It was all so strange and wonderful. I thought I'd moved to heaven. Very few of us moved back to Detroit.

But while so much was novel, there were plenty of comforting, workaday cultural parallels. We switched from drinking Goebel's to Old Style. We were happy to find Chicagoans shared our unhealthy love of paczki. No one got all judgey when you wore flannel in April — fashion taking a backseat to practicality in a howling lake wind. We had one-team superhero Al Kaline, you had Ernie Banks. We had Ernie Harwell announcing the games and you had Harry Caray (though, really, there is no comparison, sorry Chicagoans). Detroit had protopunks like the Stooges and the MC5, Chicago had protopunks like Hound Dog Taylor and Howlin' Wolf. We had Aretha, you had Mavis.

Both cities were unheralded, but irreplaceable, incubators for country music. Chicago had House, Detroit had Techno. And of course we both had our unfortunate crosses to bear. We had the Nuge, you had Styx. And for every interminable version of "Sweet Home Chicago" you've heard, there's an insipid, vaguely jingoistic song about a Chevy.

No matter how long we live in Chicago, though, the members of the Detroit diaspora never fully leave Michigan. Our heads stay on Eastern time; I've been in Chicago twenty-four years and it STILL pisses me off how early the sun comes up in the summer and how early it gets dark. Sports allegiances tend to hold, as any ballgame during a Tigers series will attest. During lean years (i.e. most of them), the crowd is easily a fifty-fifty split. Red Wings and Pistons apparel is not uncommon in Chicago, though most people keep their Lions fandom — a generations-long burden of shame — to themselves. And short haul vacations mean going "Up North."

There are many other ways we keep a sense of the outsider, no matter how long we've been here. We'll never be able say Chi-CAW-go the way natives do (nor would we particularly want to). We cringe when someone says they're picking up beeerss at da Jewels. Italian beef, tap rooms, pizza puffs, the L, and six-way intersections still feel kind of exotic. We're mystified why you put a salad on a hot dog, not coney sauce. We prefer our pizza in slices, as God intended, not squares (unless, of course, the pizza was square to begin with). We might even tell you, after a few drinks, what we really think about your cracker crusts and manhole-cover thick casserole deep dishes — though we've gotten good at keeping such thoughts to ourselves.

We remain amused (and slightly alarmed) that calling an old dude in a bar a "jag-off," more than any other insult, will send him into a frothing rage. When we moved here we thought everyone had Devil's Night. (You mean, not every city burns itself down on October 30th? This is just a Detroit thing? Ugh.)

We feel it when you laugh at us for pointing at our hand when we're trying to explain where something in Michigan is. Or when we say "party store" and you think we're talking about balloons, or when you insist Vernor's is the same as ginger ale. And yeah, we see you rolling your eyes when we blather on about euchre or try and explain a "Michigan left."

And do us a favor, don't tell us how interesting it must be to be from Detroit; how amazing the collapsed mansion you saw on Instagram looks; how compelling the installation was that some Belgian graphic artist did in a crumbling factory. This all didn't happen for your aesthetic amusement, and it all took an incredible and indelible toll. It's still our hometown and Detroiters, perhaps more than others in this country, carry a certain civic sadness of what was.

Still, Chicago's our home now and, as the saying goes, we've got more uniting us than dividing us. Beyond our shared histories and muscle memories of restless change, we are connected by something that existed long before any highway or train track.

In order to rust, you need iron, oxygen, and water, and both Chicago and Detroit have got all of that in spades. The iron ore mined in the Upper Peninsula and Wasabi Range in Minnesota, processed into taconite pellets, transported by enormous freighters, and funneled through the Soo Locks. Going southeast, down Lake Huron to Detroit to build cars and trucks, or southwest down Lake Michigan to make the railroads, trains, and early skyscrapers.

The connection to the water is powerful even if most of us have never been on a ship other than the Bob-Lo boat or the Chicago Architecture Cruise. I can count the number of times I've gone out of view of shore on one hand and still have enough panicky fingers to pull the trigger on a twelve-gauge flare gun/distress signal. But the allure of the water is real. We took it for granted that we were surrounded by three of the five largest lakes in the *world*.

If you want to see a real, locked-arms, kindred expression of commonality and community? Try and build some super water pipeline from our lakes to Phoenix or Dallas to keep their swimming pools full, or to Kansas to replace depleted aquifers, or to Oklahoma to abet extraction industries. I guarantee you Buffalo, Cleveland, Detroit, Chicago, Benton Harbor, Port Huron, and all points along the Rust Belt will sharpen their metaphorical (and perhaps actual) pitchforks and stand together. We will shake our calloused fists at industry for shortsightedly abandoning us to land fit only for snakes and scorpions and say, "We told you so."

Civilizations arise around water. They may stumble and they may recede, but they do not disappear. They reinvent and revive in time. And rust is as natural as time. Rust might make something look worn and fallen, but scratch off the surface and you'll find the strength beneath intact, as strong as the water, iron ore, and oxygen that it came from. Rust does not have to mean decay, but it does always mean change. The form might be a little different, but it might be a little better. Detroit to Chicago: the flow has slowed and who's to say it won't even reverse someday? And if it does, it'll be fine. We know we've all been built up from the same place. Plus, the Velvet Touch is still there to break up the drive on I-94.

The Last City I Loved: Chicago
ZOE ZOLBROD

*I*t depends on the definition of love, of course. You can spend a week in a city and ache at the sight of its balconies, be imprinted forever with the particular stench of jasmine and diesel. But if the intimacy doesn't last at least as long as a year, was it really love? I've always thought not. And by that definition, there's only been one for me. The last is the first: Chicago.

I grew up on a rural route outside a small town and went to college in a smaller town yet, and I pined all my young life for a big city. But it did not happen at a glance with Chicago. The buildings and streets were wider and more windswept than those of the East Coast cities with which I was familiar, the distance between the few significant points I could identify vast, and the city remained unknowable to me, unknown despite repeated trips when I came for my last time as a visitor in 1989.

In my senior year of college and on winter break, I was staying with my friend in her out-of-town parents' house in Hyde Park. Although affection lingered, our active friendship was on the wane, and the real reason I was there was that my new boyfriend was coming in to play with his band at a club called Exit on New Year's Eve. They were opening for Naked Raygun. Then they were heading out on tour. We'd been apart for a couple weeks already and were at a stage in the relationship where the thought of going a few weeks more without an alleviating consummation caused a physical pain. I would have been excited to meet him in a truck stop parking lot, let alone in punk rock majesty, and I counted the hours while whiling away time with my low-key friend, an introvert who'd grown up in the city and didn't have the impulse I did to stalk the streets like an alley cat, sniffing at cans.

On the evening of the show, her brother was supposed to drive us up north, but he was late, then later, and then we called a cab, and another one, and another one until we finally got through somewhere. But the cab never came, and neither did her brother, and I was assured a dozen times that public transportation from where we were on the South Side to the North Side was impossible at that time of night.

I had hitchhiked and Greyhounded and hightailed it all over the country and Europe during the previous few years, but there I was that New Year's Eve, trapped in a turreted home, imprisoned, infantilized, while the world raved on without me. I'd come to Chicago with open arms, but the midwestern behemoth had shrugged and turned its back. I felt I would be kept outside the urban gates forever. I believed I had failed some test set by a cruel king and would never see my new boyfriend again.

Luckily he didn't get that memo, and he showed up at my friend's house the next evening. She had been so quietly kind the previous day, in the face of my misery, and she was tactful and kind again, allowing him and me to disappear into my little guest room in the attic. We didn't come out for the next sixteen hours or so, except once in the middle of the night when hunger drove us down the three flights of stairs and into the kitchen. The next afternoon, my face sore from kissing and grinning, we set out together to make our way in the metropolis.

We took a train into the Loop and stepped off it into lit, slushy dark. I had no idea where we were, other than The City, deep in a thrilling canyon of skyscrapers, and I still don't know. But he had a vague sense. Ukrainian Village. Wicker Park. I heard those words for the first time from him. We were going to the house where he was crashing with his band mates. West, he thought it was. Barring the sight of an actual sunset, I couldn't have pointed in a cardinal direction to save my life. "West," I parroted. "Sure!"

It was warm for a winter night, the sidewalks wet, perfect walking weather — or maybe the balminess was all in my mind. I felt half afloat. We walked out of the Loop and into an industrial district, foreboding and dark, but aesthetically compatible with the Einsturzende Neubauten and Psychic TV that spun on our turntables. We saw no one. Nothing was open or looked like it ever had been. The blocks were long.

"I think this is the right way," he said. There was the frisson of unease, the tingle of walking into it, the sense of being the only two people alive in the world. We passed a warehouse that had a grey metal door flanked by three mailboxes, each bearing a label with one or more names. The label on the top box was made from red plastic tape with letters pressed into it and accompanied by signifying stickers, artfully placed, and a twist of silk flowers. We looked at each other. Smiled. We were the only people on Earth projected into the future, looking at the threshold to our someday home.

Milwaukee Avenue. He thought he recognized the name. Chicago Avenue. Now he was sure we were on the right path. A few blocks more and there was the pulse of life again. People. Shops. Signage in Spanish. A horse outside a western-wear store. There was no visible Mexican population in East Coast cities at that time, and I had spent some summers in New Mexico. I liked the combination of desert culture and urban hood. We stopped for a bean burrito at a storefront restaurant, a place blasting mariachi music and bathed in bright light. We were the only young white Americans in a country not our own. Then he called on a pay phone to get exact directions to the house, and as soon as we arrived at the neat bungalow — just steps from the Hispanic commerce but part of a row manifesting Ukrainian tidiness with clipped hedges and edged walks — we were taken back out again under the wing of a pack.

We went in and out of one bar and down another dark street. Then we were upon a one-story brick structure with painted-over windows, a hash of metal grate over one of the entryways and the other hardly more inviting, a burgundy door set back in a little alcove. Above it was a neon sign, mostly in pink: a vertical "R-a-i-n-b-o" and then the script "Club." Its seedy glow made the sidewalk brighter than the interior, where a doorman sat looking serious.

My heart started to bump. It wasn't clear to me what kind of culture we were walking into, and my boyfriend was not yet twenty-one. But we slipped by — How did we do that? They were so strict; it still seems a miracle — and slid into a circular booth. Red vinyl. Round red table. A big horseshoe bar arching around an almost rococo stage. Art hung above the dark paneling on the walls, expressively lit with inadequate spots. It was my perfect dream pairing of bohemian boudoir and wild-west saloon. James Brown blared, sounding as new and old and fantastic as anything I'd ever heard.

The bar filled up. T-shirts and leather and boots and hair. We didn't move from our booth, knowing no one and afraid of being caught as underage or just agog. But one of the women in the group kept depositing flared glasses of beer at our table. "How much?" I asked after the second or third one. I counted my few dollars carefully, was aware when someone spent any on me.

"Free when you're visiting Chicago," she smiled. And I had to accept. Chicago. Yes. It had taken me awhile, but now I was here, retrieved from banishment and inexorably bound to my boyfriend. We were in the middle of everything, right in the center of a secret world. I don't know how this fits into my theory of at least a year, but there's often an immediate clarity: You need only an evening to recognize that there will be love. At least in retrospect.

Six months later, a new graduate, I took a room in an apartment three blocks from the Rainbo Club. I would spend countless hours in a Rainbo booth over the next eight years. I would traipse up and down Chicago Avenue countless times. I would bike and walk and bus Milwaukee Avenue from the Blommer chocolate factory to the Village Thrift until I knew every E-Z terms furniture store and half-caved-in, boarded-up architectural gem. These were the parameters of my world, and it gave me joy to lay claim to them.

I admit that in the couple weeks between graduating and moving to Chicago, I sat on the living room floor of my soon-to-be-sold childhood home and pored over a street map, my heart falling as I counted out the blocks between where I'd be living and the closest patch of green. The triangle called Wicker Park looked about the size of a single backyard where I grew up, unfenced glades that sloped down to a creek. Yes, I had always pined for the city, but I hadn't exactly thought through how it'd feel to live on a permanent diet of all cement, no woods. It didn't end up mattering as much as I thought, though. I found other things to connect me to home.

Wicker Park in 1990 was in the earliest stages of gentrification, and it had features familiar to anyone who'd grown up in a crumbling Rust Belt town: decay, limitation, the creativity demanded by making do.

There were, for example, no ATMs. To get cash, you needed a check-cashing card from the Jewel. Bedrooms might have only half of one working outlet. A single space heater often did the work of warming four or five rooms. My favorite music venue, Czar Bar, looked very much like the Volunteer Fireman's hall back on Cussewago Road: the same stackable vinyl-baked chairs, tin ashtrays, starkly utilitarian lighting, and cigar smell. But this version had the addition of fantabulous scenesters collecting to see Beat Happening play a seven-dollar show. It wasn't long before I would recognize by sight most of the people in the room.

Soon enough, Earwax would move in, and a little later, Quimbys, on Damen and Evergreen before moving to North. But in 1990 you still had to make forays out of the neighborhood to buy books and records and trendy thick-soled shoes. Forays out to eat food that was not Mexican or Ukrainian or Polish. There was Leo's Lunchroom and Urbis Orbis catering to the brunch and coffee needs of arty types, but no Thai. No Indian. No Ethiopian. No bagels. Certainly no sushi. There was a feeling of expedition to get any of those things. From the base camp in Wicker Park out into the great bounty of Chicago, any adventure was possible. It was the combination of village and city made for someone like me.

That first summer I had no job yet, which meant I had no money, either, to speak of, but time to explore. When my boyfriend returned from a European tour to stay with me in my eight-foot by ten-foot room, we took train rides and walks that felt like extensions of the first one. The temperature was sixty degrees warmer, heat and stink rising from the sidewalks in waves, but there was a similar wonder and dreamlike accord. The Picasso sculpture at night. Humboldt Park for the Puerto Rican Festival. Reckless Records on Broadway. Powell's Books near Printer's Row.

Then he went back to school and I took a job in River North and beat a path in that direction. I walked north over the Chicago River on every bridge from the Loop and decided LaSalle had the most spectacular view, the best proportion of buildings to water to lights. That first year as an office drone often left me shaky and lonely — *This* is what it feels like to work for a living? What happens next? — but I'd stop and look out from that red steel bridge in the winter, and the city kept me in its thrall.

My boyfriend and I eventually moved into a loft that resembled the one we'd noticed in 1990, but the relationship faltered. My job went to seed. I met a new friend who riveted me, took to running around the neighborhood at all hours with her. We'd both ride on my bike, inebriated, helmetless, in elaborate outfits we'd scored at the thrift store the day before, the wind warm on our faces as I pedaled us from show to party to bar. Most nights we'd pass through the Rainbo, and she'd make it her project to collect quarters for the photo booth and herd us there. We'd mash on each other once the curtain was drawn, strip down or ham it up, kiss. This display for posterity felt uncontainable. We were conscious of our luck and happiness.

Then for a year I traveled, touching down once in the neighborhood for a stint to couch surf and pick up waitressing shifts and a boy while I arranged visas and vaccinations. It'd have been easy to settle somewhere else after my trip, to take up in Seattle or abroad somewhere warm — I owned virtually nothing, and I fancied myself an adventurer. But at heart what I wanted was Chicago. I returned and moved in with my friend, picked up where I'd left off with the boy.

Over the years, between moving and crashing and boyfriends here and there, I laid my head in a lot of corners of the larger neighborhood, the area between Noble and California and Hubbard and Armitage that was maybe two miles square. You could have plopped me down anywhere, drunk, at three in the morning, and I could have pointed correctly in each cardinal direction, told you what each quadrant's best bars and corner markets were. At my final apartment in Wicker Park, on Augusta and Western, a single sapling was the only tree I could see when I stood on my fire escape. By this point, when I left the city, the itch of the foliage and the scream of bugs and the depth of the dark were something that I had to get used to.

The Rainbo Club played its part in taking me out of the neighborhood. My friend went one night without me, met a man who lived up north, at Irving and Clark. He'd come in for an art opening. Once they fell in love, I was set up with his best friend, and it worked. We four participated in a red-light green-light swap of primary affection. "Where'd you find him?" a couple friends asked me, maybe wistfully. There were many more hip people and places to go in Wicker Park by this time, but in some ways it felt smaller, too, to those of us who'd been fishing there for years.

When Mark and I decided to move in together, we said we'd look both in his neighborhood and mine, and we'd move wherever we found the best place. I tried really hard. But Wicker Park was on fire. We'd show up to a viewing and there'd be a dozen other people there, pushing past each other to look at the closets in bedrooms the size of them, waving checks in the air.

So we moved to Uptown, in between New Chinatown and Andersonville, and I found other things about Chicago to love. I had Middle Eastern, Vietnamese, and Thai markets to explore. There were fewer bars I liked and fewer friends within walking distance, but that was made up for by lakefront. And oh, the lake, the lake, the lake. Crashing and green. Frozen and regal. Mirror-like. Caribbean blue. I rode my bike along it to my job in the Loop. I walked and ran along it and thought my thoughts. I wrote a novel. I settled into interior life, and domestic life, and really became part of a pair.

Eventually we had saved enough to buy a place, but now the crowds were descending on Edgewater and Uptown, bidding over the asking price of anything we could afford, and so we migrated further north into Rogers Park. I was pregnant by the time we moved in. My son was born in the spring, and he and I explored the lay of the land together as I fell in mother love. Everything looked different to me with him strapped to my chest, dewy and outsized and new. Instead of bars, my mental map was marked off by playlots. And, more than ever, it was defined by the lake.

In Rogers Park, the beach is not cut off from the mainland by Lake Shore Drive. The sidewalk just deposits you into it. We were there in all seasons, scooching on the sculpture at Pratt Beach, finding the most interesting panels on the winding mural wall, climbing between the hills of sand banked up each fall.

Our favorite spot was what we called the "playground by the lake," a one-block park and beach at Albion, separated from the continuous stretch of the Rogers Park beaches by buildings and rocks. Albion ends in a cul de sac, and while we lived nearby, the city installed a few black benches just off the curb, facing the sand and water. Sitting there, I get the feeling I'm in Brighton Beach, or in Russia — two places that I've never been. One day someone staked Tibetan prayer flags into the sand, and their flutter reminds me of the Himalayas, the fartherest-away place I've ever reached and a symbol of what I've resisted in order to take root. Looking south, I see the outline of Chicago's shore, the sky-line of the city. The view instills me with the sense of fullness and possibility just barely tipped with melancholy. Time is passing. Time has passed. Choices have been made.

I never returned to my hometown for more than a couple of weeks once I left at eighteen, and my parents split up and moved out of state soon thereafter. Chicago is my home. I don't even fantasize anymore about leaving it for somewhere sunnier or more spectacular. A sojourn, a sabbatical, sure. That'd be great. That'd be fun. An affair. But Chicago is my home. There's so much here. The Russian shore, the Caribbean coast, that place at Devon and Maplewood where the traffic chokes and the sari shops beckon. The smell of burnt duck on Argyle. The way the bike path widens when you come up on the volleyball players around Fullerton Beach. The way Michigan Avenue slices a straight, clean edge of skyscrapers apart from the infinite lake. And the cacophony of Wicker Park.

I go to visit. Sometimes I take the Metra and get off at the Clybourn stop, where — when I lived near Wabansia — I used to get on. I walk past the site of the old Artful Dodger, where my friend and I used to go for a nightcap in our pajamas and sometimes end up dancing, past the house where we lived so happily until it caught fire, past stoops and sidewalks where I'd kissed and caroused, the sign post where my bike was locked when someone ripped off its tires. Beneath windows of rooms where I had sex and cried and read and danced and talked all night. And there's another one. Another one there. Up Milwaukee Avenue to Damen. From Damen to Division, and the glowing Rainbo sign. There are more restaurants on one block than there were in the whole neighborhood when I moved here. Dinner for two at many of them costs as much as a month of my former rent. It's been like this for years, and I come around plenty. But there's a moment where I stand like a rube every time.

"There were no ATMs!" I say sometimes out loud. "There were no ATMs!"

I'm at the age and in a situation where it seems possible that I won't fall in love again, not in that way. Except to the extent that I do whenever I walk down Milwaukee Avenue, a greenhorn once more, amazed, exhilarated, and an outdated old-timer, too, in a trance of nostalgia. Everything's existing all at once for me. The scope of a big city. The small village made good. And I love it.

PREVIOUSLY PUBLISHED AT *THE RUMPUS*.

fiction

The Book of Poems by the Lost Birds of Union Station

ANDREW HERTZBERG

To the lost birds of Union Station, what does all of this mean to you: this grand hall and this high ceiling, these sounds reverberated infinitely off of eighteen intimidating columns, anemic rows of wooden benches, the sun's reflection off the cracked marble tiles at the right time of day, the ornate lampposts, always on no matter how redundant in the lavish daytime light. The hooded figures with owl and stoic crow, the disorienting purple lights, and a vacant stage wrapped in black curtain, trying to negate the marvelous, sandy marble of the rest of the room. The crumbs and snacks left behind, discarded meals and littered trash, the coughing of the sick and healthy, tired and poor and angry, officers and Amish, the rapid stride of families and friends, of businessmen and tourists, musicians walking gracefully through the station, carrying instruments resting peacefully in their cases, but mostly these single people, lost birds in their own right, waiting for the right to leave this grand hall, to the tracks where their vessels will fly them away, perhaps only to return later, perhaps to leave this city forever.

I sit here, straddled between emptiness and movement, and wonder about the book of poems that could be written by the lost birds at Union Station.

○○○

What does time matter to the lost birds of Union Station? They need not pay attention to a quiet clock, and to them the year is 1925 or 2025, no difference. An anachronistic shoeshiner is triumphant in his victory against changing customs while tense security announcements remind you that we are indeed in the future. "If you see something, say something," yet you see all and hear all, are seen and not seen, heard and not heard. But if one listens closely, they can almost hear the call of the newspaper boy hawking the day's headlines entwined with the coos of the lost birds of Union Station.

○○○

No one represents the lost birds of Union Station. They do not vote. What would a politician say to a lost bird of Union Station? What issues would an alderman fight for to help these lost birds? What use do the lost birds of Union Station have for a state budget or murder rates? Or public art and literacy centers? Sidewalk repair and bus lines? Riverwalks and biking paths? Of music festivals or parks or beaches? Transit-oriented development? Of protests and protests against protests? The lost birds don't care about gentrification or segregation. The lost birds need only a place to rest their weary wings. But in this city, any sanctuary stands on sand: a whole white city was doomed from the start. A lakefront sanctuary can only accommodate so many lost birds, but no train can take these lost birds home.

What do the lost birds of Union Station care of Finkl and his Sons, of Nuevo Leon and a nuevoer Leon, of double doors and Lincoln Ave. lounges, dirty dives and turntable havens, vegetarian cafés, and week-long waits for encased meats? Or night clubs built in former mental health clinics? But perhaps they should be worried. Because these former sanctuaries for so many have been converted or distorted or expanded as this city becomes BIGGER and BETTER and is now no longer a welcome home for the lost birds of Union Station.

o o o

These lost birds hate violence. They avoid violence until it finds them. The lost birds are hungry. And hunger can make a lost bird delirious. These lost birds aren't jealous of other birds. They have too little energy to waste on jealousy. Not to say they would deny refuge at Lincoln Park or Brookfield. They would love to enjoy the theater, explore a museum, experience visual and musical artists, to take in a ballgame with a bird's eye view.

Jealousy is not the only absence of emotion. The lost birds of Union Station do not exhibit enthusiasm or carefree activity, save for rare occasions. It is not pity they desire, these lost birds. They do not need power, they just want visibility. But not Internet attention, no: it is disgusting to think of the lost birds of Union Station reduced to a viral meme.

It can be hard to tell the breed of bird that is lost in Union Station. Outward appearance will lead you to believe that you know this type of bird, that you have seen it before. Look closer: this is not a wren nor grackle, nor blue jay, finch nor sparrow; this bird cannot be pigeonholed. Until you fly a mile in its wings, be denied how its been denied, been lost and lost and lost, well, only then can you conclude that you have been deceived: you have no idea about this bird. I've heard with my own ears newly arrived strangers to town lament how many lost birds reside here. I try to tell them the complexity of the issue. They walk on seeing and not seeing, hearing and not hearing the lost birds.

o o o

The alarm is about to sound. The train is about to leave. And maybe the lost birds will heed the call, to rejoin their flock, their crew, their own, just as the people all know that it is time to find their own, to go home from work, to end a trip, to begin a new life with someone they love.

This train could be going anywhere. To Shreveport or Savannah. To Kansas City or Columbus, Toledo, or Louisville. To DC or Pittsburgh, Davenport, or Jackson, Mis-sip.

There are some birds that don't have the opportunity to fly away. They with wounded wings may leave this grand hall but there will be other grand halls to loiter in, to try to sleep in, inevitably forced awake, feathers ruffled by arrogant authority.

There will be other food courts to observe the many shoving food in their faces, full mouths saying "no, sorry," full stomachs shaking their heads, full bodies turning away from the birds, no different than the food courts in Union Station or Union Station or Union Station.

There will be other businessmen, other musicians, other officers. For a lost bird, leaving the station is never leaving the station. Because the lost bird watches different types of people line up at different cafés, different newsstands, different bars, different indifference on different faces, different difference between different cities, different words, different worlds, all the same, until different is same, is different is different is different.

o o o

Today is a new day. A different day. Forget the days before. Some days the birds don't try to flap their wings. Some days the birds don't write their poems. Some days they don't ask for help, they don't keep warm, they don't they just don't.

Just back to the hall, that grand marble hall, like the ghost of water towers that used to surround this station, stuck in place, without a chance to get better. Soon forgotten like so many other birds before it, a nuisance to everyone else in the station, the protesters and politicians, the newspaper boy and security guards, the shoeshiner, the quiet clock, the musicians, the tourists, the businessmen, the families and friends, the officers and Amish, the angry and poor and tired, the hooded figures, but mostly these single people, these lost birds in their own right.

Without the chance to fly away.

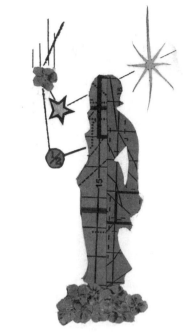

the BUILT CITY

It Is Not Waste All This, Not Placed Here in Disgust, Street after Street

KATHLEEN ROONEY

The city is dangerous and cannot be trusted.

We are making our way through the city to find a knife, but I don't know that yet. So far we are drifting, the destination a surprise.

"We" are my flâneur friend Eric and I; "the city" is Chicago, grey with an azure tinge and snowy.

The knife is not because the city is dangerous, though. It will turn out to be tiny, the size of a single Cheeto, a classic Swiss Army knife, half-red, with its Victorinox cross-bearing cover long ago cracked off, aluminum alloy and brass rivets exposed. A one of a kind — like the city here, now. And the knife will actually come to prove the opposite: that the city can be safe and the city can be trustworthy.

The city is dangerous and cannot be trusted is something that we — Eric and I and everyone, really — are told all the time.

In *The Death and Life of Great American Cities*, Jane Jacobs says that "cities are, by definition, full of strangers." How one feels about strangers and their strangeness probably determines how one feels about cities. Me, I love them — strangers and cities. So did Jane Jacobs. Eric loves cities too, and strangers — but only as strangers.

We are taking the Red Line from the far North Side — Rogers Park for him, Edgewater for me — and I know we are heading to the Loop, but I don't know why. He has told me only that we are looking for something of his that he left in public a long time ago and he doesn't know if it will still be there. He is "confident but not hopeful." He refuses to tell me what the object is, or where, because that would spoil our trip for me, turning it from flânerie into just another holiday errand to accomplish in haste.

My father is a hunter and so am I — spending hours on icy days traversing the snowy scapes in search of.

My father's terrain is rural Nebraska — mine, urban Chicago. My father carries a gun — I, an iPhone camera.

Though my walks are year-round, I think of my father's hunting only in winter because winter is the season for his target animals: pheasants and quail. Feral cats, too, which he shoots when he sees them, hating the way they decimate the songbirds, the way the cats kill not just to eat but also for sport (hypocrisy, yes, but don't try to tell my dad that).

What I'm hunting for today — the day of the knife — and every day I walk is a certain sensation of being in the city, being like total presence, and a certain sensation of being out of time. Not like running out of time as with a finite resource, but existing *outside of* time, floating above it or flowing with it, being aware of and seeing it, but from the perspective of a bird riding a thermal above a river. Affected by time, but not how most humans are; not how I am for most of the rest of my non-walking life.

We emerge from the subway at Lake Street, in front of the Macy's that for 154 years was Marshall Field's, where a Salvation Army bell ringer is ringing and ringing because it's almost Christmas.

The city is dangerous and cannot be trusted is something you are told all the time because somebody benefits by having you think that.

Because of their capacity to encourage frequent serendipitous interaction between large numbers of extremely diverse people, cities have always been engines of radical social change. Fear slows the engine. People and institutions who oppose radical social change benefit by manufacturing fear of the city: corporations that want cheap labor and profit from people's distress, municipal institutions that justify their existences by their claim to control and protect.

Fear Los Gallos, trust Chipotle. Embrace the Bed, the Bath, but never the too far Beyond. Division Street, yes, but only east of Roberto Clemente.

A flâneur knows that the wrong way to use the city is actually the right way. That to journey to the elevated-train-circumscribed financial heart of Chicago during business hours on a Monday neither to work, nor to shop, nor to sightsee is to move against its efficiencies and capitalistic tendencies. That to use the city incorrectly is to correct some of the city's undeniable imbalances.

Flâneurs never run — late or otherwise.

Flâneurs never get lost because they're not going anywhere.

Flâneurs like Eric lead you from the sidewalk up the wooden stairs to the overhead platform, still at Lake but now above the street itself, where the Pink, Purple, Green, Brown, and Orange lines all converge. The Orange Line has just arrived. The platform is flooded with shoppers, commuters, holiday tourists.

Flâneurs thread you through the crowd to the edge of the platform, where a large, locked, metal newspaper-recycling box sits. They crouch, remove their mitten, and reach around and behind and under the container. They scratch into rotted wood crusted with grime and ice. Is it here? Has it survived? Then they smile and hold up the object, the unknown thing you've come to find: the palm-sized red Swiss Army knife, all its attachments still intact, unharmed, and unrusted, just as they left it.

City as time capsule, to be opened before or after our demise, in a month, in a decade, in an hour. Now, here, or never. This patch of sidewalk has been waiting for our eyes since 1948. That stone might be older than ancient Egypt.

Even the skies above the city are dangerous and cannot be trusted, which is why Eric had to think fast. He was on his way, November 23, the week of Thanksgiving, to Midway Airport and aware that they might not let him take the knife aboard his flight, so when he transferred from the Red to the Orange Line, he stowed it.

In the Loop, out of the Loop, the city is ours. We help build it with our eyes, our ears, our minds, and our hearts. Across the river from Ozinga Concrete. Under the Dan Ryan. On the Metra tracks. Cermak west of Western. Ogden south of Cicero. Milwaukee north of Belmont. Thirty-fifth east of Wabash. The sublime wasteland stretching south to Chinatown from Roosevelt Road.

The city is multi-functional and opens like the knife. The knife is a weapon or the knife is a tool. Fear lets you see only the weapon. Unfear lets you see and trust the tool.

The truth is: you can hide something in the city, in the broad light of the public eye, abandon it for weeks of dark nights all alone in the winter, and then return to it.

The city hides itself, waiting for you to return to it.

And the city is not your enemy. The city is nobody's enemy. It is something that rewards respect and grace and careful attention. At our respective ages and demographics, Eric and I are ninety-four times more likely to die from being run over by a texting driver, from heart disease, cancer, liver failure, suicide, or AIDS—than by murder.

The hidden knife. The strangers swarming. The ice floes on the river like an invitation to a crazed and likely fatal game of hopscotch. None of these would you be able to truly *see* were you not drifting on foot with open eyes.

LOCATIVE

ANDREW CANTRELL

::

So this café was here 15 years ago. You know, there weren't a whole lot of those hippie hangout kind of places you might think when you have this really social, politically active community. This was the first one. I remember going in here and suddenly I was like, "Oh my god there are artists living here." It was a totally different reality. There would be these guys in here just holding court. Definitely the artists, the muralist guys in here with big beards, and they would round-table and people would go around them and talk. It was intense.

::

To see where everyone walks in the city
     You didn't grow up in this city either?

Where they've traveled
     Well I came here because I had to live

::

That looks like a house right out of my hometown. Milwaukee? No, Menominee, Michigan. The UP. My dad is a contractor and one of his jobs was through the state. Weatherization for economically distressed people. So we would end up spending a great deal of time in houses like that sealing windows and stuff. So I have this weird I would say imperfect or inaccurate memory of my hometown as being all these dilapidated structures when really it's not.

::

I just started thinking about all these places
     These habitations in the city

You can live in a place for years and years
     So you have this constant sense of lost places

A nowhere history transmitted against the grain

Do you think of that every time you walk by here?
    Yeah, they took everythin

::

Last week I worked on three separate freelance gigs that had to be out in a day of each other and a gallery opening and I was going out of my fucking brain. Do you ever think that all these things that we do just distract us from having to commit to our own work? But what you were working on was your own work, right? Yeah, for the opening. But I can say the three freelance jobs were not wise. It's a fine line because some of it is to avoid your own work and your own fears but some of it is also because you need fucking money to eat. Freelancers have to take the jobs when they come because they might not show up for a while. That freelance mentality is so — I hate it! It's right under my skin.

::

Each of us is two
Each has a qualitative character

Each one is defined
By not only each situation

But also its participants

Each time
Each other

::

Have you ever come by this place at night? It's a loft apartment and there's no curtains on the windows and it's super lit-up at night. That's their dinner table. I have sat and watched them eat dinner for 15 minutes just because it was so interesting. They're lit up and the environment around them is dark because it's night out. They're sitting there like this perfect little couple and I'm telling all of these stories about them and thinking about how they really hate each other.

::

There were other places I'd walk around town
    Where other places exist

Like a whole other hidden neighborhood
    There was a farm and some other things

The other part of it was the neighborhoods
    The theft that's called development

        They don't just evolve into other things

::

It seems like a monument to victory by that Russian artist. He started making things that look like big speakers. I can't not touch things in museums. They just evolve into other things. It's part tunnel part spaceship part whale. You could walk by and not even notice that. The letter up there too. What are those things called? From the print shop? Letterpress trays? It's almost like a fairy tale object. Does it remind you of the things they are talking about? This has that feeling like that. It has this sort of fantasy feel to it. He had these crazy constructions made out of paper. These constructions that would never fly.

::

Used to be a bunch of people
Used to be a big diner

Used to live right there
Used to head down

Used to ride around
Used to be social clubs

Used to be dancing
Used to belong

Used to get used
Used to really bother me

::

Have you ever been in the Dominican shrine to Saint Jude Thaddeus? Did you leave a little offering? I do every time I go in there. Then there are murals behind us. These are the ones I remember. I love how he doesn't romanticize the family. They look like they are about to get into a fistfight. There's something ambivalent and weird about the poses. The little disembodied hands above the father's head.

::

Look at all our
        [Inaudible] talking
We wanted each other's company
        A chorus?
We yearned to get there next
        Knows no leaders

So here the Other
        There's a chorus

Courses toward being
        Uncountable

::

I've been disrespectful to the ideal people across the street. Is that dancing? The ones with the really big skirts? I like how that guy is rearing up on a horse and he has a microphone. I wonder what the horses are? He's talking or singing into a microphone. I've heard you can get horses with really good speaker systems. Oh, Jesus — he's up there. Jesus of course is an ideal man. He has a see-through chest. I look for that in all the men I go out with.

::

There's always houses behind the houses
        You look down all the alleys

And there's always another little place
        All this material is somewhere

::

People don't do much graffiti or anything where I live. Every once in a while someone hits a dumpster. Very polite graffiti. It's even pretty. What's cool about the graffiti here is that people put up some really great tags. Really artistic ones. People never tag murals because it's this unspoken rule. There's just so much respect for the murals. A few of the murals got painted. *Cyber Mission Gun. OneWorld, One Dream. Cyber Nation. Ultimate Weapon.*

::

Occupation is
        Yeah, it's a chorus

I remember I guessed it must
        Be a chorus

But this is only a little bit
        Of a whole bunch of the names

Where 0 is State Street

CLAIRE TIGHE

The only way I can explain is by map.

I've been homesick lately. It comes out of nowhere, crashing over me like a wave against the lakefront breakwall. It threatens to topple me. To stop it I begin listing: places, names, addresses, lake. I'm making sure I remember home, its small elements, the streets and sites ingrained in me since day one, that grid navigation system that says 0 is State Street. Everything oriented around both number and name, eight blocks to a mile. Life squared by Harlem at 7200 West, Howard at 7600 North, down south by the hundreds, each street name assigned by the eponymous number. I recite names to numbers to make sure I still have it.

Everything oriented east, to the lake, the body so big it asks visitors to question if it really is only a lake. Always to the east, contrasted by flat land to the west, the view of lights to the north, the way the water curves down in an arc to the south toward the border of Indiana. See, what happens when you orient to the water, baby, your whole world becomes dependent on direction. Lake is always the locus. Whenever I come up out of the ground, I find east first, where the buildings end and the water begins. When I come up, up, into the city from the south, seeing the skyline growing is like coming home and landing. The flatness is reassuring.

The homesickness hits me hardest on the subway, underground, especially when we're stuck because this is no elevated train. There's no sense to the numbers.

o o o

Born and grown in the city, Dad memorized the map, matching moment to address. He held the wonders of every city corner in his mind and would narrate them to me while driving me around in his car. Always driving. Memory layered on family layered on grid layered on land.

North Side. The Brown Line train rustles the neighborhood leaves while gaining speed toward Damen. Every morning I'd wait facing east, looking over onto Ravenswood Avenue, the tops of the old industrial buildings peaking over the elevated tracks. The local favorite: the Degan Building's green tower. And my favorite: 4433 North, the old electric factory built by the company that employed Dad's dad for more than half of his lifetime. I knew it by the big square above the door where the company's mosaic rested in its infancy. How fitting their building was demarcated by a big square, because that's what they manufactured, big green boxes.

South Side. Where Mom's mom got teary eyed as her curtains dirtied from the city air. She pined for home, somewhere else. Grandpa was devising something big, something major, working at a lab that would have big consequences, for all of us, the big collective global we/us. While he was in the middle of it he didn't say much. Now we live with his story but say little about the legacy of war within us, shaped right here at home, and the consequence of science and whatever else we inherited, too, even when the government sent an apology for the effects his body endured in the years afterward.

West Side. Supposedly, Mom sang to me, one dark night, when we were all in bed, Mrs. O'Leary put a lantern in her shed and her cow kicked it over and blinked its eye and said it'll be a hot time in the old town tonight. She bounced us on her knee, singing this song no one else ever knew when I asked, but she had a tune that must have come from somewhere. Also, Dad's police beat, for those few short years he was in the force as a twenty-something. Memory made block-by-block and street names remembered by number.

o o o

In high school, my teachers took us around the city, casting questions about the dynamics of changing neighborhoods as they gentrified. When I told Dad I was learning about gentrification, he made a point to drive out of the way from where we were headed, political history lesson at the ready. He wanted Chicago to be my living laboratory. Together we walked down to one of the last remaining high rises of Cabrini-Green. I stood under its tall shadow, looking up, the Chicago sky so blue. I felt small, so small. A man sat across the street on the stoop of one of the low-rises, holding his T-shirt in his hands. He looked at me looking at the building. In just a few years the high-rises were gone. The city left a small grid of low-rises. In the mornings, I would take in the expanse of open land as I passed by on the Brown Line to work every day. I burned the space into memory, refusing to let history be erased by new condos and a big box store shopping center.

There are few other physical markers of the old regime. The Lathrop Homes are one, those brown buildings on Damen and Ashland, hidden behind the brick fence. There too live the city's memories, behind the boarded-up windows of the half-empty neighborhood. But more important, folks still live inside the other half, holding space, holding our humanity, on the same plot of city tied up in a conflict of rights and redevelopment.

I barely know what this city has seen.

o o o

On my bike I stained addresses into my memory too, where 0 begins at State Street.

Dad always says to be careful, to watch out for doors, because drivers can't see us bikers. And to beware using my phone on the train. I'm skeptical. Then I'm on the L and a man enters the car, intimidates us all to steal someone's cellphone, and runs away, and I think maybe I should be more careful. I'm twenty-five and it's the dead of winter and I love it hard but damn this city is violent. There's the ugliness.

o o o

There are churches. One in particular. Me and Grandmother, at the gates of one in Rogers Park, arches of white stone casting shadows from above. She's remembering. "When I was a little girl we used to play right here," she says as she gazes into the half-light. I'm small enough to slip through the iron.

We're down the street from where my dad grew up, in a yellow brick flat on Arthur Avenue, around the corner from the Loyola L. Every morning, from the window, they'd wave their grandpa goodbye as he left for work and boarded the train. The back of the L was still an alleyway then.

We're just down the block from my high school friend's house and just a few more blocks from Albion beach, where we'd jump in the waves all summer long, catching a breath from the unforgiving heat, just a few blocks down from the campus were Dad went to school and would look out onto the lake, deep in thought, where the Madonna della Strada opens up onto the water. Churches are contemplation places.

o o o

I memorized bus numbers, too, categorized by their routes from east to west and south to north, through the Loop and back. Belmont, the 77. Chicago, the 66, or as we'd called it, the 666. Crosstown traffic always made it feel like a bus ride from hell. I loved riding the 9 because we got to cross the Ashland Bridge, my favorite view of downtown. I always strained my neck to get a glimpse. On cloudy days I imagined what the skyline looked like, through the red industrial arms of the bridge, over the spot where the Chicago River bubbled strangely, like a washing machine.

The river, curving through history, through architecture, past the very first settlement at the mouth of the water that runs backward. I walk over, drive over, bike over it daily. One of those days I jumped, startled, when I heard the mouth of the carp clashing down on the water, creeping up on their prey. A passerby said, "Nasty, ain't they?" Because they were, their big eyes, seeing me see them. That river stunk so badly when it was hot. One night, when Dad was driving me home I complained about it. He looked over at me and said, "Oh, honey. Eventually, you'll get used it. You'll start to realize that's just the smell of Chicago in summer." Shikako, historians say the Miami and Illinois people called it. *Striped skunk or wild leek*. Chicagoua.

o o o

He held the mysteries of the city in his pocket. The old post office was one of them. As a kid, I'd sit in his car's front seat and lay back to look at the midwest sky as we drove through downtown. I was amazed when we'd drive under the old post office, speeding

— 52 —

through the bottom of a building, lights blurring in my eyes as we passed. I pictured letters flying out of tubes above my head.

o o o

The river meets the boulevard in the neighborhood where I live for more than a year in a historic home with old doorknobs and ghosts. That year I become obsessed with the boulevards. I spend Friday nights walking Logan to Kedzie to Palmer Square to Humboldt, thinking of old beer barons who wanted big homes and the wheelmen clubs who would race bicycles around the Palmer green. One night when I'm riding alone on the boulevards and a car follows me too closely for too many blocks. There's the darkness.

o o o

Chicago was his city and I was to love it, too. I felt it in the way he talked. He was passing it on to me. I could feel that he would miss me when I would go, because leaving Chicago was leaving three generations, leaving Dad.

Red Line to Howard, 7600. The edge. Dad lived just past the cemetery on the border, on the water, where he could see the white caps of the waves from his window, beyond the trees, especially in winter.

o o o

I'm home for the holidays and I've only been gone three months. We're driving home from a family gathering and get rerouted by midnight highway construction. We're around the corner from my old apartment and I try to give us directions and instead I get us lost. It's that restaurant sign on the corner that always throws me off. It looks the same from the east as it does from the south. From the front seat, Dad, looks over at me: "You're turned around, honey." My heart sinks. Only three months and it's already lost? I'm ashamed at how quickly my memory faded.

o o o

In my new city I get an ID card as proof of my new address. It's been a few months since I've had a haircut and my hair is shorter in the front than the back. When I see the picture, I'm startled. I look like Dad.

— 53 —

DATABASE

RACHEL Z. ARNDT

Past the rosemary on the windowsill
and snow-ticked glass   past the four
lanes graveled and salted
uphill   past the river pocked with hardening
floes and ducks too confused

to leave now   past the flagpole and letters,
the tv-static fields, the pile driver's
autocratic metronome   past the rush

of wheels through melt and   past unstrung hills
and unsung maps yet plotted
across suburban curvature   past
no crosswalks pedestrian enough
to pop into mall lots

and cheap density   past
chainlink reinvented pastimes swung
all around magnetic   past private
browsing and franchised waves
    past computer-beige
acres of forgotten cash   past

the immemorial cache
of tiled ground lifted to breathe
and receive water, give runoff
    past the place where you swear
the horizon curves if I
paraphrase embodied promises
to foreshorten our lines   past slipshod

hills crammed
up between ditches and tubes under
roads, flat deer stenching

shoulders   past dressed-up
willows, arms sagged with lowlight
abandon by the furnished border's
perforation   past

manmade   past permanent effort
    past the landmark decision's
envisioned subplot   past dropped-line
power lines' rut of metal on asphalt   past

the interview question —
is it better to be brave than sirened? —
and   past the answer, the texture,

the finger-greased screen laid over
the state, dragged zoom-level
great, pinched out into data-
slicked plain   past the greatest
smile scar, open the earth
    past the archaic bend in
telekinetic time   past dilapidated
diagonals   past tire tread
displays of all-American
possibility, there furnished
direction: "A parade is an arrow."

Chicago by Water

CAROL GLOOR

After a cleansing rain and slow September sunset:
then stars, lighted towers to the west,
the black Lake upholding
this small yacht,

and for now the hustling streets,
sodden garbage, nervous briefcases,
outstretched begging hands, all disappear
into glittering skyline, dark waves.

The Great Lakes contain a fifth
of all fresh water on Earth.
Were all humans to vanish this night
all traces of the towers

except their ceramics, their plastics,
would be gone in fifteen thousand years.
But still tonight, where once was only
an onion field, now this architecture,

these fluorescent trains clattering
between buildings, this peninsular planetarium,
these hundreds of small harbored boats,
masts tinkling, waiting for dawn.

Beyond the Michigan Sea

GARIN CYCHOLL

Each day in leaving work, I head north on Broadway in Gary, Indiana. In a couple of blocks, I have two choices: east to Detroit or west to Chicago. These cities would seem to offer sharp alternatives within the Rust Belt, Great Lakes cities whose economies offer stark contrasts to the outsider's eye. Detroit, the great, shrinking American city, as narrated by Charlie LeDuff. Chicago, as chronicled by Edward McClelland, "the place where we're all going to end up." But with the towers of Gary's remaining mills in my windshield, why? How does one measure Chicago's sense of place within the Rust Belt against prevailing northern and American geographies?

The Rust Belt city is where things get (or got) made. Commerce of solid things — first, ore slipping down from the north and Pontiac bumpers, then steel rods and bars — all as real as a Chicago pothole. Chicago is also composed of things of "substance." What is more "solid" than the defining cuts made in the region's wetlands, a Board of Trade margin call, the promise of a patronage job, or the arithmetic of the CBOE's "volatility index"? Chicago is a city that has made things — candy and steel, telephones and sausage, the McCormick Reaper and the Playboy Man. But following an established trend from the 1970s, the city lost 30 percent of its remaining manufacturing jobs between 1990 and 2010, and like the other cities of the American Rust Belt, Chicago still looks for new things to make. Sure it remains a crossroad for rail and air. Need a bunch of tulips? More pass through O'Hare than through any other city in North America. Roughnecks ride Amtrak's northern route from Chicago to North Dakota's oilfields on a regular schedule. In terms of made things though, how about a slice of Lake Shore real estate? A piece of property hung in the sky over the South Loop? What does Chicago make now?

The answer to this question may be wonderfully reflected in the shift a decade ago in Chicago postcards. Prior to the opening of Millennium Park, the Water Tower had been the city's most photographed image. A hard relic of the 1870s fires, the Water Tower represented a city founded on its ability to define itself against the terrain — overcoming the realities of lowland, mud, and the region's attendant ailments to become an engineered metropolis. A self-made city, "capital" of the American hinterlands.

With the opening of Millennium Park and the Cloud Gate ("The Bean") sculpture though, a new image dominated the city. Tourists' most popular image of Chicago became the one that was reflected in "The Bean" — an overturned, distorted version of the skyline. A mirror for selfies in a city that saw the number of service jobs steadily rise over the past two decades. A self-produced city, where 426,000 Chicagoans are employed in the "leisure and hospitality" trade. What Chicago "makes" is itself. A city, in the terms posed by Nelson Algren, on the constant "re-make."

New Polonia and Grand Avenue. Little Village and Chiraq. The city has offered waves of (im)migrants the opportunity to reinvent themselves against and within its grid. Chicago has been the workshop for making these new Americas, remaking itself against shifts in the cultural landscape. As the Great Lakes city fought to define itself in new eras of migration and economic stagnation, Chicago reinvented its own story. The third largest Mexican American city, it's a place that seems constantly aware of how its image reflects an invented America.

At times, Chicago is a Great Lakes city; at other times the city works tirelessly to connect itself outside its prevailing northern geographies — prairie, lake, and Iron Range — to the geography of "made things." A historical city of distinct midwestern values, but also a global city open to new lines and letters of trade. In his history of twentieth-century Chicago, Thomas Dyja unwinds how storytellers and journalists found new means of seeing themselves and their city mid-century in television's emerging screen. Later, the loops of relentless gun violence retell the city in the nightly news — images that seem at the core of American "self-production." (Even though Chicago's statistical murder rate has generally declined since the early 1990s.) After his election as mayor in 1955, the image of "urban order" was remade by Richard J. Daley out of federal dollars and all that steel. Leaving his physical imprint through the cuts made by all those expressways, Daley himself is one self-made leg of the Chicago Trinity — Daley, Michael Jordan, and Al Capone. Father, Son, and Holy Ghost.

But it's a strange "faith" that's made along the lake here. Through its boosters, Chicago has seen itself as the center of an unfolding American Empire; a city that exists beyond its lake-bound geography. It maintains a tenuous connection with any sense of the place itself. Louis Jolliet first mapped the region mistakenly at floodtide. Milwaukee Avenue, which parallels a Native American trading route and makes it arguably the oldest "road" in the city, is a chronicle of immigrant journeys and remade economic schemes on the realtor's map. Chicago is both substantial and insubstantial in its own making. Sadly, it often leaves residents stranded mid-narrative, a real estate wave crashing just a couple of blocks east. In the transition to "real estate," a neighborhood becomes "nowhere."

Reflected in "The Bean," the city exists within the Rust Belt as a postmodern "funhouse" of the twentieth century. What the city has made here is an "America" — that place that exists within its economic, ecological, and geographic shifts. In a city that has seen home values decline on the order of one-third over the past decade, Chicago now sells economic opportunity and its impact like McDonald's "sells" cheeseburgers; both the city and burger "maker" are in the "real estate" business, selling franchises and space. In the midst of a Great Lakes economy defined by its natural resources and migrating labor, Chicago was always a city that could "get you things" — a place, a terminus. But as the twentieth century slowly unravels, what substance defines this Rust Belt city's means of production? What's for sale?

Yet, there's a moment if you continue your drive north through the city on Lake Shore Drive, where you cross the bridge over the Chicago River and Lake Michigan spreads out at your right hand; Traverse City, Hudson Bay, and even the Midnight Sun lie just beyond the reach of your right hand. The city then offers you another version of its Rust Belt self — the habitation perched at water's (and an American) edge. A city defined by its waters.

How "solid" is that water in defining the city's future geographies? Does "water" offer an elemental redefinition of the Rust Belt as a defining American geography — Chicago at or near the center of a renewed Great Lakes region? In December 2008, states bordering the Lakes signed the Great Lakes Compact. This agreement put in place studies for economic and ecological cooperation in protecting the Lakes, but also marked the Lakes themselves as a territorial resource. No water could be "diverted" from the Lakes without common agreement. The agreement also forged links with Canadian governments to extend the definition of this freshwater territory to the St. Lawrence River Basin, as new issues regarding environmental integrity and invasive species emerged. Here, the Compact defines a renewed northern geography — a Rust Belt region in which Chicago is a full participant. Also, a geography in which water is perhaps the central resource.

Chicago's track record here is not good though. As a capital of the hinterlands, the city has profited and lost on regional exploitation. Boosters saw the city at the center of a growing American empire in the later nineteenth century. Chicago left a legacy here. Deforestation in the north, and sewage pumped southwest. The stockyards' Bubbly Creek and its offal as the city's true offering to the region. As Gabriel Gudding argues, the city's slaughterhouses have turned Illinois into a "factory floor," a regional agriculture stunted on industrial corn. The stockyards, padlocked and now just prospective real estate on South Halsted, Chicago maintains its distance in futures trading.

Similarly, to the east, Chicago does its best to separate itself from industrial Gary, Calumet City, and East Chicago — "factory floors" in a more graphic sense.

Chicago pretends to be an "American city" (the "most American" of cities?), but tries to set itself apart from the other industrial cities of the Rust Belt. Chicago is stung by the same challenges of other Great Lakes cities — declining population, rooted deindustrialization, entrenched segregation, the same seemingly intractable socio-economic measures that wind in a circle of cause and effect — but Chicago thinks that it's "won" where other Great Lakes cities have "lost." The city has attempted to "retell" itself out of the economic realities here.

In a wider sweep of the Americas' geographies, how "American" are these Rust Belt cities? They have participated in the United States' stunning industrial growth — steel and automobiles and shipping. However, in the trough left by that flurry of steelmaking in the mid-twentieth century, it might be worth it to reconsider the geographies here. Whereas New York's endless transformations and William Faulkner's Yoknapatawpha may be more representatively "American" narrations, the Rust Belt cities seem more "northern" in their geographies — a "postcolonial America" left in the Empire's wake, perhaps closer to postindustrial northern England or a refigured hinterlands defined by the "Great Remigration" as African Americans move back to the American South.

Chicago has lost upwards of 20 percent of its African American residents in the first fifteen years of the twenty-first century — mainly to cities like Atlanta and Houston. (83 percent of the city's lost residents over the past decade are African American.) People have moved through Chicago; this is another tie that unites it to the Rust Belt — displacement. Chicago imagines its geography closer to the nation's "center," while it remains on the "edge." The northern history is still being written. If Chicago has "won" here, the game seems far from over. The stakes might be more in how Chicago is able to recognize itself as a Rust Belt city, how it recognizes the geographies that continue to define it in a world of collapsing boundaries.

Rahm Emanuel's Chicago depicts itself as a "global city." Perhaps so in the sense that it still anticipates trends and adapts itself to the financial instruments, looming reorganizations, and "employment pockets" of the newest economy. The city has leveraged its operating expenses against rentals of its parking spaces and tollways, its pensions within the politics of a protracted state budget conflict. The city continues to re-produce itself — albeit in deals signed in red ink. Economist John McDonald points to the reality that per capita civic debt in Chicago has increased from $700 in 1990 to $2600 in 2010. With declining population and a broken school system, that number appears to be growing.

Where are the boundaries of the Rust Belt drawn here? Leaving Chicago offers a few routes south. The tail end of the South Side's Dan Ryan Expressway promises I-57 to "Memphis" as one route that many have already taken. The other option is I-90/94 to a ubiquitous "Indiana." Chicago does not have a sign for Gary.

Spectral Shorelines

CHLOE TAFT

"**I**f I see that once, I see it a hundred times."

John Stengel, self-described pile driver, tugboater, and watchman, was at home on the water in South Chicago. At night, between jobs, he'd go fishing. But starting in 1881, he began to notice something unusual. Despite the evening chill, steam rose from the shallow waters of Lake Michigan just off the shoreline. It was a ghostly marker of the marshy coast, an eerie signal that he should keep his distance. Still, with the untamed industrial growth in the area in recent years, he had become accustomed to otherworldly smells, noises, and apparitions.

Once thick with juniper and huckleberry bushes and an outlet for butchers and brewers to dig ice, two miles of the South Chicago coastline now had been fenced off by Illinois Steel. The company's South Works plant joined a massive national network of U.S. Steel holdings amidst a huddle of steel plants in the Calumet region.

At the turn of the century, however, South Works was involved in a prolonged legal dispute over its spectral shoreline. The company insisted that hundreds of acres of new land had emerged out of Lake Michigan as a result of the storms that regularly sent sand swirling into the banks. State prosecutors claimed, and John Stengel helped affirm, that Illinois Steel had in actuality deliberately dumped a byproduct of steelmaking called slag into the water — forty feet high over time — as a way to expand its plant with "made land." The company avoided paying taxes on property that, according to outdated assessors' maps, simply did not exist.

Asked by the state to purchase the land it had reclaimed from the lake bottom, Illinois Steel threatened to shut down the South Works plant and invest in Indiana facilities instead. In 1909, the parties agreed that Illinois Steel would pay $100 per acre, a bargain that would presumably preserve local jobs and spur economic growth. But the tension between mobile capital and grounded commitments continued to define this landscape for the next century.

Slag, salamanders, cinders, boulders. The courts had grappled with names for the composition of the South Works coast. Today, punctured by industrial remains, the land is a clear material marker of South Chicago's long legacy of corporate control.

A decade after South Works locked its gates in 1992, one of a series of plants to close in South Chicago in a devastating wave of industrial disinvestment, U.S. Steel entered into a partnership with Chicago developer McCaffery Interests to transform the roughly six hundred acres of now-vacant lakefront into a residential community and marina.

In the fall of 2013, I boarded a small bus with other curious Chicagoans to tour the property. We bounced along dirt roads, peering out at the brownfield as McCaffery representatives elaborated on their plan to "reprogram" the landscape with amenities like waterfront cafés and "dynamic uplighting" that promised to draw professionals from the Loop or Hyde Park. I could only imagine the odd feeling among community residents in our group that they were trespassing on their own front yard, land off limits to the public for over a century.

We stopped and got off the bus at the most visible reminders of the absent steel factory that once dominated the horizon, ore walls next to the slip where boats had unloaded raw material for storage. Their sentry status is less deliberate than fortuitous. When demolition crews tried to tear the walls down along with the rest of the plant buildings, the massive reinforced structures had firmly rebuffed the wrecking cranes.

Our camera flashes encroached on another era as we walked into the remains of a tunnel system at the base of the walls where steelworkers sought refuge from the sun or snow. The 20,000 workers that crowded the plant at peak production during World War II now linger only as ghosts. The steelworker neighborhoods that sprouted around the factory and flourished at mid-century with union wage gains and protections are increasingly shadows of themselves, isolated from the city's much-touted postindustrial rebirth downtown. Over the course of the twentieth century, the population shifted from Eastern European to Mexican and African American. Like the walls, generations of South Chicago residents display a stubborn refusal to be left behind.

The Bush, Millgate, Irondale, Slag Valley. Even the names of the neighborhoods around the city's steel mills exude grit. Back in 1909, amid Illinois Steel's threats of abandoning the plant, hundreds of South Chicago businessmen had filled Saenger Hall, a venue down the street, to affirm their faith in the community and the company's role in it. "We have come here and we have made our homes here. We have invested our money, we have put our labor and time here, and this is our home," one citizen proclaimed to applause. In a sprawling and fragmented metropolis, the men adamantly asserted that the city's economic future was here, on its fringes. "Chicago," they pointed out, "runs to the Indiana line."

More than a hundred years later, anxieties remain but take new form. Over time, heavy industry made good on its threat to leave South Chicago. Poverty and unemployment increased significantly beginning in the 1970s. Some former steelworkers see new development along the lakeshore as a golden ticket to increase their home values and allow them to sell and escape a haunting landscape of decline. But many locals insist that they will not be displaced by new economic activity. In more recent community meetings, packed to capacity in church basements, residents sought commitments from McCaffery for local employment, affordable housing, a community center, and a steelworkers museum.

Other ruins of this layered landscape, like the foundations of the factory buildings that were torn down, are buried deep in the ground, more firmly out of sight. The developers decided that the shoreline slag, an inert but jagged reminder of the industrial past and its betrayals, would need to be covered as well. In 2004, the slip welcomed barges again, but instead of carrying ore, the boats brought 232,000 tons of topsoil dredged from the bottom of Lake Peoria. Workers unloaded the dirt and spread it along the coast to transform twenty-five acres of rocky shore back into parkland.

"We're entering fall so the grass is starting to yellow," our guide noted. "It looks much better when it's warmer." On other parts of the site where the bank plunges abruptly into the water, industrial remnants, sweet clover, and prairie grass are all that pierce the gravelly waste.

As in the nineteenth century, "nature" at the South Works site is unstable, upended, and often surface deep. Indeed, on the spectral shoreline of South Chicago, nothing is as it seems. Sandy banks are covered in slag and lake bottoms are reclaimed with grassy tops. It is an in-between space where past, present, and future messily blur.

In 2016, after twelve years of false starts, the partnership between U.S. Steel and McCaffery Interests ultimately collapsed. Like the postwar guarantees of the industrial workplace and achievable dreams of owning a home with a yard and a boat parked out front, another set of promises for new economic development evaporated like steam rising from the water.

As John Stengel might say, "If I see that once, I see it a hundred times."

CYCLING

SCOTT WILSON

Starting from my north side apartment on a boulevard that once marked the edge of Chicago — a cute but too modest border, merely five miles from downtown — I ride my bike due east towards the lake, passing first an elevated railway that's in the process of becoming an elevated sidewalk, then over a river with a half-sunken barge sticking out of it like a lopsided tombstone, and eventually rolling into the Finkl Steel Plant (1902-2014). Inside its open doors I watch people in what look like aluminum foil space suits guide a vat of glowing orange goop over channels carved in the cement foundation. The vat tips and the glowing liquid, molten steel, spills into the channels, then flows off beyond my sight.

The workers in the plant are no doubt aware that they're carrying on one of the oldest traditions of human civilization. The beginnings of modern metallurgy began with bronze, which is an alloy of tin and copper. It's great for making complex tools — hinges, pulleys, and agricultural implements — because it resists excessive corrosion and is easily worked and molded. At the Art Institute of Chicago they have bronze figures that have outlived the civilizations that made them by 4,000 years, but still look good. The downside is bronze isn't very durable, so if a bronze tool sees regular use, it'll need to be beaten back into shape every so often. These days bronze is used in statues and totems that commemorate one lost thing or another, but not much else. Industrial anthropologists often see bronze as a step on the ladder to more advanced metal usage.

One such "advanced" metal is steel. Unlike bronze, the production of hard, strong lightweight steel requires a tremendous amount of energy (this is also true of cities). You can't just throw iron in a pot and smelt it over a campfire; you need a processed fuel to get it flowing — an example of which is charcoal. Made by slow-roasting the moisture and volatile elements out of either wood or the bones of those enemies with inferior metallurgy, the leftover matter burns at twice the heat required to melt iron. The Anatolians, it is believed, were the first to harness the potential of charcoal with the creation of a "crucible," a ceramic tomb that held the melting iron above an insulated flame and allowed the precise control of heat by blowing in oxygen with a primitive pump called a bellows, which is still used in domestic fireplaces, unchanged for 6,000 years. When the iron reaches a certain temperature, impurities like lead and mercury separate and float to the top to become slag. Carbon remains in the mix and bonds with the iron to make steel.

Over time, the increasing need for steel production forced bellows to grow in size, requiring men to pump with their hands, then legs, then in groups, then with horses — until the 1860s when Philander and Marion Roots developed a corkscrew-like fan that compressed and focused air by the simple turning of a crank. This new, highly efficient device, the Roots Blower as the patent calls it, allowed blast furnaces to grow from the size of rooms to the size of buildings in less than a generation. The crucible went from a ceramic pot filled with a handful of ingots to a molting cauldron lifted by cranes and pulleys, controlled by teams of men who smoke cigarettes on the sidewalk, watching me shift gears and dodge road debris.

This half-mile stretch of eastbound road is a busy, dangerous place to ride a bike. Old scrap trucks on their way to the recycling smelter, loaded down with tons of salvaged metal bits, are followed by boxy yellow machines with magnets on the bottom to pick up whatever the scrappers drop. City buses and tractor-trailers stop and go on the hot pavement, sinking in a little deeper every time. In the winter these dents fill with water that freezes and expands to make Chicago's iconic potholes. There's an ambient smell of diesel and tar. A hotshot in a new Mercedes is swerving around all these various obstacles in a desperate race against nobody to be first to the lowered barricade at the train crossing. The wind off his passenger side mirror strikes my hand. It's just the lightest touch, but coupled with the speed and noise of his pass it's enough to make me careen over the low curb and onto the sidewalk. I curse both him and his car's grandfather, Gottlieb Daimler, who, nearly a hundred years ago, set his mind to solving the problem of the outlandish growth of the internal combustion engine, allowing gas-powered cars to assume the master role in transportation.

The curb has done some damage to my front wheel. The pneumatic inner tube, an invention pioneered by bicycles that we've graciously allowed other machines to take advantage of, popped in a way that bike mechanics call a snake bite: two little holes right next to each other at the spot where the rim and curb struck, pinching the tube. The bike shop where I work is two blocks away, so I trudge north on Clybourn, guiding my bike like an injured pony.

The mechanic on duty is my mentor George. He's the patriarch of a large family that he's been supporting by fixing bikes for thirty years. He knows by the back-and-forth wobbling of my rim that I've broken a spoke.

Bicycle wheels are held together by tension. Under normal conditions each spoke will have about 1200 newtons of potential energy between the hub and rim, keeping the wheel suspended in a rigid state of equilibrium — a symptom of which is a wobble-less rim. A newton is roughly the same as the force exerted by the weight of an apple. For comparison, it takes the concentrated weight of 1100 apples to split an inch-thick block of concrete in half. So when a spoke suddenly snaps, it transfers a lot of energy throughout the wheel, affecting all the other spokes unequally. If a mechanic is to measure the tension on each spoke of my wheel, they will find that some of the spokes have two or three times the tension of other spokes. When the broken spoke is replaced, the lopsided tension will continue to affect the wheel, even if the rim wobble looks to be cured. Therefore, it's important that the repairer use care to tension and de-tension each spoke, employing secret audio, visual, and tactile cues to ensure that the wheel returns to a state of harmony. However, modern shops have figured out it's more cost-effective to replace the spoke without checking tension, then wait for the wheel to implode, then sell a new one, eliminating the shop's need for a master mechanic and his costly salary.

I've righted the wheel using a spoke that was made in Belgium by a machine that — legend has it — was recovered after being buried in a field. During the onset of the Second World War, many Belgians, afraid of being overrun and losing all their worldly possessions, took to burying everything of value. The spoke company wrapped their precious machine in a tarp and hid it under a football pitch along with the neighbor's art collection. After the war they excavated the machine, but the art is still down there somewhere; the owner died and took with her the exact location of her treasure. My friends who travel abroad tell me stories like this are not uncommon outside the U.S. Native Belgians I've spoken to on the subject warn me that the forests are filled with unexploded ordnance that could go off if disturbed. A likely story. Seems like the kind of thing I'd tell a would-be treasure hunter if I were a few potential shovel strokes from my big score.

While I'm finishing my bike repair, George encourages me to check out the new velodrome, a type of cycling arena, on the South Side. He says the racers competing at over forty miles per hour on the banked walls of the wooden track break parts with violent regularity, and they'll pay a premium for somebody who can make repairs quickly and correctly.

My grandmother, eighty years before this conversation, embodies the customer end of this sentiment while writing to the Schwinn Corporation of Chicago, requesting that they make her a racing bicycle suited for her feminine frame. She is a velodrome racer, a respected athlete of the most popular sport in America, up until the war that caused the Belgians to bury everything. Up and down the Great Lakes and in every metropolitan area with the guts to call itself a city lives at least one velodrome; post-Depression Chicago has six. This is during a time when women have the newly obtained right to vote and are launching ever more successful campaigns for equality. Doris Kopsky is winning championships on the eastern seaboard and soon Lyli Herse will set speed and endurance records in France. So, it's a shock when one of the bosses of Schwinn writes back to my grandmother something to the effect of: "Mam, we make the best bicycles in the world for the greatest racers in the world, not women."

Schwinn will go on to cede its manufacturing base to Japan in the eighties, before folding entirely. Other, more equitable bike builders will take their place. Not to be deterred by the dinosaur chauvinists of Chicago, my grandmother writes to her friends William Harley and Arthur Davidson in Milwaukee, and asks if they'd make her a bike.

"Sure thing Elfreida, come visit in six weeks."

These family histories are always shrouded by the fog of the oral tradition, but there is a photographic history of at least this much: Harley and Davidson make my grandmother a bike, and a good one, designed exactly for her body type and aggressive riding style. Though whether through miscommunication or some other confusion, the builders constructed the wrong type of bike. Instead of fabricating her the sort with pedals and skinny tires, they make her the sort with a roaring engine. My grandmother takes up the new motorized version of cycling, calling her bike the "Buzz Machine."

My grandmother's shifting interest towards the convenience and quick thrills of motorization foretells the sporting preferences of the nation: as of the closing of the Finkl Steel factory, NASCAR is America's most popular spectator sport, and one where men and women compete as equals.

On the ride down to the velodrome, I pass the wreckage of a steam ship called the *Silver Spray*. It caught on fire and sunk one night while ferrying some college kids to a casino, south of the city. Zebra mussels, an alien mollusk species without natural predators or nutritional value, who can out-compete the native invertebrates — which are the basis of the Great Lakes aquatic food chain — surround the *Silver Spray* like chocolate sprinkles on a cupcake. From roosts like this their filter feeding helps to make Lake Michigan's waters cleaner than they've been in thirty years.

When the lake was at its dirtiest, Nike missiles were installed along the lakefront trail, ostensibly to defend us from the Soviets, but also to give jobs to the wards of the most powerful aldermen. The carcinogenic chemicals they used to wash the launch pads killed many more citizens than any foreign threat. Somewhere in a playground near one of the far southern parks that nobody ever visits there's a plaque about it. The contaminated sites are all fenced off these days. My path takes me along the western border of one, which they've turned into a bird sanctuary.

Past that, in a spot that used to be a beach, the parks department has designated a "native plants revitalization zone." Chicago's shore was once a prairie wetland, but it's hard to play beach volleyball in waist-high grass, so they scoured the sand until it turned raw. But now that much of the population has left the South Side, and the beach is mostly unused, the earthmovers lay dormant. Ecology experts wearing cargo pants and wide-brimmed hats plant seeds one day and spray poison the next, selecting their targets with scholarly precision. This is how a pristine ecosystem is sculpted.

The land the velodrome is on has a history of machines and sweat so old and persistent that it has eroded the topsoil away. For years they've been replacing it with trucked-in dirt from downstate, slowly covering the old steel mill foundations and toxic slag heaps left over from iron smelting. I pity the archaeology graduate students of the distant future, and the premises of their thesis papers: "Deadly Concrete: Why Ancient Americans Chose to Build on Lead-Infused Foundations."

This place is marked for "urban renewal." Three locked layers of fence protect the vacant velodrome, despite George's confidence that it'd be open. The racetrack is the first lonely triumph of those that would have the south shore of the city be inhabited by the types of people that make up the north shore: brave warriors of commerce. Competing groups have pledged hundreds of millions of dollars to make this lakefront property great (again). There will be a marina, an organic grocery store, a private school, four trillion square feet of retail space, dog parks. The row houses of the area — some boarded up, others not — will all be razed. As is the custom in America, the original residents will be vaulted to the highest pinnacles of society, and lauded for their pioneering spirit, as we send them away to make some other frontier fashionable.

All that remains and all that will remain of this ancient landscape are the giant red walls that run along a prehistoric shipping slip, in the heart of what was the center for American steel production. These walls, several thousand feet long, a couple dozen feet wide, and taller than anything within a mile, used to hold the raw iron ore brought down by ships from what are now ghost-infested mines surrounding Lake Superior. Too massive to be destroyed, there's a spot where it looks like somebody tried and failed with dynamite. Instead they managed to make a crack that allows climbers to negotiate their way to the top. From this perch, with my bike resting below, I can touch elevated train tracks: a crane on rails used to work up here. It would lift the ore from the ships and put it in the space between the two walls. Then trains (first horse powered, then steam powered, then turbo-diesel-electric powered) would come to pick up as much as they could fit and schlep it over to the smelter. I think I can still smell a vague metallic odor mixed with the lake's fishy scent.

From the lakeshore, Gary, Indiana, whose smokestacks still exhale flame, looks like a long, black birthday cake. Thousands of acres along Lake Michigan's southern tip are now uninhabitable, marked by the poisonous scars of one industry or another. The great sand dunes of Indiana that blocked northern winds since the ice age are now glass, melted and spread thin across the world by the once thriving window industry; the apple orchards of Michigan are turning fallow in response to a changing climate; even the lake is disappearing, flowing away out of the Chicago River, whose course was reversed during the era when the *Silver Spray* sank — or the lake *would be* draining, if it weren't for excessive runoff caused by the ever-expanding lakeside housing subdivision business and their pristine lawns, driveways, cul-du-sacs, and unhampered drainage.

I can see from where I stand, going on towards the horizon in every direction: empty lots and overgrown graveyards, rusting bridges and vacant docks. People lived, worked, and died here. They were experts in their trades. Their labors made Chicago one of the greatest cities on the continent. The poisonous land is their poltergeist, stuck in a cycle of warning to the next generation. In memory of these people, the lands they came from, and the land where their bodies now lay, the city has erected a statue at the foot of the great red wall. It's an eight-foot-tall figure of a faceless man clutching a woman, with two faceless children standing at his feet. It's made of bronze.

Mornings with Sarah Jindra

EILEEN FAVORITE

There's a sunshine delay on eastbound 290.
There's a bumper in the road on the Edens.

It's all due to a semi and a crashed car and a fire.
Southbound 294 is still suffering.

Starting out, with 90 as the trouble spot
But the outbound's doing OK.

All is well on the Reagan.

We have no Indiana issues.
Pretty heavy from the Junction on in.

The Ike is 30, in and out.
It's shaking up to be a pretty normal rush hour.

We've got a semi stuck under a viaduct.
Reports of people tobaggoning on Lake Shore Drive.

Got some troubles in the Niles area.
We have no Indiana tie-ups.

Residual delays from a rollover crash.
Count 41 long minutes to get you out to O'Hare.

Broken-down freight train at Archer.
Southbound, we're jammed.

Tough morning in Batavia.

We have a fatality crash.
They just reopened all the lanes,

after a helicopter landed.
IDOT's on the scene.

The Reagan's bumper-to-bumper.
Watch out for some fire activity at 96th and Ashland.

Solid on the Stevenson.

An earlier broken-down car is now off
to the shoulder.

64th and Kedzie? That's blocked
due to a bus hitting a building.

All four Illinois tollways looking decent.
Watch out for a fender bender at Grand.

The Edens hits a snag at Dempster.
The high-speed chase on the south-bound Ryan

has come to an end off 57.
Avoid 167th and Pulaski.
It's still a very active situation.
On the Ike, just a slow pocket at Harlem.

And public transportation is running on time.

U.S. 41

SANDRA MARCHETTI

On the second full
of the second season,
the rose-blue moon

stops Chicago
like a cork.
Bicycles chase

the lake. I ride
the starred Drive,
a carpet vacuumed

up to the Drake,
to lakeshore condos.
It's a scape

of bracken beaches
punched through
with legs.

Water begs
them, pedaling
to the lume.

They wait on
the lozenge
to flick and plume.

Come, otherworldly
and complete—
a wheel of flaked

stars, a dock
off a manicured
sandbar.

The city
erodes outside
my pillbox car.

Tonight the waves
thin in the moon,
cast my pink skin blue.

PREVIOUSLY PUBLISHED IN *SUGAR HOUSE REVIEW.*

the DIVIDED CITY

NORTH SIDER, SOUTH SIDER, BI-SIDER
BILL SAVAGE

I don't have to tell anyone here about the great divide in Chicago identity, North Side versus South Side. (To any West or East siders in the room, my apologies for your irrelevance.)

As a lifelong resident of the city's most northeasterly neighborhood, Rogers Park, I have always identified as a northsider. Encounters with southsiders — from four years at St. Ignatius to working with, or for, various White Sox fans and University of Chicago types — only reinforced my North Side identity. When confronted with your opposite, it's easy to hunker down into yourself.

My identity as a hard-core northsider began to change — for me, at least — in the summer of 2006, when my sweetheart decided to stop renting. Economic and personal considerations led her to buy in what, for the sake of pride and privacy, I'll call Greater Beverly.

OK, Evergreen Park, just over the border from Chicago.

Suddenly, I was living part-time in the vicinity of Ninety-fifth and Kedzie, much farther south and west than I'd ever regularly ventured on the South Side (where I mostly knew Comiskey and Hyde Park). I rode my bike the twenty-five miles down and back during good weather, or I took the Red Line between Ninety-fifth Street and Loyola, or caught the Metra out of La Salle Street.

How much of a northsider had I been? I hadn't even known there *was* a train station at La Salle Street until I first took the Rock Island District Line. I thought "Rock Island Line" was just a Johnny Cash song.

I began to get to know various parts of this alien-to-me area by biking through it and procuring the necessities of life.

The South Side, I saw, was all right.

Back north, I began to brag on certain South Side places: donuts at Beverly Bakery on Western, good sushi at Sesame Inn on Ninety-fifth, microbreweries at Horse Thief Hollow and Blue Island Beer Company. Friends, familiar with my North Side parochialism, gave me no end of shit about the fact that I was spending so much time south of the Loop — and apparently liking it.

I half-joked that I had become a Chicago freak: neither northsider nor southsider, I was a "bi-sider," at home in both parts of town. In each hood, I had the things I needed to feel at home.

By which I mean a bar, a butcher shop, a local grocery store, and a coffee shop. I found them all, and then lost each of them, one at a time.

First, I required a local tavern, something low-key and quiet. An Evergreen Park native (neither the Unabomber nor Norm) recommended Bleeker's Bowl as a joint I might like, and he was right. After biking down on summer Fridays, I'd stop in, re-hydrate and carbo load, read the paper, do the crossword. At first, the regulars — a mellow, older after-work or retired-with-little-to-do-but-drink crowd, just looked and nodded when I came in. As in any real neighborhood bar, they'd all known each other forever, and I was the new guy who sat at a table in the window and read the *New York Times*.

And who seemed to have ridden there on a bicycle.

On the South Side, I learned, if you were an adult male on a bicycle, people presumed that you couldn't drive due to your multiple DUI convictions. This assumption was especially, and understandably, common in various saloons.

The regulars and bartenders were friendly, and one guy started calling me "Lance," in honor of the bike, I assume. Soon we hit that perfect level of casual barroom acquaintanceship: we'd say hi, make some small talk about the Bears, Cubs, or Sox (the bartenders were mostly Cubs fans, the patrons mostly Sox rooters), I'd pretend to give a damn about golf or hockey, and then we'd let each other be.

When I disclosed exactly where I rode my bike from, general incredulity ensued. How on earth could I get to Ninety-fifth and Trumbull from 6500 North Sheridan . . . alive? Passing through . . . those neighborhoods? I replied that I never had any problems in African American or Latino neighborhoods, but sometimes in Bridgeport (presumably) Irish drivers didn't respect bike lanes as much as they perhaps should. I detailed my different routes and emphasized the danger I faced came from careless drivers rather than any particular neighborhood's demographic makeup. As the years went by, any time anyone had seen some helmeted white guy with a beard on a bike, they asked if that had been me. Apparently, only one guy can ride his bike down Damen, Halsted, or California.

Then I got word: the owners of Bleeker's were selling. To Binny's. A soulless corporate liquor store replacing a bowling alley and saloon? Gentrification in Evergreen Park?

That was the first blow.

Then the butcher's closed. As soon as I began spending time in the EP, some northsiders who were fans of Petey's Bungalow recommended AJ's Meat Market at Ninety-ninth and

Clifton Park. Best pork chops in town, I was told. Excellent pork chops, for sure, as well as rib-eye steaks cut to order. But the real winner was their homemade Lithuanian sausage.

This sausage? Outstanding, world-class. What didn't sell when fresh they smoked, which created the Platonic ideal of smoked sausage. If they have Slim Jims in Carnivore's Heaven, they'd be AJ's Smoked Lithuanian. I brought them back to the North Side for years as Christmas gifts, and people clamored for more. Where had I gotten this stuff? Ninety-ninth and where?

Northsiders. Such limited worlds they live in, I thought.

In 2014, the first warm weekend in the spring arrived after our brutal polar vortex winter, and I planned to clean up the Weber, hit AJ's for meat, and grill. Only then did my sweetheart tell me the bad news: AJ's had closed. She'd known for a while but hadn't wanted to shock me till she had to. Who knows what I might have done. The older man who owned it was retiring, his family and the part-timers (including a fireman who made the tastiest lamb burgers) didn't want to continue the hard work of running a local butcher shop.

It's been replaced by an Irish bar. Just what this section of Chicago was crying out for.

I've yet to find an equal to AJ's pork chops, and I despair that I will never taste that smoked Lithuanian sausage again.

Sometimes I dream of it.

The third strike came soon after: the local grocery store succumbed to the corporate giants. Lagen's, at Eighty-ninth and California, was a typical little Centrella-ish Chicago neighborhood "super" in-scare-quotes market. The place was in a time warp from 1975. Not someplace you go to stock up, but for that emergency run for bread or potatoes, well, they carried Gonnella, and the produce was OK. Some cans of chicken soup if you had a cold. Cat food, milk, butter, eggs, orange juice, the papers.

Well, in 2013, a Meijer opened in a vast ugly-as-bad-urban-planning-can-make-it mall at Ninety-first and Western. Naturally, the joint was mobbed, and though we tried to avoid shopping at it, it was cheap and had better selection. Then a Mariano's opened on Ninety-fifth, and Lagen's went from an every-few-weeks stop to an every-couple-months stop.

Then it closed. We blamed ourselves, rightly.

During that same time period, Hardboiled Coffee had a café on Western that all too briefly supplied my need for caffeine, wifi, and solid conversation about baseball that wasn't just call-and-response Sox-rule/Cubs-drool nonsense. But it too succumbed to the physical reality of Beverly, the lack of density and the high-volume streets, that makes a café a hard sell. At least the brew is still available at County Fair, Wolf's Bakery, and some other cafés. But I'd loved that place, and it was gone, though now the space has been taken over by a local coffee roasting empire — though not Intelligentsia or Metropolis from up north — Bridgeport Coffee.

Who ever thought that the South Side would have competing artisanal coffee empires?

Nonetheless, I'd lost another essential place.

And then I felt like a true southsider.

Over these last ten years, I've learned that the sense of belonging to a neighborhood in Chicago isn't just about where you were born, or how much time you spend there, or how many neighbors you get to know, or how many formal or informal institutions you interact with.

Now, I don't just like the neighborhood. Just as I miss the parts of Rogers Park that are long gone — Hamilton's, Bornhofen's butcher shop, Dominick's, Ennui Café — I lament the parts of the South Side that I've lost.

In Chicago, on either side of town, maybe you only realize something is yours when it's taken away from you.

1964 Red Buick

ELAINE HEGWOOD BOWEN

It's 1965, and it's time again for my father to purchase an almost-new car. My father walks less than a mile from our home to Crown Buick Company at Sixty-third Street and Throop and buys a fire engine red Buick Riviera. He had previously marveled at this beauty in the showroom. As he negotiates a price, my sister Audrey and I take advantage of a warm October day to walk to Coney Island at Sixty-third Street and Ada, just west of Crown. Coney Island is the neighborhood fast food joint (I guess it was named after the famous New York attraction).

Well, let me correct that: Coney Island is the place where the youngsters hang out. Nan's on Sixty-third Street and Loomis, and later Red Apple on Sixty-third Street and Ashland, which was owned by a former Sixteenth Ward Committeeman Jim "Bulljive" Taylor, and the Walgreens restaurant on the other corner catered to the mature crowd of this Englewood neighborhood. You see, during that time, as is now, the political machine in Chicago was in full throttle. Years earlier, Chicago was one of the first cities where blacks attained great political influence. Oscar DePriest became Chicago's first black councilman in 1915 and in 1928; he became the first black elected to the United States House of Representatives in the twentieth century. As a matter of fact, blacks had won the official right to vote in 1965 with the Voting Rights Act, and local politicians and their cohorts were taking full advantage of this. It was common to have folks canvass in the community for whatever election was coming up, and my folks were active citizens in the process. It was a big thing to go up to the polling place with them, which was then located at the local elementary school.

People would mill around, talking about one candidate or the other. So Taylor's restaurant was always crowded, with folks ordering fried chicken, chitlins, and whatever was the featured "bean" of the day, along with cornbread muffins, while discussing current political issues. After the grown folks ate at the restaurant, they could walk a couple of blocks and further enjoy themselves with liquor and other "packaged goods" from the Rothschild's, which was located on the southeast corner of Sixty-third Street and Loomis. There was always some brutha in front of Rothschild's, who seemed to be drunker than the customers going in, who served as the doorman — in hopes of getting tips to buy more liquor. One such doorman was a man whose brother had recently been killed. When asked one day about his brother's murder, he shrugged his shoulders and said, "He's gone, but I'm still here."

My usual order at Coney Island is a burger and fries and, of course, a "suicide." A suicide is a soft drink made from a variety of the fountain flavors. My preference is more coke and orange flavors; something that I still order at the movie theaters even to this day. "May I help you?" the clerk asked from behind the counter. "Give us two cheeseburgers, please," my sister and I both answered in unison. You see, we weren't twins, but we often behaved as such. The burgers came with fries at no extra charge. Most of the beef to feed the free world was being slaughtered right here in Chicago, so it was easy to come by.

As my father proudly deposits $400 on a nearly $3,163 debt — leaving him with a thirty-six-month, $77.60 note give or take — we reluctantly clunk down what seems to be a life's savings of change for our food. As he drives past the Del Farm grocery store, also at Sixty-third Street and Loomis, reality hits him. He has to give my mother money for food. That's alright. We may have to eat beans and cornbread for a couple of days, but we are sure gonna look good in that red Riviera. That intersection is busy at this time of day. The rush hour buses running up and down the two streets take passengers either south on Loomis or west on Sixty-third Street from the final stop on the L line. Sixty-third Street is the business district of this neighborhood. (Yes, this is the same Sixty-third Street that the late Marvin Gaye sings about in "Hitchhike.")

Between Halsted to the east and Ashland to the west are a myriad of shops and restaurants that blacks are welcome to patronize. Throughout the years, Thompson's Barber Shop has also served as the local polling place at election time. A Mandl and Sons Cleaners advertises a "plant on premises." One of their specialties is blocking hats, and my father uses this service to clean his Dobbs hats that he most likely purchased at Howard Style Shops, down on Maxwell Street near Halsted — or what at that time was called Jew Town (to recognize the many shop owners who were Jewish). The shirts, suits, and dresses would always be so nicely cleaned and pressed. If you peered past the front counter, you could see the guy operating the pressing machine. This glimpse into the dry cleaning business would further manifest itself a few years later, as one of my father's brothers would open his own dry cleaning business over in the Gresham neighborhood. As teens we would hang out on a Saturday, placing garments on hangers and pulling the plastic over each order to keep the clothes fresh and crisp. When you drive down Eighty-seventh Street near Halsted you can still see the sign, "Hegwood Cleaners," in the window.

Then there is Sarah's Beauty Salon, which is always filled with women vying to look beautiful, especially on the weekends. There are even two banks within this short area — Chicago City Bank and Trust Company and the Ashland and Sixty-third State Bank, as well as a hospital named Englewood Hospital. The neighborhood to the west of Ashland is entirely white and even though our money is green, we are not welcome to shop there.

On our way back from Coney Island, with small, greasy brown paper bags and over-filled, brimming paper cups, we would spend the rest of our pennies on candy at Big Mama's grocery store. It takes us a while to arrive home, but it takes my father even longer. Although we live only moments from the car dealership, my father takes a leisurely drive home, beaming with pride every block of the way. This fond memory of the Englewood community will always remain in my heart, just as memories of my father and his new Buick always bring a smile to my face — a smile as wide as the grill on that bright, red Buick Riviera.

PREVIOUSLY PUBLISHED IN *OLD SCHOOL ADVENTURES FROM ENGLEWOOD: SOUTH SIDE OF CHICAGO* (LULU PUBLISHING, 2014), BY ELAINE HEGWOOD BOWEN.

poetry

seven years
QURAYSH ALI LANSANA

eight hundred miles away for two thousand
five hundred and fifty-five days blanketed
in the melanin rich cocoon of the south side.

jacob squatted in hollow of tree for one hundred
sixty-eight hours til slave catchers passed. only
duppies, good and ornery, vex me here

where it is possible to function, to dream
and never interact with a person of non-
color. more black owned businesses in

my neighborhood than my hometown. can
be thug, threat, teacher, artist, arse, poet
professor, writer, worrier. but sad nigga

in enid, my view obscured by headstones
prison and ferguson. the fools gold of distance.
damp musk of time. grief decomposes on I-44

weather lovely, the politics fucked. fracked up
earth twitches, spits greed. we drive by anyway
led by dollar signs. an uneven stretch of lonely road.

PREVIOUSLY PUBLISHED IN *REVISE THE PSALM: WORK CELEBRATING THE WRITING OF GWENDOLYN BROOKS*, EDITED BY QURAYSH ALI LANSANA AND SANDRA OPOKU-JACKSON (CURBSIDE SPLENDOR, 2017).

Fun Town: Chicago's Last Amusement Park

JAKE AUSTEN

Marcie Hill was seven years old when the fun died. In 1982, Fun Town, the last amusement park within Chicago's city limits, ended its thirty-two-year run of thrilling south-side children. For Hill, warm memories of spending time with her mother in a dynamic communal space in her own neighborhood linger every time she passes the strip malls that now occupy the real estate at Ninety-fifth Street between Stony Island and Jeffrey Boulevard.

Upon realizing her memories were murky (she recalls the pride of being able to go on small-scale rides by herself, but not the exact rides), Hill began researching the park for Shorty, her South Side-themed blog. Though her search turned up a treasure trove of information about Riverview, the massive North Side amusement park that enchanted Chicago from 1904 through 1967, there was virtually nothing about Fun Town. One of the only mentions of the park in the *Chicago Tribune* was a tiny obituary of the park's founder with wildly inaccurate information, and the Newberry Library's *Encyclopedia of Chicago* documents numerous amusement parks, but omits her favorite one.

"As relevant as Fun Town was to my people, there should have been more press and more information available," Hill laments. "This was an important part of Chicago history and black history. To see no record of it... it feels like people just don't value the South Side."

It's not too surprising that a modest eight-acre park, which at its peak had a couple of dozen rides, has been given history's cold shoulder. One of Chicago's defining achievements was hosting the grandest carnival imaginable, the 1893 World's Fair (followed forty years later by its modernist sequel). And Riverview was spectacular: 140 acres filled with over a hundred attractions, including the massive Fireball rollercoaster, and a full sideshow. Yet it's understandable that southsiders who held Fun Town dear, and who have come to expect patterns of second-class treatment, feel slighted every few years when yet another PBS special casts a nostalgic eye upon Riverview's tattooed ladies and world-class coasters.

Despite its size Fun Town was important. At its birth it represented the baby boomers' early influence on American amusements. In the 1960s when radical shifts in the racial demographics of the South Side took place, it peacefully transitioned from a majority white park to a majority black park while recreation spots around the city and the country were experiencing riots and protests. And during the seventies, thanks to black management, a funky jingle, and doors opened by Riverview's doors shutting, it became a source of community pride in the heart of the black pride era. By ignoring the action that took place at 1711 E. Ninety-fifth Street, history has been missing out on some serious fun.

o o o

In 1950 Harold "Cookoo" Greenwald, a South Shore entrepreneur, built the park, originally called Kiddy Town, from the ground up. Prior to that endeavor, Greenwald (who lettered in football at the University of Michigan in 1926 and was recruited by the NFL's Chicago Cardinals, but did not make the team), managed the Lion's Club downtown, worked as a store detective at Goldblatt's, and owned taverns. His son, Ted Greenwald, doesn't recall what motivated his father to go into the amusement park industry, but at that time, "kiddie" parks (with smaller, tamer rides than standard amusement parks) were a burgeoning business thanks to the postwar baby boom. Though the idea was not new (Kiddieland in Melrose Park, a northwest Chicago suburb, opened in 1929), in the fifties these parks rapidly proliferated. A 1953 newspaper ad (refuting a rumor about deadly rattlesnake attacks at local parks) listed fourteen Chicagoland members of the Kiddie Park Operators' Association.

In the 1950s the park established many of the features it would proudly host for most of its run, including pony rides, go karts, trampolines, a small roller coaster, mini golf, and merry-go-rounds (including the Kiddie Tank Ride, with World War II-era tanks in place of horses). Though tiny compared to Riverview, for the tiny ones in the region it was paradise.

"The best part of my life was growing up on the South Side," recalls Dianne White, who lived in South Shore in the fifties and sixties. "Kiddy Town was so exciting, right off of a busy street, just this colorful place in the heart of the South Side. If we got good grades, we were allowed to go. It was a place we really considered to be our own. Riverview was for the North Side, but this was close to our house."

At the time the demographics of the park clientele reflected the population of the area, which had many Jewish and Greek Orthodox families (the Nation of Islam's Mosque Maryam on Stony Island was originally a Greek Orthodox church). Some Hispanic and black families visited the park, but the customers were overwhelmingly white.

Some time in the Sixties, Alan Carvell, Jr. and his wife June Marie Carvell took over park ownership. They also owned the Rainbo ice skating rink on the North Side (later the Rainbo roller rink), which briefly doubled as the Kinetic Playground in the 1960s, a rock club that hosted Jimi Hendrix, Led Zeppelin, and the Who.

Around 1968, presumably in reaction to the closing of Riverview, Kiddy Town acquired a Wild Mouse roller coaster, a Rock-O-Plane ride, and other attractions aimed at older kids and teens. The name was changed to Fun Town (sometimes written as Funtown), and the park's phone book display ad now boasted a whopping eighteen rides (to go along with go karts, batting cages, and a "swinging gym"). The patrons, by then predominantly black, enjoyed a park that was often bustling, but never overcrowded. There were rarely long lines to board the Moon Rocket, take a spin on the Trabant, or go down the Astro Slide. And the prices were fair, with no admission charge, cheap ride tickets, half price coupons from Jewel supermarket, and (according to a 1971 ad) all day ride passes on special days for $2.

The park's chain of ownership has been difficult to verify, especially in the later years when it may have changed hands several times, and ownership/management groups may have been involved. The park leased out various sections, receiving rent and a percentage of receipts, so the arcade, for example, had a separate owner. Keith McDonald, who worked at the park from 1973 to 1975 stocking the food stands with cotton candy, corndogs, and sno-cone fixings, told me he believed several police officers, including Ira Harris, were park owners, but that does not appear to be the case, though Harris was in upper management, and did most of the hiring. David Dines, a ride operator and park marshal from 1975 to 1982 believes the Carvells maintained ownership until 1977. He attributes the park's decline to the 1977 takeover (either as owners or managers) by Jack Thompson Shows, an out of town interest that ran the park like a low-grade travelling carnival. After several years of bad management, he says, a well-intentioned man named Bob Johnson became the final owner, renaming it Big "J" Funtown, before the park gave its last ride in 1982.

o o o

Perhaps contributing to Fun Town's low historical profile was summer after summer of uneventful amusements. Though Riverview's long tenure saw several ride-related deaths, and seventy-two riders injured in a 1937 roller coaster accident, no such excitement occurred on the South Side. Ted Greenwald, who worked part time at his father's park as a ride operator ("he promised I would get to run the Shetland pony concession, but I never got it,") doesn't recall any serious accidents in the fifties, and the only lawsuit he remembers involved a child being slightly bruised after falling off a train ride. Bob Gas, whose father was the maintenance manager from 1965 until 1982, and whose mother worked in the kitchen (Bob worked concessions) is pretty sure there were no serious injuries or deaths (not even from snake attacks) during his years there. "My Dad took great pride in making sure that every nut and bolt was checked and double tightened, especially on the larger rides."

The countless kids protected by Mr. Gas's busy wrench included many groups of underprivileged children brought on trips by a variety of organizations. The Chicago Defender newspaper documented a 1965 free day for a thousand West Side kids sponsored by the Chicago Commission of Youth Welfare and the Chicago Committee on Urban Opportunity. The Englewood Urban Progress Center brought seven hundred kids to the park in 1970. The Defender announced the Twenty-first Police District-sponsored

Fun Day bringing in three thousand kids in 1971. Jesse Jackson's Operation Push also hosted events, and Mayor Richard J. Daley bussed in kids from city day camps.

Like many southsiders, Keith McDonald's childhood visits to Riverview made deep impressions, but ultimately he felt more of an affinity to the park in his backyard. "On the South Side you didn't see people outside of your ethnic group, but at Riverview you saw everybody," he remembers. "It was so big, and they had the guy with the bubble eyes and the lady with the beard…but Fun Town was in my neighborhood. Seeing excitement on familiar faces, hearing James Brown music at the batting cages, having a place for all the teenagers to hang out…we had cotton candy back then, we didn't have shootings."

ooo

Unlike legendary parks like Riverview and Brooklyn's Coney Island, Fun Town is rarely cited as a cultural reference (Chicago rapper Common makes a brief mention in his nostalgic 1994 song "Nuthin' To Do," and one book from Arcadia Publishing has a photo from the 1950s mislabeled as "Kiddyland"). However, a different Funtown looms large in American culture. In Dr. Martin Luther King's powerful 1963 "Letter from Birmingham Jail," the Civil Rights leader recalls his daughter's excitement at seeing a TV commercial for a local amusement park, followed by "tears welling up in her eyes when she is told that Funtown is closed to colored children." That story (most recently revived in Martin Luther King III's 2013 children's book, *My Daddy, Martin Luther King, Jr.*) was about an Atlanta park with a far different history than Chicago's Fun Town (despite both operating a Wild Mouse coaster). But the story does bring up two subjects that make Chicago's Fun Town so important to Southsiders: promotions and racial politics.

In contrast to Atlanta's park, Fun Town in Chicago didn't advertise on television (though in the fifties when TV personalities like Two Ton Baker made park appearances, their fee also paid for an announcement of the event on their show). But mention Fun Town to nearly any Chicagoan who listened to black local radio in the 1970s and they likely will respond in song, wistfully recalling the popular jingle, "Fun Town, Fun Town for the kids and you / Ninety-fifth and Stony Island Av-e-nue…Fun Town!" Though the park also advertised itself with a small fire truck with "Fun Town" painted on the door (which would pick up kids for birthday parties), by far their most successful promotional activity in the seventies was placing this infectious jingle on Chicago black radio stations WVON, WJPC, and WMPP (the East Chicago Heights station that also served Gary, Indiana's R&B needs). Though Fun Town's radio commercials changed over the years (they sometimes featured mascot Suzy Funtown, a character resembling Stephanie Mills's Dorothy from *The Wiz*, who also made live park appearances), the joyous jingle remained the same.

The song was the handiwork of Richard Pegue, an iconic figure in Chicago radio. As a teen in the late fifties, like many of his peers, he had a high school vocal group. But Pegue didn't just want his songs played on the radio, he wanted to understand every aspect of radio and music production. The teen tape machine tinkerer began working behind the scenes writing, producing, and engineering music, as well as deejaying neighborhood parties. He eventually gained fame as one of the "Good Guys," the legendary disc jockeys at WVON ("The Voice of the Negro," the influential station owned by the Chess Brothers). Less prominent was his music production career, but as Numero Group's 2011 compilation of his productions argues, Pegue was a special talent. In a town famed for sweet harmonies, he arranged and recorded some of the sweetest, and his compositions and arrangements were groovy, whimsical, and memorable.

But after his failure to produce a hit record by the early seventies, his record producing dreams were put on the back shelf. Pegue, however, never stopped recording. He had a knack for jingle writing and over the years he produced memorable local spots for North Grand Auto Parts, Wallace's Catfish Corner (featuring soulman Otis Clay on vocals), and his most enduring promotion, the Moo and Oink meat warehouse ads that he continued to record weekly in his analog home studio until he passed away in 2009. "His commercials weren't slapped together," recalls disc jockey PJ Willis, a Pegue protégé who sometimes helped on the spots. "He had a personal touch you don't usually hear in commercial work."

That was the touch he applied to his great 1970 Fun Town jingle, the recording that started his alternate career. "I was working at WVON," Pegue told Chicago soul historian Bob Abrahamian in a 2009 interview, "and one of the salesmen had an account for an amusement park...I heard their commercials and they were rather blasé. So I struck up an association with the people who ran the park, and they said they need something, and I said I need something...money!" Pegue's first jingle borrowed a backing track from a 1969 studio instrumental he produced called "For Brothers Only" by the group The Brothers & Sisters, though the vocal act has little to do on the lyric-free song (a serial recycler, in 1981 Pegue would add jingle bells to the track and use it again for a radio station Christmas single). After adding professional singers emoting the catchy couplet, and a voiceover by a young WVON newsman, Larry Langford, Pegue's production was solid but needed something extra to appeal to the Fun Town crowd.

Eight year-old Lorenzo Modeste and his ten year-old sister Lisa Ramirez were brought by their mother, a friend of Pegue's, to the WVON studios. They put on headphones, got behind the microphone and did the spoken intro ("Hey mama, hey daddy, let's go to Fun Town...") and then sang along with the pre-recorded vocal tracks. Pegue paid their mother enough to buy the children a dresser for their bedroom, but the real compensation came when the song hit the WVON airwaves less than a week later. "Within a few days," Modeste (now a dentist in Virginia) recalls, "we became instant celebrities." The song remained on the air until he graduated high school. In addition, the "Fun Town Kids" received free ride tickets for the rest of their childhoods.

The popularity of the jingle was proven on the days Lisa and Lorenzo mounted the Funtown Stage (not to be confused with the short-lived, Pegue-programmed Funtown Disco Stage, a thirty-five-foot flatbed trailer precariously parked on the inclined concrete of the former batting cages). The siblings sang along to their "hit" as the crowd cheered the youngsters, thrilled to see the radio stars in the flesh. (Pegue fans should note that Lisa was also the juvenile voice declaring, "You got a funny name," at the start of each of his radio shows.)

Though that jingle remains the most memorable facet of Fun Town, the park's real legacy may be the way it survived and thrived during the seventies when urban amusement parks were disappearing. Specifically, Fun Town, unlike so many amusement parks around the country, did not disappear because a black populace took over the neighborhood. Instead it flourished, becoming a point of pride for teens holding down their first jobs, parents appreciating affordable family entertainment, and kids able to experience something special without leaving their corner of the city. In an era when an ethos of self-sufficiency was profoundly important to the black community, Fun Town was something Southsiders felt belonged to them.

That narrative is unique, according to University at Buffalo professor Victoria Wolcott, author of *Race, Riots, and Roller Coasters*. As racial populations shifted in the twentieth century, urban recreational facilities wary of desegregation were often sites of violence and protests. Midwest unrest ensued in Cleveland (where a Euclid Beach security guard shot an off-duty black police officer during a desegregation protest), in Cincinnati (where protestor's spent nine years picketing, blocking gates, and going to jail to fully integrate their Coney Island amusement park), and four and a half miles from Fun Town at Rainbow Beach, the site of a 1961 "wade in" demonstration, in which black and white swimmers entered the water together, and were subsequently attacked by white youth gangs throwing rocks. At Riverview Park, black patrons were admitted, but were likely uncomfortable with the "Dunk the Nigger" dunk tank attraction on the midway (later re-named "The African Dip," and ultimately shut down after NAACP protests in the late 1950s). Many parks (including Atlanta's Funtown) closed rather than dealing with integration. According to Wolcott, the massive suburban parks that replaced them used high entrance fees (as opposed to cheap per-ride tickets) to filter out undesired populaces.

Fun Town avoided these tensions, in part because white flight was so rapid in the area. In 1968 there was only one black girl in Dianne White's eighth grade class but by 1970 hers was one of only three remaining white families in the neighborhood. The amusement park's demographic shift followed suit. The park may have also avoided some of the tensions that plagued other sites because it catered only to small children during much of the fifties and sixties, the influx of "threatening" black teens coming only after the 1968 shift to the Fun Town name, when white families were already leaving the area. One disturbing urban myth that plagued Riverview claimed it was a space for black teenagers to rape white girls.

In contrast, instead of damning black youth with dangerous stereotypes, Fun Town presented them with models of success, and not only with visiting celebrities like Pegue, fellow Good Guy Herb Kent, and athletes like Ernie Banks. Because Fun Town was closed in the winter, and only operated weekends when school was in session, the black managers and concession owners were moonlighting at the park, and many had successful outside careers. Leo Ammons, who owned the carnival games, also had his own construction company. And Ira Harris was one of the more prominent African American police officers in Chicago. He would go on to be president of NOBLE, the National

Organization of Black Law Enforcement Executives, and also served as Chief of Police of the Chicago Housing Authority.

Fun Town represented opportunity for many local teens. Terrance Morris, now Operations Director for CAN-TV (Chicago's cable access network), managed carnival games at the park from 1972 through 1976, starting when he was barely a teen. "Working there taught me responsibility, and showed us it was possible to make something of ourselves. A lot of what I do in my job today I learned working at Fun Town."

One anecdote McDonald wistfully recalls says it all for him in terms of what Fun Town meant to the South Side. "One time I had to close and didn't leave until after eleven, and while I was waiting for the bus at Ninety-fifth and Stony a policeman approached and asked to see my ID. But then he saw my red and white Fun Town shirt, and that was ID enough. That shirt was iconic in the neighborhood, if you worked at Fun Town everyone knew you were OK."

o o o

By the early eighties, Fun Town was not OK. Mismanagement chipped away at the good-will associated with the park. Increasing poverty in a neighborhood where once everyone could work in the nearby U.S. Steel mill, which laid off half its workers by 1980, led to increased crime. Gas recalls overnight break-ins which resulted in German shepherd dogs patrolling the park at night. "Sadly," he says "several of them were found dead, some poisoned and some shot." The increasing popularity of the suburban mega-amusement park Great America, which opened in 1976, was the final nail in Fun Town's casket. "There were some nights," David Dines recalls, "where there might have been five customers in the park. It was really sad and hopeless." In 1982 the rides were auctioned, the land sold, and Chicago's last amusement park was no more.

"Places of urban recreation were such important spaces for residents of these communities," Wolcott reflects. "It's sad they no longer exist."

Terrance Morris concurs. "Fun Town did a lot for the neighborhood in terms of giving kids a safe environment. It was a meeting place, not a lot of riffraff hanging around. If there were something like that today maybe we wouldn't have so much of this violence."

THANKS TO Bob Abrahamian, Bill Dahl, David Dines, Bob Gas, Ted Greenwald, Al Greer, Marcie Hill, Cynthia Plaster Caster, Lisa Ramirez Martin, Keith McDonald, Lorenzo Modeste, Terrance Morris, Erica Rizzio, Rob Sevier, Mario Smith, Richard Steele, Gary Tyson, Alex White, Dianne White, PJ Willis, and Dr. Victoria Wolcott.

PREVIOUSLY PUBLISHED IN *BELT MAGAZINE*.

Rogers Park *Botanica*

DAVID MATHEWS

For Robert James Russell

It was off of Clark Street. I am not sure if it is still there. It
was not far from a sighting of a Christ image on a tree near a
bus stop on Touhy Avenue. I was with someone who I wasn't
sure was my girlfriend or not, on what would have been our
third date, if someone was keeping track. She came in often
and wanted to stop in while we were passing by. We waited
among the shelves stacked with sentries of *Santeria orishas*
disguised as my familiar saints, for Estella, who would tell us
our fortunes. Her *nietos* spoke Spanglish and flipped between
afternoon talk shows in the old storefront's backroom-turned-
living room. Estella eventually sauntered in with six Sears
shopping bags, three in each hand. To my companion she
greeted, *"Hola, bienvenida de nuevo,"* to me, *"Mucho gusto,"* to
us both, "I be right back."

Once she settled in, she read for my friend first, then for me.
Estella would not let my friend come in to translate — they
spoke seriously about it. After putting her hand up and
giving her a stare down, Estella simply told her, *"Esta bien."*
We prayed together in a combination of broken Spanglish
mixed with Latin, before she went about her card-work,
with her *abuela* poker face on. I could sense she could sense
that gypsy blood brought over with my ancestors. I was not
a mark anymore — she liked whatever magic was in me,
in us to share. She did not speak English well, but I could

understand what she was trying to say. Estella started to tell me things she shouldn't know, like the fire I felt coming that I stopped before it burnt my work, and I wondered, *perhaps she has the sight*, Just then she gave me a freebie, "Your friend is not worth your time. The spirits are uneven in her house." She warned me, "You have all the papers all about the house, cherish them as if they were your namesake's psalms." Then she hugged me, the way my *Babicka* would on Christmas or after long absences or before long goodbyes.

She tried to up-sell me on some candles and incense sticks explaining they would help quicken her predictions, as I started to smell grilled cheese sandwiches while hearing *reggaeton* music videos from the show Estella's *nietos* decided finally to watch.

PREVIOUSLY PUBLISHED BY *CHEAP POP*.

ALL SALES FINAL

SHARON BLOYD-PESHKIN

It's a cold, grey, blustery March morning on Chicago's near North Side. Taxis, delivery trucks, and luxury vehicles swoosh along Grand Avenue and Orleans Street, kicking up road salt, honking and jockeying for space as they pass condo buildings, self-storage facilities, coffee shops, and investment firms.

River North, promoted by the city as "the go-to district for those who appreciate fine art and design," has undergone an almost complete transformation in the past four decades, from a place of manufacturing to a locus of consumption. Long gone are most of the factories and the blue-collar workers who once gave this part of the City of Big Shoulders its brawn; in their stead, the neighborhood now warehouses workers of a white-collar sort, and the shops, restaurants, bars, and services that supply their more patrician needs.

But in the shadow of the new construction, an older, three-story building remains: Clark & Barlow Hardware, a business that served Chicago's construction, manufacturing, and railroad industries for more than a century. It's a hardware store where men in Carhartts who actually wear them to work line up at the counter to request tools and parts that aren't stocked by the Ace Hardware down the street or the Home Depot across town; a place when the salespeople swiftly turn to the shelves behind them and extract those obscure items; a place where many employees have worked for their entire adult lives because, they say, they feel like a family.

A place that is closing.

LIQUIDATING TO THE BARE WALLS
Sale ends soon

The signs outside are unmistakable, from the banners flapping in the wind to the trucks pulling up at the loading dock to cart away deeply discounted merchandise. In the front hallway, the steel shelves are for sale, $25 per section. The hard hats are $5 each, final. Interested in the wood display cabinets? Make an offer.

Angela Mucci, sixty-four, sits in the first-floor office, processing some of the markdowns. She's worked at Clark & Barlow for more than half her life, starting at the downtown location, 123 W. Lake Street, which was displaced in 1980 by the soon-to-be-built State of Illinois Center (later renamed the James R. Thompson Center). She fondly recalls the variety of tasks she performed there, from patching together phone calls on the second-floor switchboard, to sending customers their change and receipts in metal cups that sped along an overhead wire. A frame containing two black-and-white photographs of the Lake Street location hangs above her desk.

But she's rarely at her desk — one of the reasons she has worked here so long. Rather, the soon-to-be-grandmother spends her work hours sending invoices, ordering out-of-stock items, and pushing carts and even brooms. "I don't want to sit in an office," she says. "I want to work like this."

The other reason is the people, she says, starting with Joseph J. Sullivan, who owned Clark & Barlow for forty-six years until his death in 2010. "It was a good place to work, and he was a good boss," Mucci says, pointing to Sullivan's photo on the wall. "It was a place that you really wanted to stay. It was like family."

In fact, for many people it really was family. Two of Sullivan's six children, Teri and Judy, worked at Clark & Barlow for decades. Mucci applied for a job because her sister, Sophie, worked at Clark & Barlow. Sophie met her husband, Marty, there. Many employees worked alongside their siblings and cousins. People stayed until they retired, and sometimes until they died.

Now long-time employees who once worked together to stock the shelves are endeavoring to empty them. "It was a great work environment," says Michelle Diaz, forty-five, who began at Clark & Barlow in 1991 and is now a manager.

Diaz, whose mother, sister, daughter, and cousin followed her to Clark & Barlow, is one of six remaining employees, down from twenty-three when the building and company were sold in 2012, and more than fifty when she started working here. She recalls her first boss, John Patdu, who came from the Philippines in 1972 when he was twenty-four years old. Patdu walked into the Lake Street location and saw "a bunch of old guys working there," Diaz says, but he applied for a job anyway and was hired in accounts payable. Patdu stayed for forty years. "Clark & Barlow was my first job and my last job," says Patdu, now sixty-eight, who retired after Joe Sullivan died.

The *Chicago Tribune* obituaries tell similar stories. There's Herbert Christiansen, who worked for Clark & Barlow for seventy-one years until his retirement at age ninety; and Harold Schroeder, who began as a stock clerk right out of high school, became a buyer, and retired at age sixty-five. They and other former colleagues are fondly remembered by the employees who remain during these final days.

Check it out.
70% OFF BOX PRICE
ALL SALES FINAL

"I've only been here fifteen years," says Don Schelberger, sixty-two, who works behind the counter. It took him about a year to figure out where everything was stashed on the shelves, but now, when a customer requests an item, no matter how unusual, "I can go any place in the building and know where it's at."

Over the past decade, he's watched the clientele change. At first, most customers were contractors, railroad laborers, and construction workers. Then the people who lived in the newly built condos started coming in. But the main client base remained those in the building trades.

"Hey, Dan. What time do you leave in the morning?" he asks Dan Mogan, who commutes in from the south suburbs before the store opens at 6:00 a.m.

"Five," replies Mogan, who has worked for Clark & Barlow for thirty-three years. "There's always someone outside waiting to buy something."

Mogan, too, applied for a job because his brother worked there. "I didn't know much about hardware," he admits. But after stints on the dock, at will call, and in shipping, he learned where everything was squirreled away and started working behind the counter.

The counter at Clark & Barlow was the front line for finding all manner of uncommon hardware. "There is no other place you can go and say, 'I need this screw,' and they know exactly where it is and will sell you one of them," Diaz says, pantomiming a customer holding up a singular object. "We were still one-on-one. We were more personal. We were known for our customer service."

Now customers poke around areas that previously were restricted to employees like Schelberger and Mogan. "It's strange watching people wandering through," Diaz says. They paw through the shelves, brush dust off old boxes, squint at unfamiliar parts. They ask whether they can still get a particular tape or tool or trowel. "We've been pulling things out that've been buried for the past twenty years," Schelberger says.

Sheldon Holden, fifty-five, an airport baggage handler who lives in Chicago, came in when he saw the signs outside. "I drove past here a week ago and I thought they were just having a big time sale," he says. "Then I looked at the signs real good and thought, 'Wait a minute; they're going out of business.'"

Holden recalls visiting Clark & Barlow with his father when he was a child, and becoming a regular customer when, as an adult, he owned an older home. "If you had something in your house that dated back to the forties, fifties, sixties, you could probably go in there and get something to replace it. You can't do that at Home Depot," he says. He also came in for advice. "If you was tackling a project you thought was hard, after you talked to them, it turned out it was simple."

"I'm going to miss the service," Holden says. "This was the Rolls Royce of hardware stores. It was the Last of the Mohicans."

That kind of customer satisfaction is what made working at Clark & Barlow attractive to Teri Sullivan, one of the owner's daughters, who worked for a car rental company before taking a job at the store in the mid-1990s. "The hard-to-find things, oh yeah, they'd come in and say, 'I was told you have everything,'" she says of the store's customers. "We totally cared about them and took it personally when they needed things and went out of our way to find them."

But the bread and butter of the business were contractors and construction workers. "I would say our business was 80 percent with contractors and 20 percent retail," says Patdu, who worked as Clark & Barlow's comptroller from 1975 until 2012.

Now construction trucks and vans are at the loading dock, and men in sweatshirts and work gloves who don't want to talk to reporters are hauling away what they can salvage. A group of Amish men from Ontario, Wisconsin, who stand out in their white shirts and brimmed hats, drive away with a load of axe and scythe handles along with miscellaneous hand tools and hardware.

"I know for a fact there's nothing like [Clark & Barlow] in the city," Teri Sullivan says. "They're going to have to go to a Home Depot, where they're not going to find those things, or online. They're not going to be able to go in and ask a person who can help."

"All the contractors are like, 'Oh my God. Where are we going to go?'" Mucci says.

$10 each
SOLD
Watch Your Step
Sale/Sale/Sale

Upstairs, past the hot pink and fluorescent green posters partially obscuring the neon "Decorative Hardware Showroom" sign, the dim lighting and the soft sound of an AM radio station create the atmosphere of a theater set. Track lighting illuminates a room full of boxes, most open and exposing sinks and toilets. A few bathtubs rest near the doorway, and some mirrors lean against the wall. You almost expect Willy Loman to come in and offer to sell you a bidet.

Judy Sullivan, another of Joe Sullivan's daughters, worked in the showroom for more than two decades. "We had everything, and if we didn't have it, we would get it," she recalls. Those were the days before the inventory was in computer databases, when sales were written up on paper and stored away in file cabinets. She left in 2012, about the time that Studio 41, a home design retailer of kitchen and bath fixtures, hardware, and cabinetry, purchased the business.

Across the hall is another room where floor-to-ceiling industrial shelves are crowded with lock sets, hinges, and cylinders. A poster of Miss Makita 2002, Amber Goetz, holding a drill, covers the side of a filing cabinet; a 1992 calendar with a tool-wielding blonde in a pink bikini is taped to a pole. A man in a backpack shuffles shelf to shelf, removes a lock set from its box, leaves both on separate shelves. The wind rattles the steel-frame windows.

The main offices inhabited a room full of beige metal cubicles, now deserted, where phone lists are still tacked above empty phone jacks. A few old IBM terminals remain, along with blank white boards and metal filing cabinets. A sheriff paid for the enormous safe, but hasn't yet come back to retrieve it. The lady who purchased the coffin carrier also needs to return for it before the building closes for good.

The basement, once off-limits, contains some of the oddest items: railroad car lifters, crane winches, scythe handles. A display board full of casters suggests the full cycle Clark & Barlow has been through over the past half century.

$5 each. Final.
All hinges $5 set
Pulls & Plates $10 each

The caster business is where Joe Sullivan got his start. He and his older brother, Harry, worked for Payson Manufacturing, selling industrial-grade casters. One of Sullivan's clients was Jack Barlow, co-owner of Clark & Barlow since 1923.

"After he worked for Payson for five or six years, he went to Mr. Barlow, who was old, and says, 'I respect you. I know that someday I want to run my own business. If one of your friends ever wants to get out of whatever business they're in, I'd be interested in talking to them,'" recalls Joe Sullivan, Jr., his oldest son. "So two years later, Mr. Barlow says, 'What do you think of this business?'"

According to Joe Sullivan, Jr. and all four of his sisters, what followed was a combination of savvy bargaining and gentlemanly behavior. The accounts differ in some of the particulars, but they agree that Sullivan got wind that someone else was interested and quickly consummated the deal, at which point the two shook hands. Then another offer was made—perhaps by Barlow's sons-in-law, perhaps by someone else—for more money. But in the end, Joe recalls, "My dad says, 'You shook my hand.' And Barlow says, 'You know, you're right. I did shake your hand; we've got a deal.'"

By all accounts, Clark & Barlow thrived under Sullivan's ownership. It expanded from one to four locations; Sullivan's family of eight moved from a three-bedroom house to a six-bedroom house. Sullivan was beloved by his employees in part because he didn't interfere too much with the daily operations of the business. Instead, he was out making connections and sealing deals, as well as pursuing his own eclectic interests, which included playing golf, racing horses, and singing in local bars. "My dad didn't live to work at all," Joe Sullivan, Jr. says. "He said, 'This is great. I don't want to grow the business any more. I'm very comfortable.' So it's not the American dream of dominating the Chicago area."

But while Sullivan hewed to Barlow's vision—stocking the shelves with everything anyone could possibly need, prioritizing hands-on customer service over computerization and cost-cutting—things changed around Clark & Barlow. Discount, big-box hardware stores moved into the neighborhood; the internet provided information about and access to hard-to-find items; competition among online retailers led to quick and cheap delivery. Business began to drop off. Clark & Barlow closed the other locations, but even in River North revenue dwindled. At its peak, Joe Sullivan, Jr. estimates Clark & Barlow did $10 million in sales. By 2015, it was down to a quarter of that. And meanwhile, costs were skyrocketing. Real estate taxes alone were $80,000. "Clark & Barlow, they're not here any more because they didn't change. My dad didn't change," he says. "They continued to do business the old-fashioned way, and ultimately that led to their demise."

After Joe Sullivan, Sr. died, his children looked at the books. Again, accounts differ a bit, but they sold the building and the land to Onni Group for $8.8 million, and the business to Studio 41 for an undisclosed amount that is rumored to have been very low. Joe Sullivan, Jr. took care of the handshake on this transaction, but it was far more formal. In exchange for purchasing the business, Studio 41 agreed to offer every Clark & Barlow employee a job and take care of emptying out decades of inventory from the building. "I look at Studio 41 as, they saved us," Joe Sullivan, Jr. says. "Studio 41 did Clark & Barlow a favor, and Clark & Barlow did Studio 41 a favor because of the name, the history, etc."

"It was sentimental. It was a little heartbreaking to see it go," says his sister, Amy Schroeder.

Make an offer
SOLD!

After Studio 41 purchased the business, most of the employees stayed on until the building was emptied. Only Michelle Diaz and two other Clark & Barlow employees accepted the offer to continue on working for Studio 41.

After that, the great sell-off began. Prices were steadily reduced; spaces were gradually cleared. Eventually the cleaning service was discontinued and the employees had to clean the bathrooms and sweep the floors themselves.

"I think the last day is going to be the hardest because it's an era that's ending and who knows what's really going to happen?" says Diaz.

Most of the long-timers have decided they don't want to find out. "I think I'm just going to call it a day," Schelberger says. "That's enough. It's hard."

Mucci, too, chose not to take a job at Studio 41. "I have my good memories, so that's it," she says. "When Mr. Sullivan passed away, to me the store passed away.'"

On a dreary March afternoon, this is how it ends, slowly, bit by bit, bolt by bolt, as the wind blows leaves around the dumpster outside.

Previously published in Belt Magazine.

THE PANTRY

MICHAEL A. VAN KERCKHOVE

"We are the opposite of Hitler."

That's how a coworker once put our restaurant job into perspective during a particularly trying shift. As in, as waiters, we feed people. And we manage to facilitate joyful experiences. Sure, we deal with needy customers, screaming children, and gooey, raw pizza dough occasionally clogging the moving parts of a service shift, but we are ultimately doing good — even as our souls and muscles squeeze through the proverbial ringer. My coworker's words offer fleeting but valuable comfort, and as I forge a creative career path that does not involve waiting tables, I in the end want my work to matter.

The Lakeview Pantry, a food distribution and social services organization founded in 1970, also feeds people and does good. The Pantry is currently nestled on Chicago's North Side at the border between the Lakeview and Uptown neighborhoods; between the condo I recently purchased with my husband Ernie north of Irving Park Road in Uptown (where prices have a helpful way of dropping) and our old apartment south of Addison Street in Lakeview. As a longtime neighborhood resident, I've walked and bused past the Pantry many times, always meaning to drop off a bag of groceries or volunteer some other day.

Perhaps the Catholic church bells across the street from our new home are in part responsible for finally getting me through the doors to volunteer. The bells, cutting through the grey Chicago winter from their early twentieth-century, arched-window tower, provide a soothing daily soundtrack. And for a moment or two, I am climbing into the back of my family's station wagon Sunday mornings before Mass, bells ringing faceless from Detroit area churches out of sight. I am at church basement potluck dinners. And I am choosing non-perishable offerings from my family's own pantry for school food drives and watching our classroom's donations box piling higher and higher with canned corn and boxed macaroni-and-cheese — which I hope stayed mostly local for the hungry people of Detroit rather than being sent to Ethiopia or Peru or somewhere else the nuns were always flying off to.

Easter is early this year, and the blessed foreheads of Ash Wednesday and the hyper hearts of Valentine's Day stumble over each other confused. I am now a non-practicing Catholic to put it politely, but this Lenten season of sacrifice has a way of sticking, and I believe maintaining "good person" status will ultimately help. Giving up ice cream for six weeks as a kid may not have exactly pushed me closer to Jesus, but this chilly time of year can still inspire me to strip away some of life's distraction and to do some good in this world.

o o o

It's 11:30 a.m. on the morning of my first day as a volunteer. A handful of us are back behind the Pantry, unloading a van full of donations from area grocery stores, primarily Trader Joe's, Whole Foods, and Jewel. I am comforted to know that not all excess supermarket inventory is wasted. From inside the van, Ray, ponytailed and maybe in his early sixties, and Luke, who's maybe in his early thirties, hand us crates of sliced bread, produce, ice cream, and flowers. We are preparing for the distribution half of our shift, which will start at noon.

A green bell pepper flies from the back of the van, smashes into bits against the open dumpster lid, and slams the lid shut.

"Nice shot, Luke!"

I laugh with the rest, both amused and horrified as I navigate my current situation. While we are finally experiencing appropriate February weather, the snow over the parking lot is either too slushy or too old, crisp, and useless. We range in age, yet there is still a sense that we are all boys on the playground discovering that green peppers make a fine alternative to snowballs.

Luke throws another pepper, but it misses the second open dumpster lid and instead smashes against the brick wall of the Pantry. Luis's failed attempt also hits the wall. Ray's pepper misses the wall altogether and sails through the open back door and into the food storage area before exploding on the floor. I laugh, despite the destruction of food at an institution whose primary mission is to fight hunger; despite my bleeding heart anguish over waste and excess. While as a waiter I regularly throw away bread and scrape away the plates of humanity at work, this still feels wrong.

o o o

I half-joke that my favorite room in our new place is the pantry with room enough for wire kitchen shelving, a coat bar, and our Christmas tree. We no longer have the rankling "first world problem" of glass vinegar bottles falling out of overly stuffed cupboards and breaking on granite countertops. Now, I can spread out my thrifty store-brand purchases, and we have room to participate in big box warehouse, bulk food culture. Before making the seven-minute walk to the Pantry, I'd thought about not eating breakfast in order to feel the pangs of our clients. To walk a mile in their shoes and all that. If I'm not brave or crazy enough to lock my pantry for a few days or experiment with shaking off my material coils of home and hearth by walking the streets for a week, then I could at least try to connect somehow. But my bravery is relative, and I'm no Method actor.

Knowing that a cranky, passed-out volunteer is no good to anyone, I fill myself with a hearty meal of oatmeal with pecans and bananas, turkey bacon, and of course, coffee.

May, a longtime volunteer in her twenties, took me on a tour. "You're allowed to eat anything you want," she said, as she pointed out open packages of cookies and donuts, the aluminum tray filled with chicken and vegetables, and the frozen pizza cooking in the industrial-sized toaster oven. I understand the concept of sanctioned, shared volunteer food, which is not unlike family meal at work. But breaking open a box of donuts while on a shift, like smashing green peppers, still feels odd. Like, shouldn't this be for them and not us?

"You'll never go hungry here," May said. And I wondered how many of the volunteers themselves depended at least in part on their time here for their own sustenance. Though maybe I read too much into May's remark, the word *hungry* taking on concentrated social significance in an institution like this, and perhaps this extra food is simply a perk of the industry.

o o o

It's almost noon, and I stand behind Counter One with Pantry veterans Jackie and Caroline, who are excited for both "my young, quick mind" and the fact that I'm tall enough to reach the top-shelf boxes some clients will need to carry (somewhere, if not home) their groceries. We take last-minute stock. I throw away a cereal box that expired in 2009 and wonder who would donate years-old cereal. I notice a whole flat of canned cranberries with their labels applied upside down. Our clients won't care about the imperfection of these grocery store rejects that have no place in our must-be-perfect retail culture.

The wall of cans behind us is awesome, and I'm thankful for my close-toed shoes. When I'd signed up, the message was clear: you don't know what dropped cans can do to exposed toes. The wall is a near half-room length of canned vegetables, fruit whose light syrup I would spoon as a kid like easygoing medicine with dinner; soups, beans, tuna, pasta, and sauce well organized but without the monotonous gleam of a supermarket or Costco grocery section. There's enough variation in size, shape, and product to give the operation a ragtag edge.

The wall summons my inner toddler, and as I wrap my hands around each can, I am also reaching into the lower cupboards of my childhood kitchen before Mom wised up and moved our pantry to the cupboards above the washer and dryer. I would take out each item with its ridged label, traceable circular ends, and tangible heft, and roll it across our pimento-loaf colored floor, the bologna brown tile with specks of red, blue, and green. Campbell's Soup cans. Fat cans of peaches. Cannonball heavy cans of apple juice. Can I roll them all the way to the edge of the dining room carpet? This early pantry brought forth not only food and experiments in how much I could get away with, but also lessons of the physical world. And of warmth.

As the shift begins, my hands try to pass on that same warmth, despite the cold from the opening and closing front door and from the frost on frozen Styrofoam packages of meats and whole, plastic-wrapped chickens. The rough, dry winter default texture of my hands amplifies, and the cans pass on a musty, metallic texture. I don't have time to wash, lotion, or warm my hands as I obsessively do in life and in my restaurant job. When the jolly, lanky mid-forties-Ray-Bolger-as-the-Scarecrow-in-*The-Wizard-of-Oz*-looking man shakes my hand and smiles as we finish up, I don't have time to worry about the mild germophobia inherited from my grandmother. His hand is not overly street-soiled, despite what my lingering prejudices may tell me. In this moment all issues dissolve, and I send him to my counterpart at Counter Two for produce, eggs, and bread.

The people gathered in the black stackable chairs waiting for their number to be called echo the canned goods' variety. They come in all shapes, sizes, colors, and ages, and I have Spanish-speaking assistance when needed. There are older Latina women, younger African American men. Young African American women, some with kids. An old white haired white man with a Union blue Civil War cap. An Asian couple who tries to return the meat they received last week because they don't eat pork. A young Latino boy either in drag or somewhere along the spectrum of transitioning reminds me that our gay-friendly neighborhood is here to serve people, not just cosmopolitans, expensive appetizers, and catchy dance remixes. As much as I want to learn all their stories, there isn't time. And they didn't come here to dwell on all that anyway. They are here for sustenance and hopefully to give and receive a smile and maybe a handshake.

Overall, my clients are happy and gracious. And the young, red-haired girl is excited that I've given her one of the few family-sized peanut butter jars because I know she has kids at home. Some take everything I lay out. Some trade items. Maybe they're not as excited about the canned plums as I am so I give them preferred peaches or applesauce, or they have health or religious dietary needs and I switch out a can of vegetarian chili for the pork and beans. A man nearing eighty with a European accent speaks in near whisper and I must turn my ear close to him: "I am a sick man...Do you have any fish?" And I don't, save for the canned tuna, which I kick in an extra can of even though I'm not supposed to. I give him frozen shrimp, though. Ground turkey's OK, and I find him as much as I can. He doesn't want many of the canned items. When we're finished, he reaches to me, squeezes my arm, and smiles. I give him the lone bag of dried apricots no one else has claimed.

I must keep my big old softy heart in check, though any "extras" I hand out karmically balance out anything I accidently short anyone in my attempt to stay organized. One African American man in his fifties says to me, "See I knew I was going to have trouble with you," as we navigate through the process. When I give him a whole frozen chicken, he argues. "That's a hen," as it's labeled, "not a chicken!" But he means that it's not been cut into easily fried parts, and I want to ask him, "Don't you own a knife?" I give in to his demands for forbidden trades between categories — like exchanging canned fruit for more beans — if only to get him off my back.

In brief down moments, I have time to look out at everyone still waiting. I want to understand who these people are. But I don't stare. I am humbled and have to fight the tears, and I realize that despite my earlier misgivings over destroying food, our parking lot hijinks offered a boost to volunteer morale worth a few green peppers. Nobody needs to see me wear my emotions on my old college-era flannel sleeves anyway. As a waiter, I've had years of practicing my game face and not expressing those inner monologues and snarky questions. It's in these moments that I realize this work does compare to waiting tables: on-my-feet and back aching. Reaching, bending, and keeping organized. And of course serving food — but while at work, I rely on them for my living, here they rely on me for theirs.

Of all the different people I see and work with, my heart gravitates furthest to the clean-cut white guys around my age — living their thirties, some pushing into their forties like me. There is the recognition of *That could be me*, and while I feel for everyone here, like it or not we have a tribal tendency to protect our own: Hey man, *we're* not supposed to end up like this. So what happened? How did you get here? How did our paths diverge? How close are any of us to changing which side of the counter we find ourselves on? The pantry stands sentry in my neighborhood, watchful as its inhabitants fight the good fight, and I did not expect when I walked through its front doors this morning that I'd be facing a sort of mortality. A reminder that nothing is guaranteed. That the fully-stocked pantry in our new home is a precarious, if still joyful, institution.

Ballast

CHRISTINE RICE

We hoisted ourselves up the limestone-block wall, through the hole in the chain link fence, and onto the Ravenswood rail line. The ballast stones dug into the soles of my Keds so I stepped on the rail and balanced like a tightrope walker. Johnny, wearing thick-soled Doc's, hopped from one railroad tie to the next until I pointed to the seam where the overpass's wall rose above the steel bridge.

"That's where I found it."

We'd lived our entire lives on Ravenswood. The long straight Metra track, the solidness of it, its steel certainty, felt more spiritual than walking into Saint Andrew's with its pews and hymnals and appraising eyes. Up on the tracks, elevated above the street, felt spiritual. I figured our neighbor Mrs. Gerber felt the same way, two days before, when she'd stepped in front of that northbound Metra.

Johnny knelt to get a closer look. "Right here?"

I nodded. It hadn't rained since the accident and a crimson smear of blood still stained the grey stones.

"The ring still on? No one saw it?"

"A clean cut." I chopped my hand through the air, "Like with a blade."

He shook his head and I noticed the frilly scar running from his eyebrow to his temple, the one he got freshman year when some delinquent jumped him from behind and dragged a pen across his face.

It was warm for mid-October, but Johnny still wore a black leather jacket, his favorite Ramones T-shirt, and cut-off jean shorts. Next to Johnny's dramatic Latin beauty, I felt pale and conventional. My auburn hair pulled into a ponytail, my skin sprinkled with freckles, my complete lack of curves, my glasses — everything — screamed *not interesting*.

Looking south, past Johnny's spiked black Mohawk, the train materialized in the distance. I loved the way it did that, how it appeared out of the haze like a speck of silver glitter at the end of a shiny string.

If we didn't hide fast, the train engineer would radio the cops, so we hurried off the overpass and ducked into the grapevines. Over the years, we had woven the vines into a tiny cave so that, even in winter after the leaves fell, we felt protected from neighbors' prying eyes. We would hide there after school, smoke weed, do homework, avoid the neighborhood assholes.

Johnny and I faced each other, cross-legged in our vine cave. Johnny pulled out his one-hitter and a baggie of weed. The train roared past. I covered my ears and closed my eyes until the dust and leaves, curling in the train's wake, settled.

I told Johnny how Oma had been walking her dog when she heard the train's warning horn and the thud.

"Shit."

"Yeah."

Johnny packed his pipe. "You think she waited *here* before she–" He ticked his head to the tracks and narrowed his eyes. They were oil black and, besides his broad shoulders, slim waist, and crooked smile, one of his best features.

"Maybe." I shrugged. "Probably."

I shoved my hand into the vines and pulled them down to peer at the Gerbers' neat little clapboard house. "She musta seen us, you know, climbing up here."

"Probably."

"But she never snitched."

Johnny shrugged. "Guess not." Then he locked his gaze on me. "Why'd you come up here alone?"

"You were in detention." I paused. "Again."

"Yeah." Johnny's nostrils flared. "But you heard what that little fuck called me."

Johnny had been walking Angelina Flores to class when Jared Zayas called him a *bat-caver joto*.

"You gotta let it go. You can't fight every asshole every day."

"Whatever." Johnny held the flame to the bowl and took a hit.

He offered me the pipe. I shook my head.

Another train rumbled past.

I tried keeping my mouth shut but the words tumbled out. "But Angelina Flores? Seriously?"

He blew smoke out the side of his mouth. "In case you hadn't noticed, she's dope."

I couldn't argue with that. She *was* dope. Long black hair, curves, bark-colored skin smoother than a Cover Girl's. Add to that: smart and kind and well-liked.

"Whatever."

Johnny stared. "So what's the problem?"

"No problem."

If I'd been honest, the problem was this: She wasn't *me*.

"So I have your blessing?"

I rolled my eyes. "Like you need it."

Johnny leaned back and changed the subject. "I can't believe I was in detention when you found it. Where'd you put it?"

"In Oma's extra fridge, in the garage."

Johnny laughed. "No shit? You better pray she doesn't find it."

"Tell me about it. But I wrapped it in plastic and hid it way in the back."

"What are you gonna do with it? Give it to Mr. Gerber?"

I shrugged.

Mr. Gerber worked at the factory a few blocks south with the other neighborhood fathers but unlike the rest of the factory workers, who walked home after clocking out at 5:00 p.m., we rarely saw him.

"Wouldn't that be weird?"

"Yeah. But it's his wife's finger. And ring. I would want it if I were him."

Johnny closed his eyes and tipped his head back just as another train passed.

The rumbling faded and we sat in silence. We could do that. Just sit together, not talking, and it never felt weird.

"Juan Miguel! Get your ass in the house this instant!" Even coming from her front porch across the street, Johnny's mother's shrill voice startled me.

"You're grounded?"

"Eternally." Johnny tapped out his pipe. "Show it to me tomorrow, OK? Meet me at the clock tower after school." He stashed his pipe. "Telling my Ma we were studying in the library. If she asks, you'll cover for me right?"

Late afternoon shadows stretched across the street as we climbed down the abutment. Johnny ran ahead of me, crossed the street, and took his front porch steps two at a time. He didn't need to wait for my answer.

We lived in the flat above my Oma. It was Tuesday, Oma's night to cook dinner, so I walked into her kitchen to wash my hands. It smelled of fried liver and onions.

Standing at the stove, she noted my disapproving glare.

"Since vhen you don't like liver and onions?"

"Since forever."

"Acht."

She and Opa had worked like dogs to buy this two flat. They were Volga Germans, their grandparents some of the first to settle in Russia until the reforms of Alexander II. That's when they left Russia to settle in Scotts Bluff, Nebraska, worked four jobs between them, saved, and finally moved to Chicago where Opa opened a butcher shop and Oma raised their eight children.

Oma was the proudest, most rigid, and most terrifying woman in our neighborhood. She wore black, low-heeled lace-up shoes, shirtwaist dresses, a navy cardigan, and pulled her grey hair into a bun at the nape of her neck. She walked Kaiser, a big mutt she'd rescued one frigid winter, every day at eight in the morning and four in the afternoon. Religiously. That dog, a sleek terrier mix with jaws that could crush a bowling ball, followed her every move. Sat obediently when she stopped to talk to a neighbor, and growled when any man approached.

Her grey eyes settled on me as I took the plates out of the cupboard. She'd terrified more than a few of my friends with that penetrating stare.

I set the table.

"Miss Paola says you and Johnny walk home from school every day."

"You knew that."

Miss Paola was Johnny's grandmother and the only non-German Oma had befriended in our neighborhood. They formed an unlikely alliance but, since the day they'd moved in, Miss Paola had joined Oma and the much younger Mrs. Gerber in an unending battle to keep the street outside our two-flats immaculate. Every day, barring rain or inclement weather, Oma, Miss Paola, and Mrs. Gerber would talk and laugh and sweep with a fervor that suggested they could get past the cement, down to something glittering beneath the surface.

"No hanky panky."

My face flushed. Under my breath I said, "I wish."

"Vhat?"

"No hanky panky, Oma. Geez."

Unconvinced, she kept her eyes on me.

My place settings looked odd. I'd put the knife and fork on the wrong side of each plate.

"He doesn't even think of me that way." I fixed the utensils.

"But you do."

It would do no good to argue, but before I could, my parents walked in.

Mama still wore her cashier smock. In the past year, her dark hair had gone completely white and, against that lack of color, her blue eyes looked faded and sad. Daddy hung his jacket on the hook next to the door, washed his hands, and kissed my forehead. They smelled of the butcher shop, of sawed bone and blood.

We sat down and linked hands to pray. At the end, Oma repeated her plea, "And vatch over Billy."

That would be the extent of the discussion about my older brother, the Vietnam War hero, the pitiful drunk. His absence, first during his deployment and now in his own private hell, felt like an open wound.

As I pushed the liver and onions around my plate, Daddy listed two more customers who'd announced they would be moving to the suburbs.

Mama looked worried. "Can't blame them. Better schools."

"They shouldn't abandon the neighborhood."

"Abandon the neighborhood" was Daddy's way of saying they shouldn't leave because Mexicans and Puerto Ricans were moving in. With the big stores as competition, our business relied on both the old timers and the newcomers. And because of this, and much to the disapproval of some of our Slavic neighbors, Daddy had hired a Mexican butcher.

Oma shook her head. "Poor dear Bertha." She impaled a leathery piece of liver with her fork. "That drecksau husband of hers."

Daddy ticked his head as if to say, Not in front of Jamie. I was the baby, a surprise, born when my parents were well into their forties. But Oma resisted their constant attempts to shelter me.

Noticing that I hadn't touched the liver, Mama heaped noodles on my plate and deftly changed the subject. "They defused a bomb at University of Utah today."

"That Unabomber's a slippery one–" But before Daddy could finish, Oma clucked her tongue and pointed a long crooked finger at Daddy. "You think my kids gave me the nervous exhaustion? No! It was that no good vater of yours."

Daddy sighed. "Here we go."

Oma's calm rarely cracked so, when it did, I listened carefully. I'd heard her reference her 'nervous exhaustion' before but I'd always figured that anyone with eight kids would need a few mental health days.

"Untreu hund."

"OK, Ma." Daddy quickly finished his food and stood. Mama did the same. They looked exhausted. Billy had called last night; his bi-weekly, middle-of-the-night beg for forgiveness and money.

Mama looked resigned, as if she couldn't take any more bad news. "Rose. Please."

"Acht." Oma flapped her hand.

Mama stood very still for a moment, probably filing through the reasons I should not hear whatever Oma was about to divulge. Finally, she and my father walked upstairs.

I cleared the table and took extra long washing each dish. Oma's anger would percolate until she couldn't hold it in. This was how I'd first heard about Billy's drinking. One night after dinner, while I helped her clean up, Oma told me how Daddy threw Billy out the back door of the shop after Billy came to work plastered.

Since then, my brother had gone from bad to worse. He lost his apartment, his girlfriend, and finally, my folks kicked him out of our place. And for them, the kindest people I would ever know, that damn near killed them.

Oma wiped the counter next to me. Her long arm swept in perfect arcs. She stopped and lowered her voice. "That Gerber...just like your grosvater. He ran around like a filthy hund until the day I threw dirt on his grave. My boys," she violently wagged her finger, "are not like that No Good."

I kept my eyes on the soapy water, at the brown bits of liver and onions disappearing beneath the sponge.

Kaiser sat attentively, waiting for the raw liver Oma surely saved for him.

"How did you know?"

"Everyone knew!" Oma dropped a piece of liver into Kaiser's mouth. "First it was some so-and-so over on School Street and then it was another so-and-so on Wellington." She circled her free hand like a revolving door. "One after the other."

I wasn't sure if we were talking about Opa or Mr. Gerber but I imagined how humiliating — not only that their husbands cheated, but that it had become common knowledge — that must have been for both women.

Oma dropped another piece of liver into Kaiser's mouth. "Hunds."

o o o

The next day, after school, I waited for Johnny below Lane Tech's crenellated clock tower. Grey clouds curdled overhead. We'd planned on stealing into the garage to look at the finger while Oma walked Kaiser, but after thirty minutes, no Johnny. I figured he'd probably gotten in trouble again so I went back inside to check the room where kids sat detention. No Johnny. Just the usual suspects — stoners and goof-offs.

I walked through the near-empty halls, accompanied by a few squirrely freshmen, nerds on their way to academic clubs, and athletes running to practice. On the east side of school, the absence of light left the halls dim and cool so I walked west where floor-to-ceiling windows faced the athletic fields. The afternoon sun, tumbling golden down the hall, warmed my face. On the field, football players lumbered around in their heavy gear. As I watched, something caught my attention, a flash in my periphery, by the cinder block building where the announcers called games. The inset doorway, hidden from view, was a favorite place for couples to make out.

I should have left right then. But I didn't. I stood there far too long; until Johnny and Angelina, their arms wound tightly around the other's waist, stumbled out of the doorway.

o o o

Walking south on Ashland, I turned east on Melrose and, fighting tears, walked quickly until I reached the abutment. I considered hoisting myself up, tucking myself into the vines, waiting for Johnny, acting like I hadn't seen him and Angelina. Instead, I dropped my backpack and leaned against the cool limestone. Nothing seemed right. Mrs. Gerber's sadness infused everything; as if she knew that her last act would remind everyone what her husband had driven her to do.

Hearing music, I made my way down our street. As I neared our house, I spotted my brother Billy leaning against our stoop, clutching a transistor radio. The side of his face looked like someone had dragged it over cement. Eyes closed, he cradled his left hand, red and swollen, against his chest.

Kneeling in front of him, I palmed his cheek. He felt hot and clammy. I shook him gently until he opened one eye.

"Hey, Jaybird."

"Hey, Billy."

He took a deep breath. "How's my lil' sis?"

"Better than you."

"A few scrapes."

Oma would be back soon from walking Kaiser. I'd been warned against engaging with Billy in any way, told that we had to stop *babying* him, but I couldn't help it.

"Let's go inside."

Billy's eyes rolled back. "Can't. The Old Man says no."

I sat beside him. The radio played John Lennon's "Watching the Wheels." Billy mumbled the lyrics. He smelled sour and unwashed, of stale beer, and cigarettes.

He suddenly stopped singing, sat forward, and brought the radio in front of his face. He held it there for a moment, staring into its dial, his breath short and sharp. "Fuck you John Lennon and Yogo-ono and peace and–" Just then a train roared past and swallowed his words. Into that vacuum of sound, he heaved the little radio. It hit the pavement and exploded in an arc of plastic.

He fell forward onto his hands and knees. "Playing your goddamn guitar…no one forced *you* to shoot a guy in the face." He looked up at me, eyes wild, breathing heavily.

"Let's go inside, Billy."

He swayed on all fours. "Wait. Gotta tell you something."

I knelt beside him.

"It's like, I can't–"

I hooked my arm around his shoulder. "Come on. Get up. Tell me inside."

"Listen!" He shook his head as if trying to clear it. "I have to tell you. You need to know." He paused. "There's nothing holding me down."

"OK, Billy."

"You understand, Jaybird?"

"I'm trying."

"Everything's shifting." He spread his good hand wide on the pavement. The terror in his voice stunned me. The only thing I could think to do was try to help him up. Just as I did, Johnny came bounding around the corner.

He stopped abruptly when he saw us.

I should have ignored him. Instead, I called, "You gonna help or just stand there?"

He came loping up, his long legs carrying him quickly to Billy's other side.

"Johnny's gonna help me get you up the steps."

"Johnny?" Billy turned to Johnny, "Shit, man. Ya' look like a–" Billy tried focusing on Johnny's Mohawk, "a fuggin' Egyptian or some shit."

"It's punk, man."

Billy smirked. "Whatever."

I dug my keys out of my pocket. "Let's take him in Oma's."

Johnny's eyes widened. "You sure?"

"Yeah. Doubt we could get him up the steps anyway."

We steered Billy into Oma's bathroom and helped him into the tub. I turned on the shower and Johnny held Billy up while I undressed him and scrubbed off the grime.

Billy's head rested on the salmon-tiled wall, eyes closed. We shared the same wide-set eyes and long, dark eyelashes. With his face so relaxed, he looked like his old self and I decided, then and there, that I wouldn't let my folks kick him out again.

By the time we'd finished, Johnny and I were both soaked and, just as we hoisted Billy's naked body out of the tub, Oma walked in. My breath caught in my chest but, without a word, she grabbed a towel and began drying him off.

When she finished, she told us to put him in the spare bedroom. The thing about Oma: she could be simultaneously terrifying, efficient, and gentle. She told me to run up and get a pair of Daddy's underwear and a T-shirt. By the time I returned, she had dressed the wounds on Billy's face and wrapped a bag of frozen peas around his swollen hand. After we dressed him, she tucked him in a thick down comforter, pulled up a chair, and settled next to Billy with her Bible.

She looked at me. "Tell your parents I have a sick headache, that I'll eat by myself tonight." She laid a hand on Billy's forehead and shifted her gaze to Johnny. "Go home. Dry off...and don't tell no one."

We walked outside and sat on the stoop. A train flashed past. Its cabin lights glowed behind green-tinted windows.

"You ever wonder about all those people? Where they go?"

During the day the train's windows reflected the sun but, after the sun set and the cabin lights lit the train's interior, I imagined the commuters — their still, dark silhouettes like ancient scarabs — frozen in amber.

But I didn't say that so Johnny continued, "I think about where they live. Abuela says that, up north, the streets are so clean you can eat off them."

Johnny's front screen door slapped and his mom walked out. She ignored Johnny and addressed me. "How ya doin', Jaybird?"

"Fine, Mrs. Montero."

A cigarette dangling between her fingers, she leaned over her railing. "Why you two wet?"

"Water balloon fight after school."

"Hmm." She narrowed her eyes at Johnny. "You have memory loss?"

"No."

"You forget you're still grounded?"

Johnny sighed. Before making his way down our stoop, he leaned into my ear, "Show me the finger tomorrow?"

Nodding, I ran upstairs to change.

The next day after school, after making sure that Oma'd left for her four o'clock walk, we stood in the corner of Oma's garage next to the ancient fridge humming in the corner. A row of horizontal windows separated the fridge and a door that opened into the back yard. Through the windows, I could watch for Oma coming down the gangway. I didn't have to worry about my parents barging in. They would be at work until they closed the shop. As I unwrapped the finger, Johnny stood close, shining a flashlight beam on my hands.

"We gotta do this quick. I wanna make sure Billy's OK."

Johnny shook his head. "You used cellophane?"

I rolled my eyes.

"Seems like Reynolds Wrap woulda worked better."

I stopped. "What do you know about it? When you find a finger you can wrap it how you want."

"OK. Chill."

I peeled the last of the cellophane off Mrs. Gerber's finger and laid it in my palm. The garage smelled of motor oil, and the peat moss Oma used to winter her dahlias. The bone, sliced cleanly, stuck out slightly from where the flesh had shrunk. The skin had turned powdery, dry, pale, the nail bed greyish. A cheap wedding band, shoved up to the first swollen knuckle, didn't gleam but looked dull and malleable.

Johnny leaned in to get a closer look. "Damn."

"Yeah."

"It's not fake?" Johnny pressed the knuckle with his index finger, then took a sharp breath as if confirming its authenticity.

The finger held us rapt. A shuffling of footsteps startled me, I flinched, and the finger fell to the garage floor.

Just as I knelt to pick it up, Billy walked in. Johnny switched off the flashlight and we froze. Billy didn't see us in the shadowy corner but moved slowly along the side of the garage, placed a foot on a crate, and hoisted himself up until his hand reached the seam where the rafters met the wall. He groped around, shifting his hand between two rafters until he breathed "*Bingo*" and stepped off the crate. He held a pint bottle in his hand.

He leaned against the wall and unscrewed the cap. He was just about to tilt the bottle back when the gangway gate slapped shut.

"Billy–"

Startled, he dropped the bottle and it crashed to the cement. He looked around frantically until I stepped out of the shadows with Johnny behind me.

Kneeling, Billy picked up the bottle's broken bottom and tilted it over his mouth. "God damn!" He heaved the shard against the opposite wall.

"Oma's coming." Oma always hung Kaiser's leash on a hook just inside the garage door.

Billy sat down, dropped his head into his palms.

The finger in my fist, I positioned myself between Billy and the door. When Oma opened it, she would surely see him and the broken pint at his feet.

Just as she opened the door, I stepped forward. "Oma."

She took a sharp breath, "Jamie!" She paused, locked her gaze on me and then narrowed her eyes. Kaiser nuzzled my knee with his big wet nose, then sat as if waiting for events to unfold. Without taking her eyes off me, Oma hung the leash on its hook. "Give me a heart attack."

I tried to block her view but she wasn't the kind of woman whose attention could be easily diverted. "I–"

Oma's eyes ticked around the garage: to Billy sitting on the crate, the glass now glittering in the open door's light, to Johnny standing behind me. She held up her hand, her signal for me to be quiet.

Panicking, thinking she might throw Billy out, I brought my open palm, the finger curled on its side, into the light.

"I found Mrs. Gerber's finger. On the tracks."

At this, Billy slowly pushed himself up and shuffled over to stand beside me.

Oma stared at the finger and brought her palm over her mouth. With her free hand, she gripped Billy's forearm. "Her..." she began, but stopped and remained silent for what seemed like ages. "Ah," she finally gasped, shaking her head. Her grey eyes welled with tears. "I keep thinking...if I had come back just a few minutes sooner...I might have seen her. I might have stopped her like before."

"Before?"

"Once before I caught her climbing up. And I joked with her like I didn't know what she was going to do." She shook her head as if trying to erase the memory. "I should have not joked. I should have done something more."

I imagined dark-haired and plain Mrs. Gerber fitting a toe between the limestone blocks, finding a smooth handle between the stones, pulling herself up.

Oma took a deep breath and looked at her watch. "Well. Ya." She nodded as if she'd made a decision. "He should have it."

"Oma?"

Before I could protest, she plucked the finger out of my palm, grabbed Kaiser's leash off the hook, and stepped into the backyard. She stood in the shadow cast by the garage for just a moment before hooking Kaiser's leash and disappearing into the gangway.

We followed. I helped Billy along, his face pale as candle wax, his hand clammy and shaking. Johnny clomped beside us, his Doc Martens scuffing the pavement.

Mr. Gerber worked at the lamp factory three blocks south. Oma led the way with the single-minded gait of a soldier going into battle. We crossed Belmont and walked along Ravenswood accompanied by the whoosh of rush hour trains traveling to and from the city.

Gerber would get out at five o'clock sharp and we arrived just as the factory's front doors opened and men in grey work uniforms streamed out. We stood beneath the overpass, kitty-corner from the factory entrance. To our west, the slanting sun shimmered down Wellington. Gusts picked up leaves and tossed them around in tiny whirlwinds. Billy shivered and leaned against the limestone. Johnny stood ramrod straight. Kaiser sat obediently at Oma's side.

Gerber walked out with a cigarette shoved to one side of his meaty mouth. He took a few steps, pulled a book of matches out of his pocket and struck a match. Just before lighting the cigarette, though, he spotted Oma across the street. He froze, the match's flame centimeters from the cigarette. His gaze locked on Oma, he slowly leaned into the flame. Turning west, he flicked the match to the street.

Oma crossed the street to meet him just as he reached the underpass. He stopped, took a long drag, blew it out the side of his mouth. The rumbling and vibration of an approaching train drowned Oma's words as she extended her fist toward him, as she turned her palm up, as her fingers bloomed open.

As the train roared overhead, Mr. Gerber reached out to steady himself against the limestone wall as if something that insignificant could hold him in place ever again.

SPORTS BREAK

HARD HAT, LUNCH PAIL: THE MYTH OF TOUGHNESS IN CHICAGO SPORTS

DAVID ISAACSON

I t was not by accident that F. Scott Fitzgerald's big-shouldered Tom Buchanan was "Tom Buchanan of Chicago."

"Not even the effeminate swank of his riding clothes could hide the enormous power of that body," wrote Fitzgerald of *The Great Gatsby*'s leading jerkface. Long Island had its froufrou effects on a man, for sure, but the brawn of Chicago could not be disguised: "…you could see a great pack of muscle shifting when his shoulder moved under his thin coat."

It's no surprise that Fitzgerald is channeling Carl Sandburg's 1914 identification of Chicago as the "City of the Big Shoulders"; after all, it is hard to imagine a city as collectively obsessed with a single poem as Chicago is with Sandburg's "Chicago." San Francisco has its Beats, yes, and New York might sometimes tune itself to the lyrical sentiments of George M. Cohan, Comden and Green, Kander and Ebb, or Nas, but Sandburg's poem — with its emphasis on the manly and macho — became Chicago's imbibed creed, an unconscious template for the city's cops and gangsters, union bosses and anti-labor thugs…and its athletes. "Here," writes Sandburg, "is a tall bold slugger set vivid against the little soft cities."

The fictional Tom Buchanan was himself a jock — "one of the most powerful ends that ever played football at New Haven" — and as the twentieth century progressed, Chicago's most heralded professional sports teams were ones deemed to be most possessed with the sweating spirit of Sandburg's "husky" and "brawling" proletarians.

There have been exemplars of this mighty, striving figure across all Chicago sports — "Man of Steel" middleweight Tony Zale, scrap-happy hockey hunk Keith Magnuson — but the most indelible model was the Chicago Bears football team of the early 1940s, dubbed "Monsters of the Midway." Even their intra-squad scrimmages were opportunities (echoing Sandburg) "to be alive and coarse and strong and cunning." Or, quoting a *Chicago Tribune* headline of the time: "Bear Practice Makes Trench Warfare

Mild." The franchise star was Bronko Nagurski, whose very name seemed to epitomize the bone-crushing power of the man. This was an Iron Age of iron men, and Chicago teams ever since have strived to live up to the brutish standards of their fore-Bears.

The second coming of these "Monsters" came — or so the narrative goes — with the 1963 championship edition of the Bears. The ethos of this oh-so-prototypical Bears team? Grind it out on the gridiron, a no-nonsense approach in marked contrast to the flash and sizzle of, say, New York Jets quarterback "Broadway" Joe Namath — a man known as much for his fur coats and the effeminate swank of his pantyhose ads (definitely worth a YouTube search) as for his Super Bowl victory in 1969.

The legend continued. A key member of that '63 Bears team, tough-guy Mike Ditka, went on to coach a third — and the most famous — iteration of the "Monsters": the 1985 champs. Firmly within the tradition, this team eschewed the emerging pass-oriented "West Coast Offense" popularized by the San Francisco 49ers, preferring a more pounding, ground-based style.

Ditka emphasized the contrast between a Chicago team and a coastal team when he told the *Chicago Sun-Times* (in an article printed under the bizarre headline "Bears' image ethnic classy") that:

> "There are teams that are fair-haired and there are teams that aren't. There are teams named Smith and teams named Grabowski. The [Los Angeles] Rams are a Smith. We're a Grabowski."

The city's myth-makers were enthralled. Paul Galloway followed up in the *Tribune* with the thesis that Chicago — the city itself — was a Grabowski.

> "Grabowski means people who come from a working-class, immigrant background, people who work hard and have nothing handed to them, people who have struggled against discrimination, people who are honest and tough, people who persevere and prevail...
>
> "It's the shot-and-a-beer, hard-hat lunch-bucket guy who gets his muscles through toil versus the white-collar, white-wine, striped-tie stuffed shirt who tones his in a health club."

The Bears's star defensive tackle, Steve "Mongo" McMichael (nicknamed, yes, after the character in "Blazing Saddles" who punches a horse), proved himself well-inculcated with the local civic literature when he (or, OK, perhaps his ghostwriter) wrote in a memoir:

> "Carl Sandburg was close when he titled Chicago as the City of Big Shoulders [*sic*]. He just didn't go far enough; Chicago is the City of Big Shoulder Pads. Chicago fans want to love their Bears because the Bears are much of what Chicagoans like about themselves: Big. Tough. Champions."

Let us now pause a moment in our narrative to acknowledge that: No.

Any reasonable census of the city's citizenry would find several residents who are neither big nor tough, and whose sense of self-worth might in fact be based on factors beyond hat size and hardiness. This census might even reveal a few who don't care a whit about the city's professional sports teams. Or about Carl Sandburg.

Yes, because Chicago is flat and far from any salt-water sea, it is easy to imagine its people as down-to-earth. Because it was once home to International Harvester and Zenith Radio Corp and the Industrial Workers of the World, it is easy to conjure the image of boulevards filled with muscled stevedores, boilermakers, welders, and tanners. And because of a capable poet's sound-bites, it is easy to encapsulate these mythologies in newspaper columns, sports memoirs, and — to be sure — in this essay.

Let us also acknowledge that Chicago — with its historical dependence on its financial markets and tourism industry — has had no greater share of Galloway's "Grabowskis" than its midwestern rivals. And that plenty of large American cities — even those "little soft cities" on the coasts! — have their own proud-and-not-so-proud histories in industrial manufacturing, their own beleaguered working classes, their own Golden Gloves competitions, their own propensities to see their sports heroes and working-class heroes as "tough."

Furthermore, let us acknowledge that there was much about the '85 Bears's cast of characters that did *not* fit the white working-class "Grabowski" model:

- Three of its four First-Team All-Pro players were African Americans from the South (Walter Payton, Mike Singletary, and Richard Dent).

- Key defensive back Gary Fencik was (uh-huh, like Tom Buchanan) a Yale man.

- They were total big-media darlings. First and foremost among these nascent TV stars was William "Refrigerator" Perry, a 325-pound rookie defensive lineman occasionally inserted — in a bit of Ditka gimmickry — as running back or receiver. His success on *Monday Night Football* led to appearances on Letterman, the *Tonight Show*, and *The Bob Hope Christmas Special*.

- Their embrace of Hollywood-style glitz was consummated with the mid-season release of the single and MTV-style video "The Super Bowl Shuffle." ("Well, they call me Sweetness / And I like to dance / Runnin' the ball is like makin' romance.") It hit number forty-one on the Billboard charts.

The falseness of the Grabowski characterization, however, did not stop new generations of sportswriters from reviving it whenever they had a chance. The Tom Thibodeau-coached Chicago Bulls (2010-15), were justifiably praised for their hustle and hard work on the basketball court. Thibodeau, according to *Grantland*'s Andrew Sharp, "built a team that brought every blue-collar cliché to life. The Thibs Bulls were everything Chicago likes to imagine about itself." The Bulls's television color commentator, Stacey King, was a ready-and-willing sloganeer for this sentiment: Center Joakim Noah was "heart, hustle, and muscle." Forward Taj Gibson's stalwart play was "hard hat, lunch pail" — a phrase that echoed Galloway's "Grabowski" essay and embodied blue-collar pride: the hard hat versus the homburg, the lunch pail versus the three-martini lunch.

But in 2015, Bulls's management tired of the bristling Thibodeau, and replaced him with the mild-mannered and decidedly fair-haired Fred Hoiberg. Almost immediately, an existential Grabowski crisis ensued: "We just get out-toughed sometimes," star guard Jimmy Butler told the news media. "You can call it being soft, whatever you want to call it."

The city's incipient self-doubt is exacerbated by the fact that its most accomplished basketballer is not *manly* at all. In fact, she is a woman: the Chicago Sky's Elena Della Donne. And while no one who has seen the WNBA's reigning MVP in action would question her toughness, it is — predictably — not the focus of the local media: a recent *Chicago Magazine* profile leads with her "gliding through the glitterati" at "a swank TriBeCa gala." No hard hat or lunch pail in sight. (Females, it must be said, have always been sidelined in this vision of a team or city of Grabowskis, just as they were sidelined in Sandburg's poem. They appear in "Chicago" only as "painted women under the gas lamps luring the farm boys" or in the line: "On the faces of women and children I have seen the marks of wanton hunger." In other words, as whores or mothers, sirens or victims.)

Meanwhile, Chicago's top sports story in this year of 2016 was, of course, the World Champion Cubs. They were extraordinary, but were they Monsters of the Midway? Let's see:

- Their president, Theo Epstein, is a Yale-schooled technocrat known for a "Moneyball" approach; whereas baseball teams of yore were assembled by tobacco-spitting old-timers with gimlet eyes for baseball talent, Moneyballers prefer to base personnel decisions on computer algorithms.

- Their coach, like Mike Ditka, hails from small-town Pennsylvania. But Joe Maddon is no Ditka. He's a tie-dye-wearing, self-proclaimed hippie. He drives a van which he calls his "Shaggin' Wagon."

- Pictures of their young star, National League MVP Kris Bryant, blanketed the interiors of dozens of L train cars; he looked dapper as all get out in the luxury cottons of his sponsor, Express Inc.

- Their newly refurbished clubhouse hardly has the vibe of a blue-collar hang-out. Says the *Tribune*, "The space is replete with polished chrome and mood lighting, exuding a nightclub feel without the bar." There's even a fog machine.

- Their owner is an investment banker.

In other words, the Cubs's image is neither husky nor brawling. Recent Bears squads, too, seem less than monstrous. They made it to the Super Bowl once more, in 2007, with a style again emphasizing running and defense. But that team's coach, Lovie Smith, was replaced with Marc Trestman, a man with the look and demeanor of a downtown architect or Mercantile Exchange exec — one of the white-collar professionals left out of the Grabowski version of the metropolis, and decidedly omitted from Sandburg's vision of hog butchers, tool makers, freight handlers, and stackers of wheat. Trestman was known as "The Quarterback Whisperer," a man who could unleash the skills of his under-achieving (and reputedly *soft*) quarterback Jay Cutler. A coach who *whispers?* In *Chicago?*

Trestman's tenure as coach was mercifully short, but still enough — along with the listless Bulls and flashy Cubs — to undermine the city's tough-guy bona fides. Pundits wishing to invoke the Chicago-versus-the-Coasts narrative were forced now to rely on historic precedent rather than current exploits. 2016's iteration of the theme, then, pitted the Golden State Warriors — who won seventy-three of their eighty-two regular season basketball games — against the memory of the 1996 Chicago Bulls, who held the previous high-water mark, having won seventy-two.

Partisans of those Bulls — predictably — invoked "toughness." The game in 1996, we were told, was a rougher affair, with rules that allowed more contact, and enforcement policies that left egregious, violent fouls unpunished. Those Bulls collectively played what was known as the Doberman Defense. ("Fierce as a dog," went Sandburg's "Chicago" metaphor, "with tongue lapping for action.") This physical style contrasted with the "Showtime" Lakers of coastal Los Angeles, the team that these Michael Jordan-era Bulls had supplanted as dynastic titlists.

Jordan — acclaimed the greatest basketball player ever — had a blue-collar background, the son of a General Electric forklift operator. The Warriors's lithe star, Steph Curry, on the other hand, lacks a working-class pedigree. His father — Dell Curry — was himself an accomplished and moneyed professional baller. Steph's success on the court is based not on overpowering his adversaries, but on the ability to launch parabolic shots from improbable distances. Surely, Chicago's pundits said, the fey artistry of this Golden State team (its name — Golden — standing in sun-splashed contrast to the drear greys of Chicago) could not withstand the aggression of the '96 Bulls.

The supposed dichotomy between the two teams' style and substance evaporates under any real scrutiny, of course: the scrawny Curry, it turns out, is sneaky-strong, and can deadlift 400 pounds. Conversely, Jordan was (and is) a pitchman for Hanes undergarments, while his teammate Dennis "The Worm" Rodman made a splash by appearing in public in a wedding dress.

Surely, any sports iconography based on rigid assumptions about strength, power, and gender is ripe for debunking. And yet the Grabowski iconography persists, defying its own contradictions. So we exhume a Bulls team from two decades ago in order to overcome our anxiety — perhaps an anxiety with Freudian undertones — over our present *softness*. This exercise in rhetorical resurrection mirrors other attempts to recover a supposedly triumphant blue-collar past: "It is critical that we bring back manufacturing jobs to Illinois," tweets Illinois Governor Bruce Rauner. And of course, "Make America Great Again," says Donald Trump.

Like the sports fan nostalgic for MJ and Scottie, we reminisce about the days when we could stroll down Cortland Avenue and see men smelting vats of molten metal through the open doors of Finkl & Sons Steel; we boast of the city's former industrial grit and grime (before Mayor Daley the Younger prettied up the North Side with roadside flowers and European-style newspaper vending boxes). We are borne back ceaselessly into the past.

No matter that Chicago's resumé in manufacturing is inflated; no matter that our honored Monsters were not really so monstrous: Our politicians will feed our nostalgia because feeding nostalgia is good politics. They will invoke Sandburgian imagery in a futile attempt to brand Chicago as a ready-and-willing player in heartland economics. They will emphasize the town's (or the state's, or the country's) masculinity in the hopes that it will — in the eyes of voters — enhance their own. They will don the hard hat for photo ops, they will invoke the lunch pail at editorial board meetings, they will indulge in sports clichés. Because, after all, when the going gets tough...

Postscript, March 2017. Elena Della Donne has been traded, Donald Trump is president, and the themes of coastal elites, heartland virility, and white, working-class Grabowskis have never been more destructive, nor more ripe for deconstruction.

DiSCO DEMOLiTiON, JULY 12, 1979

KEVIN COVAL

*White males... see disco as the product of homosexuals,
blacks, and Latins, and therefore they're the most likely to respond
to appeals to wipe out such threats to their security.*
Dave Marsh, *Rolling Stone*

Steve Dahl donned a helmet
a military uniform, drove the diamond
in an army jeep. Dahl was white
and middle brow. his listeners white
men in the middle of an america
factories were packing up.
the world promised began
to look other/wise.
      Dahl and white
sox management made a promo
night to attract a dwindling fan
base in a sub-par season.
it was 98cents to get in
if fans brought a disco record
to be blown up in center field
after game one with the Tigers
in the middle of the summer reagan built
his stride toward the white
house.
           Disco was dance music
           for the generation after Vietnam.
           sped up ethereal soul dreamt in Gay
           clubs, Black and Latino and more.

and the whites came
and the whites came.

tonight they came, disgusted /aroused
tens of thousands brought beer and weed
and records to burn. a bonfire of vinyl.
ensure Black records aflame. erasure.

comiskey park
in Bridgeport is home of the dick
daleys. they fell in love with their mother's
corn beef and cabbage and an architectural
appreciation for viaducts. the city was rigid.
the Robert Taylor homes an eastern border
a Black tombstone. Lenard Clark was not
a glint in his parents' eyes. his skull still
unbashed and embryonic.

white men hopped turnstiles, ticket lines.
more bodies crammed in comiskey
than there'd ever been. Chicago was playing
Detroit. cities dwindling like the white
majority. the last vestige of light
crept over bakeries and bar stools.

Dahl, a ringmaster, a comic imp
a cowardly warlord set the fire.
a small pop and boom! fans
stormed the field. grass littered
with bottles and concession debris.

records sliced the air like weapons.
long hairs in lee jeans and cut-off
t-shirts slid into second. they stole home
/ again. a crater burned into center
field. a mob of white on the diamond.
the game postponed, forfeit, rigged
from the beginning. Harry Caray couldn't
control the crowd or get them back
in their seats. the police were called:
uncles and fathers returned to chase
their sons. so the force restrained.
no one was shot or beat to death.
there were scoldings, a few arrests.
no felonies. Steve Dahl walked free.

> Chicago
> would grind disco in a steel mill
> run it thru electric sockets till it bumped
> grimy. til it was House and jacked
> the body. til the technology developed
> in Japan displaced white disc jocks.
> made them obsolete, old machines
> dancing on their own graves.

PREVIOUSLY PUBLISHED IN *A PEOPLE'S HISTORY OF CHICAGO* (HAYMARKET BOOKS, 2017).

THE CARNIVAL

PAUL DAILING

When I was a kid, I thought Chicago was a perpetual carnival.

It was a place where the Cubs lost and the Sox won, but I didn't care because the Sox were pooey dumb-dumb heads who smelled like poo. And I loved the Cubs.

I loved the Cubs because of ivy and piss troughs, because of Ryne Sandberg, Mark Grace, and Andre Dawson. I loved the Cubs because the Cubs meant a two-hour drive out of my hometown to that place I thought was a perpetual carnival of sports and fun and a pre-1:20 lunch at that novelty fifties diner downtown where the waiters were paid extra to be sassy.

My hometown was not a carnival. It was the worst city in America.

That's not me saying that. That was *Money Magazine*'s yearly ranking of the nation's 300 largest cities. Year after year, that damned magazine would look at our shitty schools, high unemployment, high crime, and low prospects and name us the worst place to live in the nation.

We lived at the bottom of that list so long, *The Daily Show with Craig Kilborn* did a snarky segment congratulating us when we moved up to number 299.

Not Detroit, not Flint, not Gary, or East St. Louis. Rockford, Illinois, was the worst place to live in America.

"Rockford, Ill. — so named because it was founded at the site of a ford across the Rock River — is a pleasant, tree-smothered city 90 miles northwest of Chicago," *Life Magazine* wrote about us in 1949.

"A hardscrabble town in the middle of America, the place is not much more than an intersection of interstates and railway lines," *Rolling Stone* wrote in 2008.

We never really recovered from the factories closing. A Chrysler factory in nearby Belvidere is still a major employer, as is Woodward Governor, which makes airplane controls. But the furniture companies and — this was the big one — screw factories linger on as shadows of what they were.

In the early eighties recession, Rockford's unemployment hit 21 percent, the highest in the nation. The *New York Times* did a story on us.

The *Times* came back in 2011 when we hit 16 percent, the highest in the nation during that economic slowdown.

"Parking meters line the streets of the shopping district. A fleet of cabs lines up at the station to meet the seven daily passenger trains. On Saturdays farmers pour in from the surrounding county to shop while their children go to the movies or roller-skate at a rink across the street from C.I.O. headquarters." — *Life*, 1949

"Finding a meaningful target to blow up in Rockford isn't easy." — *Rolling Stone*, 2008

But then there was the carnival.

Two hours away there was a red and blue Terra Magica at Clark and Addison. Smiling men tried to sell T-shirts and tickets the moment you stepped off the Red Line and everyone was, whether the team won or lost (but usually lost), happy.

When Harry Caray thrust the mic out the press box window in the middle of the seventh, we all sang with joy.

My life in Rockford was sadly good. My father was executive director of a legal services nonprofit. Free lawyers for people who couldn't afford it. The Reagan years were tough at times — I'll never understand Bonzo's post-mortem canonization — but I grew up aware of poverty without suffering from it.

After afternoons of basketball and taunting each other, I went to sleep each night in a lovingly-restored, early Victorian manor in a historically protected district. My friends Dale and Tyrell had to cross the rickety bridge literally to the wrong side of the tracks to their beds at the Jane Addams Housing Projects.

I went to college. Dale and Tyrell went to prison. Because I was a rich kid in a poor town and that's the only thing that can happen.

"Furniture industry…American Dream…as nearly typical of the U.S. as any city can be." — *Life*, 1949

"Backwaters…sad-sack…the lone claim to fame of being the hometown of Cheap Trick." — *Rolling Stone*, 2008

But this isn't about my sad-sack hometown, which has improved by leaps and bounds and strides and where I would move in a second if there were still such a thing as a job there.

This is about Chicago. And the Chicago Cubs.

In the years, yeah, decades since, my dream became my home, I realized Chicago wasn't a carnival but a deeply troubled and divided city. I realized I wanted to write about Chicago, not party there. I realized that if I could do one thing for this city it would be to fix it.

But I still loved the Cubs.

I grew to see the economics that took the bleachers from the bums to the richies. I see the owners' donations to Donald Trump and the cushy cabinet jobs they're tossed as recompense. I grew to see the political favors and aldermanic oneupmanship that made my childhood carnival happen in a bleeding town. I see every complaint you're about to lodge against the Cubs and Wrigley and I find it difficult to care.

Because the Chicago Cubs taught me to believe.

They didn't teach me to believe in the goodness of the world or that stuff just works out or any of those terrible life lessons that give the warm fuzzies. The Cubs taught me to believe that, with enough work, even legendarily bad things can be fixed.

My hometown's poverty, my new town's segregation, a lack of investment in the battery — all could be worked on, tinkered with, given a deeper pitching bench, and fixed.

My childhood carnival is my troubled, bleeding home. And now the Sox lose and, as of the moment I typed the first draft of these lines, the Cubs just won it all. A World Series for Wrigley.

The obligatorily snarky will tease and prod about if it'll be another 108 years till the next one and to grow up because it's just a ball team, but we know better. For me, the Cubs were Chicago and joy via piss troughs and ivy. The Cubs were my first step toward what would become the new broken midwest town I want to fix.

I can never thank them enough.

SIXTH CITY

PAUL DURICA

For the final game of the 2016 World Series, being played in Cleveland, I went to my neighborhood bar in Chicago. The Skylark would be a safe place, I reasoned. Sheila, one of the owners, came from the Cleveland area, and Dmitry, the bartender and a Chicago White Sox fan, hated the Cubs. Most importantly, the bar was known for not having a TV, so no one would think to watch the game there (although Sheila had propped one up on the photo booth near the back and played it with the sound turned off since the Series began). I was right: three people sat by themselves at the bar, a young couple talked quietly in a booth, and the whole place, with its high ceiling and low lights, had the feel of a wake in contrast to the collective joy filling the city, reaching even down here to the South Side.

The week had not been easy. In the Loop, where I work, I'd pass streams of people in Cubs blue, wearing oversized Harry Caray glasses or singing "Go, Cubs, Go." A "W" flag appeared pinned to every office window. Even the sculpted lions outside the Art Institute wore jerseys. The Chicago Cubs had not won a World Series in 108 years, the Cleveland Indians in '68, but the math didn't matter. That week every American, it seemed, cheered for Chicago. As my father said, on the phone, early in the week, regardless of how it ended there would be only one of two national headlines the following morning: "Cubs Win" or "Cubs Lose." The team from Cleveland was a minor obstacle to be overcome on the way to making history.

That night at the Skylark, I wore my Indians hat and a "CLE" T-shirt. I'd brought along a friend from the East Coast, and we sat close to the TV. I came in with a plan: three beers for the night, one every three innings. Even the sips became measured, a calming gesture between outs as Cleveland fell behind early in the game. It was just baseball. Both teams had rosters of interchangeable millionaires — but the Chicago papers that day had told stories of cash-strapped Clevelanders selling their tickets to wealthy out-of-towners and as the cameras cut to Bill Murray, John Cusack, all the Chicago lovers cheering and clapping in the stands in Cleveland — the game got to me.

People often think I'm a Chicagoan because of the local history work I do. I've lived on the South Side of the city for eleven years, but I spent my first eighteen years in Cleveland, in a neighborhood near the zoo. The cities are similar — formerly industrial, midwestern, built around where a lake meets a river, with cultural institutions of international acclaim, and a troubling history of segregation, crime, and inequality. Chicago, the younger of the two, has always been the more ambitious, the Second City, the "tall bold slugger," as Sandburg wrote, "set vivid against the little soft cities," like Cleveland. Critics called it the Mistake on the Lake, and the best we could ever do was the Sixth City — but when is one ever proud of being the sixth of anything?

From time to time, as the game progressed, as the Cubs lengthened their lead or the Indians chipped away at it, Dmitry would step from behind the bar to shake his head at the score on the screen or give me a thumbs up. He knew that the other Chicago team, the White Sox, had won the World Series in 2005; this was nothing to be excited about. My friend tried to comfort me: at least Cleveland would play a part in breaking a century's old curse. Near the middle of the sixth inning, while I sipped my second beer, a Chicago fan walked into the bar. He wore a Cubs bandana and jersey and looked like David Foster Wallace. He sat beside us. Not a minute passed before he muttered something to me about how television hadn't been invented the last time Cleveland won a World Series (not true). He then made a joke about the Cuyahoga River catching fire.

The river burned long before I was born, and in the sixty years my father's been alive, Cleveland lost half a million residents — where did they all go? Summer afternoons, as a child, watching the Cubs on cable, I never dreamed of moving to Chicago. The South Side, where I live, reminds me of the former Sixth City. During that same childhood, I spent a lot of time with my father's parents; they'd take me to the Cleveland they knew, on trips to the West Side Market for groceries; St. Procop, their church now shuttered; and, on special occasions, to the May Company downtown where my grandmother tried on a new hat or pair of gloves. Often I stayed in the car, a beige Crown Victoria, with my grandfather, who'd tell me a story for each place, about the vanished streetcars and steel mills, the silver lights that once hung from the Soldiers and Sailors Monument in Public Square. I never disliked Cleveland for what it is because he showed me what it had been. Chicago still thinks itself the "tall bold slugger" although that moment too has passed.

Cleveland lost the game, the country celebrated, but before that, something unexpected happened and I shamed myself. I wish I could share the Cubs fan's joy, but ten years of burning river jokes, that cloying song, Bill Murray weeping in the stands — when in the bottom of the eighth inning, a two-run home run by Cleveland tied the game, stunning the man beside me and the whole city, it seemed, into silence, I stood up, turned to him, and bellowed, "Chicago sucks," drawing out the "s" for what seemed like decades. All the color drained from his face. He knew loss as a possibility, something I've always known. He got up quietly and left the bar.

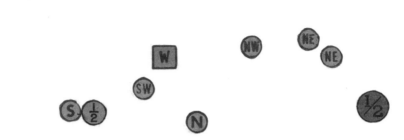

the CONFLICTED CITY

VICTORY AUTO WRECKERS, MOO & OINK, AND THE FREE WILSON BASKETBALL

ROBERT DEAN

Hey kid,

There's a fifty-fifty chance your dad didn't finish high school. Many fathers down here didn't. Said it wasn't worth it, said was easier just to get a "good job" if you knew some folks. They could read a ruler and knew how to rewire a two flat in same time most kids are figuring out who they were. You took a good job when one was offered to you. Why get an education when you can earn an honest buck working with your hands?

Who needed school when you could craft, build, and create something from nothing? Be a bricklayer, or millwright.

Screw college, you can go to trade school down on Forty-fifth and Halsted and learn to be a plumber. Who doesn't want the prospect of making $25 an hour right out of high school? Join the union! Learn a trade and you're set for life. Pride comes embedded in your knuckles, in your work ethic. Don't wanna swing a hammer? Be a cop or a firefighter — most kids understand the concept of furlough by the age of ten around neighborhoods like Beverly or Lawndale.

No matter your hood, your kids are screwed if they go to public schools. Because public schools are broke. There is no infrastructure for success. There is no after-school club, and there's no finding that subject that changes your life. Instead, kids in public schools are met with closings, crumbling buildings, and teachers navigating a classroom with barely the tools to make it through the day.

So, what do parents do? Either work themselves to the point of exhaustion to send their kids to private schools, or they ship off to the burbs where the kids can go to school for free, thanks to that tax money. Many parents choose the latter. You may have grown up around Fifty-fifth and King or Forty-third and Union, but a whole hell of a lot of south-siders went to high school in Lemont or Tinley Park because mom and pops got tired of high taxes, police sirens, and Catholic high school tuition.

After-school activities don't exist, there are few community centers, and the folks who want to build a better community are handcuffed by typical red tape — just what we're known for, aka where the Windy City got its name, from politicians with a lot of talk.

But, you keep moving kid, you keep on swingin'.

Ever heard of the Chicago Board of Trade or the Chicago Mercantile Exchange? You'd be kidding yourself if you thought that joint wasn't run by the South Side. Sure, the rich guys from up north were in the pits flashing cash. But, it was a smattering of kids from off Western Avenue who pushed the paper and made sure Mr. Rich Guy slept in his fine feather bed at night.

o o o

College was a dream your parents chased for you. Some of em' made it; many didn't even come close — those guys have hard hands, just like their fathers. Chicago is working class; it was founded on sweat, iron, and pig's blood.

Hard work built this city, these alleys, these streets — rivet by rivet. Your grandparents, the greatest generation, fought in some wars and went right back to work in the stock-yards. Your fathers saw the bloodstains on their father's boots, and you? You're thankful they laid the ground for you.

Our parents wanted better, but no matter how optimistic the plight, it was a plight none-theless. Such as with a Picasso, trying to explain the social proclivities of the South Side of Chicago takes patience, and a will to grapple with parallels beyond the pale. Nothing is easy on the South Side. Life isn't handed to you, and if you don't understand the trappings of your environment, you'll never make it out alive. It's a harsh reality, but it's built into your DNA.

When the city you're from looks at you with doubt you'll ever make it out alive, you'd better be ready to fight on your toes because it's never going to be easy. But you have heart, and you're never not proud, never not ready to argue that it's not a wasteland and you won't die when you cross the street.

Maybe reality comes a lot sooner, but you at least know where you stand in the game of life. If you're not willing to work for it, it won't happen. For many it's a hard pill to swallow, but on the South Side, you're born with that pill in your fist.

Most of us were born at Mercy Hospital, in the shadow of downtown Chicago. Despite the prominence of location, Mercy has always been one step away from the charity ward. It's dingy, dirty, and current only by necessity — Mercy has seen a fair share of births by the unwed and white sheets placed over a gunshot to the head. Mercy sits on the edge of the cash money business world known as Chicago's Loop, while being a kissing cousin to Chinatown, and is a quarter toss from the projects. Mercy is only a few miles from the Italian and Irish Grabowski neighborhoods, Bridgeport, and Canaryville. Mercy is a juxtaposition of an attitude, but never without its own ghosts, too. Mercy doesn't exist; it looms over the edge of Lakeshore Drive, letting you know life is always watching with expectant eyes.

When you're a kid coming up, you learn a lot of truths. Many of them shape you, but many scar you, just the same. On the South Side, you're taught to value work ethic, to get up earlier, grind harder, and make everyone jealous of the shit you've earned. Keyword: earned. You must achieve these things by sheer will to take a punch, but never throw one when it comes to talking about one's achievements, or salary: you must showcase through grace, through rough hands and tired eyes.

If you didn't have a work ethic, the South Side wouldn't have an identity. While the North Side boasts the cute houses and the higher incomes, the South Side prides itself on sweat equity and being able to be counted on. Everyone wants to be known as a "good guy" or "a great gal" — that's a label that sticks with you for life, it's a form of currency worth more than any line of credit. Being known as a hard working, good human being is paramount because it opens you up to jobs, social circles, and always a beer in the local tavern.

You want everyone on the block to know you as "That Jimmy, good fella. Salt of the earth, give you the shirt off his fuckin' back, and never ask for anything in return. That's a good guy right there." Then, that guy buys Jimmy a Jameson for being a good dude. You'd say "mensch" but most of us didn't know a single Jewish person till out of high school. It ain't ignorance. It's just the way the neighborhoods work out.

Growing up, every kid you knew was one of four and a half designations:

Irish, Polish, Italian, or Mexican. That's it. Sure, you saw a lot of black people but didn't know any. Sure, you shopped together, went to the grocery store together, sat in line at the doctor's office, but not until high school did you *know* any black kids.

The neighborhoods on the South Side are like mini strongholds, no new kinds of people suddenly move in, and it's chic or affordable. It's the same people, breeding with other people of the same ethnic groups to create the same cultural dichotomy and, in most cases, it's Irish Catholic folks. And Irish Catholics breed like goddamned rats. Every family was at least three kids, and a cousin living with them whose dad was a piece of shit who walked out on his mother, who had her own thing going on.

Being Irish is a massive deal. Being proud of your bloodline is everything. When you meet people who don't care about their heritage, it's hard to understand or relate. What's being an American when you can't take pride in what your great-grandfather went through to get over here? Aren't you proud to have the last name McMannus or Reilly? You're a Sullivan, a Hilliard — take pride in your family! You'd better be, or your grandma would beat you with a kitchen spoon.

Much stock is put in the fact that families, despite having never set foot in Ireland, can name counties, know bars in Ireland, and have land in Ireland they someday plan to move to. You're born knowing all of the songs, your girlfriends wear Claddagh rings, and 99.9 percent of us are raised Catholics with an overbearing sense of guilt.

The door to your mom's house is green. You know someone who play the accordion, you have a cousin named Shannon, and most of the houses are decorated just as heavily for St. Patrick's Day as they are Christmas. Your mom cooks corned beef and cabbage every year, like clockwork. The Clancy Brothers were the soundtrack growing up. This is not even slightly unique.

You knew about gangs from the jump. Never wear a lot of red or a lot of blue if you don't want to find out if you're loyal to the Satan Disciples or Gangster Disciples. You knew that black and whatever adjacent color could send off the wrong message. You knew what team logos were en vogue, and knew someone could confront you should your hat match your jacket. The Sox were always safe, but wearing that matching Raiders hat and jacket could make some folks ask questions about your block.

You knew what gang symbols looked like, what they meant, and how to act if there was a "presence" locally. If you saw a six-pointed star or pitchfork in red, chances are you were in a part of town where cops cruised on the regular. Even in the nicer parts of town, seeing a threat like "SD IN A BODYBAG" painted on some old, lovely Polish lady's garage wasn't entirely out of the question.

You knew that if you cocked your hat to a side, it could mean you were in a gang. You knew how to make gang symbols with your hands. Everyone knew someone whose brother or cousin was in a gang. How could anyone be surprised when our cultural icon was a man named Scarface Capone? While for many, Capone is a figure of a doomed history, in Chicago, he's the hometown boy made good.

Baseball is your identity. You choose your team and let it mark you for life. There is no "I root for both" on the South Side. If you pick the Cubs, you're a traitor and will be labeled as such. Liking the White Sox isn't just buying into a team, it's buying into a team that's from your side of town — location perceives ethic. You love the White Sox, you swear by them, they are yours and no one else's. They're ours: by the park being down on Thirty-fifth, it lets people know this is a working-class team.

The North Side gets everything; they get the cool bars, the hip place to get tacos, expensive condos with a water view. They get the nice parks and the Lincoln Park Zoo.

On the South Side, you've got generational neighborhoods and places to get a Mother-In-Law off a Formica counter. The Bears feel universal, the Hawks and Bulls are in the middle of the city, but those White Sox, they're as South Side as it comes. But with that sense of identity comes a complicated relationship.

You don't love the Sox any less when they lose, but a White Sox fan punishes the team for underperforming by not going to games. There's a sense of cruel irony because the fans refuse to spend money unless the team is winning. Fans from other teams talk garbage for not filling the stadium nightly, but you lay on your sword when you're a Sox fan.

The White Sox, to so many, feels like a piece of their lives, because they're a cultural identifier: folks from the neighborhood run the park, the neighborhood loves the team, Mayor Daley was a Sox fan, and President Obama was a Sox fan. While the rest of America pines over the little blue bears and this being their year — the White Sox fans loathe the attention, the gushing of Wrigley. It gets under the skin; it becomes vitriolic that their neighborhood is a media darling and filled with tourists from Iowa. You're born hating the Cubs and you'd better stick to it. You'll always be number two, and that's basically what it's like to grow up south of Madison Avenue in the first place.

When it comes to friends, you stick by the same group of folks for life. Most of us know the kids we were baptized with or went to high school with — ask someone from the South Side how many friends they have and they'll rattle off more than the names in the phone book. It's good to know you can count on someone or when you just need to crack open a beer, a few people are always ready to walk down to the tavern with you.

You know someone who can get you a bag of weed, or always has a line on Playstations that "fell off the back of a truck." In the days before everything was built on the Internet, there was always a guy who'd climb the pole and turn your cable back on for fifty bucks. Why look in the phone book when the guy down the street made a living off selling dope and wrenching cars in his garage? And because most folks knew some cops, no one ever got busted, because why throw the book at "good cop Frankie's cousin"?

But the elephant in the room is violence. People assume that if they step foot on the South Side, they'll be murdered on sight. And yes, Chicago has a gun problem. When there's little hope and little opportunity for a basic education, what's left? The streets. The further down the street numbers go in Chicago, the worse it gets. Ain't an opinion, just a fact of life.

People get violent because there's nothing there, no hope — just a reality that cannot be solved in a few moves by a city that doesn't care. A gang is an easy place to make money; the corner is an easy place to make money. A school is an easy place to avoid because no one is going to call when you don't show up. There's no one manning the phones in the first place. These streets have plenty to say, but a lot of the time, the words are lost behind the barrel of a gun.

So, kid, what's left? Everything is complicated, and nothing is easy, but it's ours. The South Side isn't perfect, not even close.

It's not a place you can box in, because how do you explain a Rubik's cube to someone who's blind? You're taught lessons on one hand, but those who can't grasp the basics will never get what's inherent, and it's heartbreaking. But, it's a two-sided coin that smells like fresh Mexican food or seeing your cousin Kimmy on the sidewalk. It's knowing Killer Bill down at the corner store, or realizing the guys who'll carry your coffin are the same ones who toasted you on your twenty-first.

On the South Side, you have few joys: your team, your culture, and getting by with hard work. You're born to be proud of what you are, but for many, that's a hard nut to crack. You're proud to be from the South Side, but you're not proud of what it takes to exist down where the street numbers go higher the further south you get.

The Sediment of Fear

TONI NEALIE

I was afraid. The man behind the glass partition leafed through my papers and asked me something in a language I didn't understand. "I speak only English," I replied. Avoiding my gaze, the man flicked his eyes from the papers to me to the papers. His grey sports jacket shone slightly at the elbows, a middle button dangling from loosened threads. His maroon shirt was undone at the top, no tie. The room echoed, its rows of grey plastic chairs empty. This was a space intended for many, but I was the only person on this side of the barrier. I had stepped into a geography both foreign and startling.

In a corner, green prayer mats lay rolled on a filing cabinet. Separating the main room from a large alcove was a rosewood screen embedded with golden tendrils. Beyond the screen I saw a Pakistani flag and the Stars and Stripes flanking a green table, over which hung wrinkled portraits of Pakistan's founder Muhammad Ali Jinnah, the eleventh president Asif Ali Zardari, and the seventeenth prime minister Raja Pervaiz Ashraf. The walls of the broad space were decorated with photographs of remote desert valleys, mountain peaks, and ancient forts. My planned journey seemed tangible, no longer imagined, and I felt uneasy.

Moments earlier, I was being jostled along the Magnificent Mile with clusters of pre-holiday shoppers, past storefront windows full of Italian lingerie, hockey memorabilia, Disney toys, and bright candy. Tourists in puffy jackets were clustered around a plaque set against the polished granite base of the building I needed to enter. A Chicago landmark. "This outstanding Art Deco-style skyscraper helps define one of the city's finest urban spaces," read the inscription. "Its prominence is further heightened by the jog in Michigan Avenue, where it crosses the Chicago River." Peering up to where the guide pointed, I saw Native Americans, traders, soldiers, settlers, and oxen trudging in bas-relief across the limestone wall five floors up. I imagined the riverbank of yesteryear: the crop-tending, fur-hunting, and domestic routines, and the ambushes, massacres, and rifts between competing peoples. This commemorative sculpture, on the site of old Fort Dearborn, demands that we pay attention to the past. It reminds us of conquest, of what is gained and lost.

I stepped from the rowdy street into a silent, gleaming foyer. Roaring Twenties extravagance: verde antico, marble wainscots, and mahogany trim. A sleek monument to the glitter of its time, it was built only fifty years after the Great Fire of Chicago burned down what remained of Fort Dearborn. Hewn from deposits in Minnesota, Indiana, and Greece, the stone is the type used for cathedrals, cenotaphs, tombstones, and the countertops found in 75 percent of America's new kitchens. Quarried and transported across borders, these are the rocks that become a surface for our history.

An elevator with bronze birds sculptured on the doors shuddered up to the eighth floor, opening into a corridor with linoleum floor and several sets of identical opaque glass doors. At a dim end, I pressed a buzzer and one door opened. The man behind the glass examined my pile of documents: application, invitation, passport, green card, employment letter, sponsor's identification. A staccato of questions fired through an aperture:

Who is your sponsor?
My mother's cousin.

Why are you going?
To attend my mother's cousin's granddaughter's wedding. To meet family in Pakistan. To visit the homeland of my mother's father, Amritsar, across the border in India.

One moment. The man walked out of my vision. I heard a door open and click shut. I was alone in the lofty room, with the rows of empty chairs.

I stood there with my disquiet. My feet sounded tinny on the tiled floor. I tried to slow my breathing, to stop its shallow rasp and soften the sharpness in my chest. My anxiety rested on getting a visa, two visas, before I could travel to Lahore in Pakistan, then Amritsar in India, the next month. This type of paranoia bubbled up when I faced bureaucracies with changeable and inexplicable rules. I dreaded the sentries overseeing the secondary interview rooms where one could be isolated or made invisible. Recalling a train ride I took years ago, from a former Eastern bloc country to northern Italy, I saw a faint blue drift of cigarette smoke inside; a blur of damp spring fields outside. The travelers are in good spirits, a mixture of ladies wearing floral headscarves, backpackers, young men laughing in the seats behind me. The carriage quiets as several drab-uniformed soldiers, guns slung across their bodies, sway down the aisle checking documents. One stops at my seat, flips the pages of my passport and barks: "Your visa expires tomorrow!"

"I leave today," I reply. The train slows in a muddy landscape and stops at a white checkpoint station. I can't decipher its sign, written in Cyrillic. The soldiers disembark, taking with them a group of young men, including those who had sat behind me. They don't return.

My palms dampened. As much as I longed to go to Pakistan, I jittered. Bombs and kidnappings dominated the news, although my relative Rafi assured me that his city was safe. My mother worried that my emails were scrutinized. Is the CIA keeping tabs on visitors? Would traveling there impede my re-entry to the U.S.?

I was, I am, a coward. My world is small these days, a domestic sphere of children and husband and dog, neighbors who chat while I tend the garden, friends and colleagues who share interests in writing or teaching. The unfamiliar, the unknown rises up, an oppression that threatens to swamp me.

I felt uneasy about meeting a family of strangers, of answering questions and trying to shore up the rift between generations and continents. I picked my fingernails and turned to look at the photographs of immense mountains and deep gorges of rocks. I saw ravines of grey, brown, and black. Shale, limestone, schist, greywacke, feldspar, soapstone, marble, dolomite, sandstone, granite, born from the earth's thrusting and flowing. Rock created from eruptions, fault lines, folds and cleavages, conglomeration and sedimentation, displacement, and ruptures.

Years ago, my husband and sons began giving me rocks: heart-shaped stones, black and white pebbles washed up on Atlantic beaches, gems tumbled smooth, a carved green-stone from New Zealand, speckled souvenirs from the Great Lakes.

When we excavate the earth, what do we bring from the past into our future? How do the sediments connect us to our earlier selves, our heritage, our conflicts and rifts, our disrupted families?

A door clicked open. The man returned to his post behind the glass. He cleared his throat. I stepped over to the aperture. He looked closely at the Invitation For Marriage, which described the celebration ahead:

> 1. the Nikah ceremony (marriage agreement), to be performed by a religious celebrant including exchange of rings,
>
> 2. the Mehndi, for the bride, where henna is applied on the bride's hand; to be followed by a night of music,
>
> 3. the Mehndi for the groom,
>
> 4. the Marriage ceremony,
>
> 5. the Walima, a celebration of the marriage.

The letter said: "You will live in our home as a family guest. It will be a matter of pleasure for us to arrange your reception, entertainment, and sightseeing."

My sister and I shopped for these five events—she in London and I in Chicago—for different outfits, bright silky pants, tunics, and gauzy scarves embroidered with sequins and faux gems. Costumes, unlike our usual jeans and boots, so we could play the part of wedding guests without appearing alien. I explained to the man that my mother's cousin extended the invitation when he visited his siblings in Toronto, where they had migrated many years ago. I flew to meet him for the first time just months earlier. Now, I planned to meet my sister in Lahore. She would travel from her home in London. Together, we would represent multiple generations of our New Zealand family. After the wedding, my sister would fly home, while I would cross the border with my relative's friends, stay in their Chandigarh house, then travel on alone to my grandfather's ancestral hometown, Amritsar. This seemed a lot to tell a stranger.

My grandfather Abraham Wally Mohammad Salaman, a British subject in colonial India, sailed across the oceans to the Dominion of New Zealand. In the early 1900s, he married my grandmother, whose forbears had migrated from Cornwall. My grandfather died in

1945, before India's independence and the bloody separation of India and Pakistan, two years shy of a 1947 law change that would have granted him New Zealand citizenship. My grandfather was British when he died. I knew him only from photographs, an unsmiling, clean-shaven man wearing a waistcoat with a fob watch on a chain, and pince-nez spectacles in the style of Theodore Roosevelt. My mother — and then my siblings and I — were stranded from extended family in the way of so many separations, without the bedrock of history to either anchor us or stand in our way. Part of my worry was embedded in familial angst. The fossils of racism and worry about heritage — passed from my forebears and inherited by my mother — had washed up on my banks. I wanted to bring our family's ossified connection to life, to stake a claim to that part of my heritage.

Is it possible to have a multiple-entry visa?
No, it is not possible.

I wish to travel to Amritsar from Lahore.
It is not possible.

But I really want to go to Amritsar.
No, it is not possible. You must leave Pakistan and you will not be allowed back.

But I am flying in and out of Lahore.
It is not possible to provide you a multiple-entry visa. You are applying from a third country.

He pushed my green cardboard folder back under the window, making it clear that persistence would result in no visa at all. I pushed it back.

Can I have a single-entry visa?
Yes, that is possible. Come back on Monday afternoon at three o'clock.

Outside, I barely recognized Wacker Drive. The river glinted graphite as it coursed toward Lake Michigan. Disappointment scalded my cheeks. I felt inconsequential.

My quest for an Indian visa was outsourced to a global corporate enterprise, starting on my home computer and finishing at a booth in a city business center. Impersonal compared to the Pakistani consulate approach, the pursuit began with an online form. Boxes ticked: a six-page printed checklist including the visa application form, a digital visa photograph, a copy of the online order form, two signatures, my passport, my two-inch-by-two-inch photograph glued, not stapled, a photocopied proof of address, my permanent resident card. Documents paperclipped, not stapled, in order.

I rode the L to Adams and Wabash, walked a block to State Street, and through a door between a sandwich franchise and a cosmetics chain. Inside, a room the size of two tennis courts was sectioned by rope. A slow snake of people moved through the labyrinth to a row of "consultants" sitting in booths behind a long glass window. Behind them, more clerks stapled documents and checked computer records. Processing visa applications to India seemed quite an industry, like a scene from Richard Scarry's kid's book *Busy Town*. I was one in a bustle of overheated bodies peeling off overcoats, shuffling papers, nattering about forthcoming journeys to see grandparents, a yoga retreat, favorite places in a guidebook. A stranger told me about a tea plantation tour somewhere, Darjeeling? A skipping, singing child knocked over a rope barrier. In this room of bright chatter and warm lights, I felt my fear dislodging.

The consultants accepted documents under the glass and talked loudly through slatted portholes at the applicants. A young man slowly counted a pile of bank notes and slid them across the counter, but was short a few dollars and rushed off to the bank. A woman with blonde hair piled up on her head scrabbled in a very large velvet bag. Perhaps if she paid attention to the small purse instruction on the checklist, she may have discovered her missing photographs. Her visa could not be processed. She cajoled and simpered, shouted, then left in a flurry of perfume. My turn. Gleaming the kind of smile you see in tourist brochures, a woman clerk glanced quickly at my documents. She asked me no questions about my purpose or whom I would visit. She gave no indication that she recognized me as a descendant of India or even cared. But she would ensure I had a visa.

"Come back tomorrow, please. Next person in line!"

Two days before my anticipated departure and the day my sister was due to leave London, I received an email from my relative Rafi telling me of a "serious mishap."

The whole family is in such a state of mourning and mentally upset no one would be able to look after you if you come at this stage. I therefore humbly request you to cancel your tour. Since our Indian guests will also not be coming now, there will be no one to take you to Amritsar. The circumstances demand that the visit be deferred. I feel extremely sorry about all the planning and efforts you put in for this visit and the excitement that you had, but one cannot challenge the acts of nature.

Further emails trickled in. A member of the groom's party had died suddenly. Custom dictated forty days of mourning. The young people had practiced their dancing for months and the first wave of international guests had already arrived, but now flowers, food, wedding venues, hotel rooms, and club lodgings all had to be cancelled.

"It feels destined not to be," I wrote to my sister, dismayed.

"At least we are OK, alive and well!" she replied. She stayed in London. I rearranged my flight to travel direct to Delhi and then on to Amritsar alone. But there was a riot in Delhi and I couldn't shake the feeling that this journey was not to be taken. I changed my flight again and instead visited my mother in New Zealand — another trembling, mountainous land situated on tectonic fault lines. This time, the Shaky Isles felt calm and stable, and my mother felt like home.

I have my visas, one to India, the homeland of a grandfather I never knew, the other to Pakistan, home of other branches of the family tree. Like the two countries, they lie across a divide, twinned on adjoining pages in my passport. I possess a new stone heart, a consolation prize my youngest son bought at Ten Thousand Villages, a local fair trade store. The size of my palm, it is translucent rose salt stone, halite, from a Pakistani mine in the Himalayas, equidistant from Amritsar and Lahore. It sits on my windowsill.

"THE SEDIMENT OF FEAR," EXCERPTED FROM *THE MILES BETWEEN ME*, BY TONI NEALIE (CURBSIDE SPLENDOR, 2016).

Four Poems

RAYMOND BERRY

Roseland

Indiana to Halsted / 103rd to 119th street / neighborhoods: Fernwood,
Princeton Park, Lilydale, West Chesterfield, Rosemoor, Sheldon Heights,
and West Roseland / all food deserts / two public high schools: Fenger and
Harlan / 44,619 residents / 19.5% live below the poverty line / 17.8% are
unemployed / 17.4% are 25 & older without high school diploma / 40.9%
are under 18 / boys in white tees flood Chicago streets / two by four's in
hand / shirts removed / mouths water like bees for pollen / they thirst / rub
their six packs / stones bloom in their stomachs with each blow/cracking
Albert's skull / one yelling, *put him to sleep* / then the final stomp / one
serving 26 years / the others 32 / they're men now

*On September 24, 2009, Fenger High School student Derrion Albert was beaten to
death with nail-spiked railroad boards after walking into a gang brawl between
the Gangster Disciples and the Black P. Stones. Four Fenger students
were convicted of murder.*

memory

for Derrion Albert and Blair Holt

he would put his key in the door at 3:15
& spend hours on his computer
but today, he'd go out and walk into chaos

16, a mere 5-foot-7
his 115lb physique could do nothing
against planks that dented & damaged his body

recorded in a two-minute video
as others witnessed
his slight frame slowly crawling toward Agape

&

Holt
16, who shielded his friend under him
as shots blazed on a packed cta bus
youth frantically ducking under seats

lead piercing his flesh   a father wiping
blood from his son's ears and nose
apologizing to a shirt held tightly in fist

both boys honor students
their names now another stone
on a mountain

Agape is the community center in Roseland where Albert's body was discovered.
In May 2007 Blair Holt was gunned down on a crowded CTA bus.

dichotomy of Yummy Sandifer

there was a boy whose fists were too small to hold light
so he held onto crime:
23 felonies, 2 convictions
bullying, extortion
stealing then burning caddies & lincolns
his burn-marked skin
changed world of pretend
to one of gangs and dead bodies

he wanted to touch sky
but traded wings for matches
he was tough but afraid
docile, but disturbed
by two worlds:
theft, drugs, and murder
make-believe, sleepovers, and bicycles

one day his hands would be large enough
to hold any gentle thing
but maybe hands were meant for breaking

beneath a viaduct underpass

your boys moved you
between hideouts
promised a way out

you trusted, depended
the one nicknamed yummy
who loved cookies and junk food

thought you were leaving Roseland
and black disciples behind you
one of them fires, .22 in hand

blood moving like something spilled
after head and bullets meet
two casings lie beside you

body in puddle
your one palm outstretched
still reaching

On September 1, 1994, Robert "Yummy" Sandifer was killed execution style at age eleven, by fellow gang members out of fear he would snitch to police.

Ida B. Wells Testifies in the Ghost Town, 1995-2011 in the rubble of the Ida B. Wells homes

KEVIN COVAL

this is not the white city,
though perhaps, it is a city
for whites. not Mississippi
or even what Chicago looks like
west & south, when Mississippi
rushes north like the Nile.

these are the Southern Horrors;
abandoned streets, boarded buildings,
empty tumble weed lots. one can
almost hear Lake Michigan in all this
barren land where children once moved
from these blocks to prison, auctioned.
            blocks never been safe.

this is a Red Record of displacement.
what happens when culture has amnesia.
I sat on a train seventy years before
Montgomery. what'll this land be named:
ghost town, scrapped plan for poor
& Black, will it be Lynchburg
or Prisonton, New Laborville
or the white city

I witness & testify. my prose titled:
why children of Diaspora & Africa
legacied slavery & jim crow, ran out
of every Monarchs' land: daley
pharaoh. why these citizens
never included in Burnham Plans.

I stand on rhodes near Bridgeport,
astonished. prime land, my body, real
estate for the taking & dismembering
by maps & hands the shade of ghost.
my body disfigured, again, this is what happens
when a culture has amnesia, when cities tear
down its promise, call it renewal. what happens
to those blue light monitored & standardized
test tracked, those forced into obsolete industrial
training, railroaded into new slave labor, orange
suited & disenfranchised, what do we do
with the forgotten, those left   out
to
hang
like ghosts.

I witness
until the whole world does
until ghost stories are documented
& irrefutable, until America is haunted
by the spirits of those it says never happened.

PREVIOUSLY PUBLISHED IN *A PEOPLE'S HISTORY OF CHICAGO*
(HAYMARKET BOOKS, 2017).

Cotton Cobwebs: Hauntology and History at Stateville, Statesville, and Cook County Jail

LOGAN BREITBART

"The slamming of the steel doors was a signal that the iron monster had once again been fed." — Shaka Senghor, Writing My Wrongs: Life, Death, and Redemption in an American Prison

"First Principles, Clarice. Simplicity. Read Marcus Aurelius. Of each particular thing ask: what is in itself? What is its nature?" — Hannibal Lecter, The Silence of the Lambs

Statesville Haunted Prison is the most infamous haunted house in the state of Illinois. Situated in the middle of a cornfield south of Chicago, the harvest chill and moonlit barnyard entrance conjure a mise-en-scène akin to the Rust Belt horror movie *Children of the Corn*. The "officers" rattle off a list of rules to the patrons, or "meat," then send them off to the prison proper. Replete with smoke machines, flickering lights, industrial sound effects, and 150 ghouls, it's a sugary spectacle. But a more sinister terror lurks in the autumn crosswinds.

Statesville Haunted Prison is two miles west of Stateville Correctional Center, a maximum-security prison with — until 2016 — the only operational panopticon in the world.* Stateville is haunted by its past, a crypt that can be opened by way of comparison with Statesville Haunted Prison and Cook County Jail, where I work as a GED instructor.

I walk from my morning class in the jail's Division One to my afternoon class in Division Six through an underground tunnel system that connects each major building in the complex. It's lunchtime; a miasma of bologna and stale beef hovers in the humid halls. Grey liquid dribbles from the ceiling in spots where it floods during rainstorms. We call this bile "jail juice." Detainees get processed and transported through these sick intestines. Bloodstains older than Al Capone mottle the concrete floor, and eggshell

---

* IN AN OP-ED FOR THE *CHICAGO SUN-TIMES* ON OCTOBER 14, 2016, ILLINOIS GOVERNOR BRUCE RAUNER ANNOUNCED HIS ADMINISTRATION'S INTENTION TO CLOSE THE STATEVILLE PANOPTICON. IT WAS EMPTIED BY THE END OF THE YEAR.

paint coats mold and cracks like powder on herpes.

Today, a palm-size cockroach pushes through a Make-an-Effort-Not-an-Excuse poster and plummets onto my student's neck. He rips off his uniform shirt and screams. His classmates and I barely budge; it's business as usual. We squash the bug with a GED prep book, and the student excuses himself for a drink of water (with permission from the dozy guard down the hallway, of course). Besides the initial yelp, it's a clinical and quiet affair. This is an insatiable and indeed listless monster house.

In order to construct an effective haunted house, designers must pry into the mythos of horror within human consciousness. Beyond the shock and awe of a sudden movement or loud noise, the ghoul's ghastliness stems from a connection to death and decay.

Spiders, for example, tickle our flesh and remind us of our vulnerability to nefarious forces outside ourselves. Their very anatomy, their roe-like gleaming eyes and fingering chelicerae, and the primordial propulsion of their fluid creep can drive humans to tears. A clear fixture in the nexus of horror in our collective psyche, cotton cobwebs dangle in most haunted houses, and Statesville is no exception. But spiders only kill about six people a year in the United States, and they eat household pests, like flies, roaches, and disease-carrying mosquitoes. Hell, they even eat each other. The spider, as a metaphor emblematic of horror, is compelling to the extent that it's embedded in a collective nightmare, but the metaphor excludes attributes essential to a spider's existence.

It seems to me that the "inmates" in Statesville are a manifestation of the clichéd fears that Americans harbor over people who commit crimes, but there are some direct parallels between the characters in Statesville and the ghosts of the real people disciplined and punished over the years in Stateville and Cook County Jail.

According to the Statesville website, the current warden of the haunted prison is the Demon of Darkness, a djinn-like despot, whose crimes include brainwashing and conspiracy. His ostensible control over daily operations and prison personnel recalls the absolute power Joseph E. Ragen wielded as Stateville Warden from 1936-1961.

Ragen inherited a Stateville in disarray. As noted by sociologist James Jacob in his essential (and overlooked) book *Stateville: The Penitentiary in Mass Society,* for fifteen years after its opening, Stateville hired workers through a spoils system enmeshed in state politics. Governor-appointed wardens oversaw guards with low wages and twelve-hour shifts. The real power of the prison belonged to Irish and Italian gangs. Escapes and violence abounded. The state took a hands-off approach when it came to penal operations, so Ragen was free to develop Stateville in accordance with his vision.

He isolated Stateville from the outside world. When Republican Dwight Greene became governor in 1941, Ragen resigned. But Governor Greene demanded that Ragen return as warden in 1942 after Irish gangster Roger "Terrible" Touhy and six of his henchmen escaped from Stateville. Ragen agreed to return only if political influence on hiring and operations ended. He made this stipulation with succeeding governors, thereby securing complete control over Stateville.

His rules were exhaustive, extending into hypothetical situations. Ragen micromanaged every aspect of prison operations, stressing minutiae in order to prevent bigger problems.

In his *Training Manual for Guards and Officers*, Ragen writes, "If you work for a man, in Heaven's name work for him. If he pays you wages that supply your bread and butter, work for him, speak well of him, and stand by him, and stand by the institution he represents." He demanded absolute loyalty from all employees, and, according to Jacob, besides housing, clean clothes, and decent meals (that had to be lieutenant-approved with a taste-test and official statement), everything was considered a privilege for inmates, including work.

Ragen broke in new inmates with six months of labor at the coal pile, where they would move hundreds of pounds of coal in wheelbarrows from the yard to the powerhouse. It busied the inmates, keeping them sore and pliant. Like the Demon of Darkness, Ragen gave the most desirable jobs to the toughest inmates. Docile inmates worked in the basement, censoring outgoing mail, while tougher men worked clerical jobs and nursing positions. Snitching to officers helped them climb the social ladder and secure better jobs. Defiance resulted in indefinite banishments to solitary confinement and returns to the coal pile. All inmates marched in paramilitary fashion, ate their food silently, and were constantly supervised. Some inmates started "going stir bugs," becoming paranoid that they were "being watched everywhere and plotted against in every conversation."

Before it closed, the first floor of the four-story panopticon housed inmates with severe psychological impairments. Stateville's "F-house" panopticon materializes Jeremy Bentham's 1791 vision of a utilitarian and cost-effective prison architecture. It's a circular building with the inmates' cells facing the center of the circle in which stands a guard's tower. A guard stands watch; he can see out, but the inmates cannot see him. The threat of being watched (or caught doing anything illegal) conditions inmates into policing themselves. As Michel Foucault renders it, the prisoner "is seen, but he does not see; he is the object of information, never a subject in communication."

"Maniacs" litter the longest cellblock in Statesville Haunted Prison, some swinging from their cages like kids on monkey bars and others jeering at passersby, flicking around the straps of their straitjackets and licking their faux iron muzzles. It's the loudest stretch of the spectacle, as the Maniacs scream, glossolate, and giggle.

What Bentham deems superfluous, what Foucault overlooks, and what the haunted prison narrowly taps into is the noise — the excruciating sounds of insanity that bellow inside the panopticon. All the cells face the center tower, so if an inmate drops a plastic food tray all the other inmates will hear it. Add 419 inmates, and it becomes a storm.

I visit the Stateville panopticon in April 2014 and nearly pass out amid the thunder. The guard in the tower loads his shotgun, showboating his power to our tour group. Our presence riles up the choir on the rim, silhouettes in the latticed Plexiglas. Relatively new are the plastic scrims affixed to each cell on the first floor, a guard informs us. He says that they hide the "bugs," a slang term for the inmates who "refuse to wear clothes, that play with their feces, that spit, that jerk off in front of anyone." The soundscape smears together, but the primal howls from the first-floor cells punctuate. I feel light-headed, and drift away from myself, ascending toward the top of the tower, becoming one with this iron hell.

The clinically-insane population is swelling in Stateville and Cook County Jail, primarily due to the mass closure of mental hospitals in Chicago. Deinstitutionalization in the United States began in the 1950s in an effort to move treatment from crumbling mental hospitals to community clinics, but funding for these smaller efforts has been scarce. The complex historical trends that continually lead to the dumping of mentally ill citizens onto the streets (and into Cook County Jail) are elaborated at length in Matt Ford's Atlantic article "America's Largest Mental Hospital is a Jail" and include the ramifications of Mayor Rahm Emanuel's closure of six mental health clinics in 2012. A story that Martin (not his real name), a man incarcerated in Stateville, told me illustrates the problems.

Martin was originally serving his time at Menard Correctional Center for first-degree murder. After several years inside, he started experiencing nightmares like never before in his life, dreams where he felt like he was, "on the edge of a precipice." He explained, "There's a point where rehabilitation becomes institutionalization." Martin overcame a drug addiction in jail and prays for his victims' families every day. For this growth, he gives full responsibility to the isolation that incarceration provides. But the institution consumes him languidly.

Martin's final roommate at Menard was a schizophrenic man from Chicago. One night, Martin awoke from a nightmare to discover his roommate leaning over his bed, wide-eyed, gawking at him. Mortified — and unsure if he was still dreaming — Martin shoved his roommate and asked him what the fuck he was doing. His roommate wept and explained that this is what happens when he does not take his schizoid-meds. Martin warned him that if it happened again that he might not be able to control himself. It happened again; Martin pummeled him. As punishment, Martin was transferred to F-house in Stateville (making it extraordinarily difficult for his ailing mother — who has since died — to visit her son).

Insanity begets insanity; insanity begets violence; and violence — violence in these spliced histories. But, per usual, missing from predominant discourse are the inmates themselves. How are the men inside affected by the changing outside world? How do they cope with the funneling of insane people into penal institutions?

The language of rehabilitation infiltrated American consciousness in the 1950s and 1960s, as the Civil Rights movement catalyzed concern for prisoners' rights. But "rehabilitation," like all words, bears a vortex of contorted costumes. Ragen justified his paternalism by appealing to the hot topics of the times, by using the fashionable buzzwords. His preferred title became "penologist," and he writes, "The prison authorities must take [the] chronologically underprivileged mass of humanity and place it on the path of morality."

Today, inmate workers (if they're lucky enough to land such a privilege) in Cook County Jail make $2 an hour for physical labor: moving janitorial supplies, cleaning bathrooms, moving laundry, cleaning laundry, moving clothing, moving entire offices to and from the various divisions around the jail through the underground tunnels, etc.

When I ask the workers why they do it, they usually say some variation on "it's better than doing nothing." Most of the men are awaiting trial, and some await re-trial. That means this majority is technically still innocent, yet they receive a serf's compensation. When I ask them why they don't invoke their Sixth Amendment right to a speedy trial, they usually say something along the lines of, "I don't want to piss off the judge."

Both my maternal grandfather and my father were incarcerated, the former in the state of Arizona for fraud and the latter in the state of Nevada for conspiracy on a plea bargain. I think about their attempts to sew their own patch of shimmery American fantasy, the former looking for oil investors to invest in the exploration of land bereft of oil, the latter selling cocaine while wearing board shorts and muscle shirts. I think about the resources they had to survive prison, the advocacy of their families on their behalf, and about their recourses to prosperous communities for jobs after they finished serving their time. In other words, they had the means to integrate back into society that many do not have.

Inmates who already have their high school equivalency work as tutors in our GED program. They do a lot of the heavy lifting in the classroom when it comes to drilling concepts and motivating students. Tutors receive community service hours as compensation for their work that they hope will get them some "good time" from their judge, who may or may not grant it to them.

A couple weeks ago, a longtime tutor of mine joked, "Where's my paycheck?" at the end of class. It was a pithy and crushing question. It reminded me of my complicity in this system of servitude, the white schoolmaster free to roam the halls of captivity, making the jail look good through the success rates of my students. I was a privileged tourist in a rotting zoo at Stateville, and now I facilitate the production of free labor from my predominantly Black and Latino students.

I'm complicit, but we're all complicit. Even if I quit my job at the jail, the jail persists, gobbling up my tax dollars to serve me and my loved ones by purportedly making a better and safer society. Its architecture and premises for existence most closely resemble those of our public schools and hospitals.

Ragen's departure from Stateville in 1961 coincided with growing concerns about prisoners' rights in society. His successors had to take the reins of an institution that was thought to be a cornerstone example of compassionate prison ideology, but in reality they had to fill the shoes of a dictator. Black Muslims, both inside and outside the prison, advocated for an elevated quality of life for prisoners and were unilaterally suppressed in the prison; every demand was rejected and leaders were thrown into segregation.

The Warren Court expanded civil rights, and by 1971 Stateville was beholden to a new reign of bureaucracy, a chain-of-command that answered directly to Springfield. "Rehabilitation" and "humanization" were the key terms for the new administrations. Guards were expected to be pseudo-counselors to the inmates and were offered neither classes in counseling nor psychology. Prison was supposed to be "corrective," but they received no extra funding for these big ideas.

Thus, prisoners' expectations grew astronomically compared to the material circumstances enclosing them, and new wardens could not find the balance between leadership, rehab, and rhetoric. Power fell into the hands of the inmates; it was a time warp, a new reign of gangs.

But today, Stateville looks positively Ragan-esque, with frequent lockdowns and little movement. When inmates do move, they do so in formation in small groups. When I visited Stateville in 2014, silence filled the yard, save for a few people in the recreation area. After we toured the roundhouse, we passed by a basketball court gated with barbed-wire fencing. An officer in a tower on the court had his rife ready as he watched two men playing basketball.

The reversion to an authoritarian regime can be traced to one of Chicago's most notorious residents: Richard Speck.

In 1967 Speck was found guilty of murdering eight nurses in a South Side townhouse. He was sentenced to death in Stateville, where he evaded execution through judicial technicalities until he died of a heart attack in 1991.

Speck's imprisonment coincided with the growth of four powerful gang presences in Stateville: the Black P Stone Nation, the Gangster Disciples, the Latin Kings, and the Vice Lords. "Open yard" became the norm in the late 1970s, with hundreds of inmates free to move around the prison grounds during recreation times.

Recorded incidents boomed in the 1980s as gangs continued street business behind the prison walls. According to several old-timer inmates I spoke with in 2014, wardens invited gang leaders to catered lunches where they discussed tactics for decreasing violence. Assassinations between rival gangs were a regular occurrence, as were officer-inmate fights. From this chaos Speck emerged as the queen, king, and mascot of Stateville.

We know this because in May 1996, Chicago news anchor Bill Kurtis received videotapes of Speck recorded in 1988 from an anonymous source. In the video, Speck plays the shirtless guest of a talkshow hosted by a younger inmate with a calm narcotized glee. Speck shows off his cotton blue panties and snorts cocaine off the host's leg. He has full breasts, evidently grown through hormone treatment smuggled into the prison, and tells the host he enjoys being sodomized. "If only they knew how much fun I was having," Speck deadpans to the camera, "they would turn me loose."

The dissemination of this video across major media outlets was an embarrassment for the Illinois Department of Corrections and incited another time warp. Stateville now maintains order with a new authoritarian regime, this time governed by bureaucrats.

Besides the troupe of designated Maniacs, it's safe to say that just about all of the characters inside the Statesville Haunted Prison have gone mad. They perform the psycho killer in its various instantiations: there's Dr. Vierhoff, a Dr. Mengele-esque physician-torturer, his transmogrified patients, a tier of evil clowns, a bounty-hunter, a butcher, an electrician, and even a leather-faced, chainsaw-wielding-guy at the very end. Latex organs and red-dyed corn syrup remind us that these murderers love what they do and do what they love, and, in case we're still not convinced, some of them brag about the numerous murders they have committed.

What makes "criminals" so scary in our psyches is their abstractness, their hiddenness, and their one-dimensional portrayals in media and fiction. Subsumed under the blankets of "criminal" and "murderer" are father, mother, artist, cosmetologist, neighbor, drug dealer, veteran, musician, nurse, child, etc. Most incarcerated citizens are not Richard Speck or John Wayne Gacy, Jr. A vast majority of incarcerated people are not criminally insane. What struck me most when I first walked into Stateville was a feeling of imminence. If I were hungry enough, angry enough, lonely enough, desperate enough, I could, in a flash, just as easily be on the other side of the bars.

Time flows differently inside the prisons. The Stateville elders of the inmate population exist in the radical present, having traversed and lived in their death site for years and years. Whereas inmates in Cook County Jail are trapped in the past and the future, obsessed with their cases, built around a flash in the past, and the fanciful notion of "the day I'm getting out of here." They're more agitated than the men in Stateville, more on edge. And the Haunted Prison is seasonal and cyclical, a ritualistic and ephemeral theatre.

Stateville is an endless archive of itself, haunted by its past, its traumas and transformations. Functioning buildings stand next to dilapidated ones — a lively woodwork shop filled with staff and inmates, next to the ruins of an old cellblock. One can nearly admire the beauty of the ruins, but their proximity to the functional buildings constitutes an ambiguous and inspiring hauntology that unites Stateville, Statesville, and Cook County Jail with a gaze into the future. Inmates are kept in buildings slick with Clorox but eroding into the ruins surrounding them. Inevitable collapse, manifested in the detritus, infects the prison with dangerous possibility. One might call it a future haunt.

How to Win Reparations

What Movements Around the Country Can Learn from Chicago's Successful Fight for Reparations for Police Torture Survivors

BY YANA KUNICHOFF AND SARAH MACARAEG

Somewhere between his twelfth and thirteenth hour inside a Chicago Police interrogation room, Lindsey Smith decided to confess to a murder he didn't commit. The year was 1972. Multiple officers had pistol-whipped, stomped on, and beaten him, again and again. Convinced he would not otherwise live to see sunlight, Smith signed a false confession for the attempted murder of a twelve-year-old White boy. At seventeen, Smith, too, was a boy. But with one major difference: he was Black.

Tried as an adult and convicted, Smith took a plea deal and served nearly five years in prison.

He was among the first of at least 120 young, primarily Black men whom Chicago police officers would torture into false confessions. Yet while many who suffer at the hands of the police never get justice, Smith's story ended differently. More than forty years later, following the passage of historic reparations legislation, he became one of the first Black people in America to be granted reparations for racial violence.

After receiving parole, Smith moved out of the city and attempted to rebuild his life. But his struggles were far from over. Given the conviction on his record, Smith faced difficulty in everything from finding work to accessing his car insurance benefits. And he remained haunted by his experiences as a teen inside the interrogation room, and never felt at ease in Chicago again — until May 7, 2015.

On that date, the City of Chicago signed into law an ordinance granting cash payments, free college education, and a range of social services to fifty-seven living survivors of police torture. Explicitly defined as reparations, the ordinance also includes a mandate to teach the broader public about the torture, through a memorial and public schools curriculum, and a formal apology from Mayor Rahm Emanuel. The hard-won legislation, envisioned by activists, made Chicago the first and thus far only municipality in the country to pay reparations for racist police violence.

"I can sleep a whole lot better tonight," Smith told local media upon the bill's passage. A sixty-one-year-old factory worker, he has since collected $100,000 in reparations.

"I'd take that night back before I took their money any day. I can never get back that time away from my family and the things I could have done," Smith said. "But at least I can afford new shoes now."

As the national conversation around racial disparities in the United States has broadened to include criminalization, job discrimination, school segregation, and neglect of infrastructure, so has the need for a reckoning of the institutional wrongs done to African American communities. Reparations, the concept of offering monetary or social redress for historical injustices, has found a renewed life in American public discourse, and is at the heart of some social movements.

With the election of Donald Trump, it seems unlikely that reparations will move forward at the national scale anytime soon. But Chicago's ordinance provides a model for creating reparations on the local level, even in the face of daunting circumstances.

The momentum has been building for years. Reparations sparked debate on the presidential campaign trail, and, when more than fifty organizations collaborated to write the Movement for Black Lives policy platform in 2016, they put reparations front and center.

"We wanted to put forth a set of policies that show what we really want and what would lead to a transformation of our conditions," says Karl Kumodzi, a member of the coalition's policy table who is active with the organizations BlackBird and BYP100 in Brooklyn, New York. "Reparations had to be at the forefront of that."

Since then, a Georgetown University committee has recognized that the school profited from the sale of slaves and said it would "reconcile" by naming two buildings after African Americans and by offering preferred admission status to any descendants of slaves who worked at the university. Whether or not Georgetown's plans offer true recompense is in contention. "You don't admit you owe someone money and repay them with lottery tickets," wrote sociologist Tressie McMillan Cottom.

Increasingly, the question appears not to be whether reparations are needed, but what form they should take and how to get them.

Most of the time, it's still an abstract conversation. But Chicago's $5.5 million reparations legislation is a concrete exception.

According to a city spokesperson, as of October 2016, payments have been made to the majority of the fifty-seven recognized survivors; nine individuals have begun the process of potentially accessing free community college; and eleven requests for prioritized access to social services have been made. A city-funded community center dedicated to survivors and their families opened in May 2017, and a curriculum on the torture scandal was in the early stages of implementation in Chicago Public Schools as of April 2017.

FROM THE BLACK MANIFESTO TO THE MOVEMENT FOR BLACK LIVES

Mary Frances Berry, a former chairperson of the U.S. Civil Rights Commission, documented the country's first struggle for reparations, which was led by ex-slaves, in her book *My Face is Black is True*. She thinks Chicago offers a model for how to win reparations across the country.

"We often hear talk about national legislation and national responses in the civil rights community.... But a lot of things can be done locally," she says. "Chicago shows [what] can be done — and [that] other kinds of remedies for other kinds of harms can be done, like for example the harm done to the people in Flint."

Berry was referencing the ongoing water crisis in Flint, Michigan, that left thousands of residents in the predominantly African American town without access to clean drinking water.

Not far from Flint, nearly fifty years ago, the Black Manifesto launched in Detroit as one of the first calls for reparations in the modern era, penned by James Forman, a former organizer with the Student Nonviolent Coordinating Committee, a key Civil Rights group. Released at the 1969 Black Economic Development Conference, the manifesto demanded $500 million in reparations from predominantly white religious institutions, for their historic role in perpetuating slavery. The manifesto asserted that the money would fund nine key projects, aimed at building the collective wealth of black communities: a black university, black presses and broadcast networks, research and training centers, and a southern land bank. A multiracial contingent of clergy in support of the Black Manifesto succeeded in raising at least $215,000 from the Episcopalian and Methodist churches, through months of rancorous deliberation — that ultimately rendered the coalition apart.

The mantle was next assumed by the National Coalition of Blacks for Reparations in America, or N'COBRA. Centering their demands on reparations for chattel slavery, N'COBRA gained a hearing throughout the early 1990s but their demands never garnered a mainstream foothold.

Joe Feagin, distinguished professor of sociology at Texas A&M University, has a hunch about why that is. It has been difficult for demands for reparations for slavery to gain traction in the past, he says, because the direct link between slavery and the high rates of poverty prevalent in contemporary black communities is not widely understood, let alone acknowledged.

"When you focus on slavery, it's easy for whites to say all the whites are dead and all the blacks are dead," Feagin said. In other words, it's easy to dismiss the idea as water under the bridge.

"That is not true for Jim Crow segregation," Feagin said, citing a study on "segregation stress syndrome" based on interviews with 100 elderly African Americans in the South. The study revealed that 80 percent of the participants' families had suffered extreme violence in the form of lynching, rape, attempted rape, and home invasions. "They can name the white families who were involved," Feagin said. "Without knowing the whole story you can't know that whites are unjustly enriched, blacks unjustly impoverished — and that that has to be repaired," Feagin said. "What allows us whites to get off the hook is nobody knows this history, so we can make absurd statements like 'Slavery happened hundreds of years ago.'"

But with the publication of Ta-Nehisi Coates's landmark article, "The Case for Reparations," in 2014, the living legacy of white supremacy became difficult to deny. Detailing the systematic "plunder" of black communities, Coates's work tracks multiple Chicagoans living the outcomes of generations of racism — demonstrating a legacy of impoverishment that runs from slavery, sharecropping, and Jim Crow, to housing discrimination and economic hardship today.

As for solutions, Coates called for support of H.R. 40, federal legislation that seeks to form a commission on reparations.

Sponsored by Democrat John Conyers of Michigan, ranking member of the House Judiciary Committee and a founding member of the Congressional Black Caucus, H.R. 40 aims "to examine the institution of slavery and its legacy, like racial disparities in education, housing, and healthcare" and then "recommend appropriate remedies to Congress." First introduced in 1989, H.R. 40 has been reintroduced by Conyers in every session of Congress since — and subsequently mired in the House of Representatives' Subcommittee on the Constitution and Civil Justice, currently chaired by Republican Trent Franks of Arizona.

But although H.R. 40 has languished, other reparations legislation has prevailed at both the state and federal levels. In 1988, President Ronald Reagan signed a bill providing $20,000 to each of the approximately 65,000 living Japanese Americans who had been interned during World War II, prompting Congress to allocate $1.25 billion. A few years later, the state of Florida approved $2.1 million dollars for the living survivors of a 1923 racial pogrom that resulted in multiple deaths and the complete decimation of the black community in the town of Rosewood. More recently, in 2014, the state of North Carolina set aside $10 million for reparations payments to living survivors of the state's eugenics program, which forcibly sterilized approximately 7,600 people. The practice was widely adopted across thirty-three states, sterilizing an estimated 60,000 people without their consent. Last year, the state of Virginia followed North Carolina's lead, and will soon begin awarding $25,000 to each survivor.

Meanwhile, the five-point outline for reparations in the Movement for Black Lives platform broadens the conversation. From a demand for services focused on healing from trauma to access to free education and cash support in the form of a "guaranteed livable income," the policy platform was built on decades of experience, research, and values long held by the black radical tradition — galvanized further by the victory in Chicago, says Karl Kumodzi.

"I got chills," he says about the day he heard the Chicago ordinance was signed. "What they won offers clear examples of reparations being more than just a check, but rather a set of initiatives and investments that address the economic, psychological, educational, and health impacts of the harm that's been done."

HOW THEY DID IT

So how'd they do it?

According to sociologist Tressie McMillan Cottom, there are three key components to a reparations program: acknowledgement, restitution, and closure. In addition, for an offered recompense to be called reparations, it must be specific to alleviating or directing resources at the harm caused.

In many ways, the movement for reparations in Chicago started out of a lack of recognition. Communities in Chicago had spent years fighting for legal redress for survivors of police torture under Commander Jon Burge and his officers, who for nearly three decades tortured more than 100 Black and Latino men into confessing to crimes they didn't commit.

Their first effort was legal — to get Burge into a courtroom despite the fact that the statute of limitations had expired on many of the alleged cases of police torture, and to achieve retrials where possible for the wrongfully convicted people still imprisoned.

The second was to make sure the torture would never be forgotten. Attorney Joey Mogul had been litigating Burge cases for more than two decades by the time the commander was finally brought into court.

But looking around at the torture survivors she had been working with, especially those asked to dredge up painful memories for the trial, she realized the victory of his conviction for perjury and obstruction of justice was a hollow one.

"It didn't bring them peace or relief," said Mogul. She points to the case of Anthony Holmes, who was tortured by officers under Burge in 1973 and went on to serve the full thirty-year sentence before being exonerated. "Anthony Holmes...struggles with trauma to this day. There are no psychological services for him whatsoever."

The first steps toward the ordinance began not explicitly geared towards getting reparations in Chicago, but rather to collect ideas for how to memorialize the cases and make sure that Chicagoans knew of the history of police torture that scarred African-American and Latino communities in the city. Mogul and a handful of torture survivors and other people who had been involved in the movement to bring Burge to justice started the Chicago Torture Justice Memorials as a vehicle to start collecting ideas.

From there, the idea of drafting a city ordinance as a way to recognize the harm done took shape — and bringing in reparations as the answer began to form. "I feel like reparations is a really simple concept," said Alice Kim, an academic and activist whose longtime work organizing with Burge survivors was pivotal in the CTJM and eventually the reparations ordinance. "It's repairing harm that was done."

The first draft of the ordinance was sketched out in 2012, with an explicit aim of calling for reparations — inspired by Mogul's colleague, lawyer Stan Willis, who had been active with N'COBRA and first raised the demand.

The reparations package aimed to fill in the gaps where legal efforts had fallen short. It included key practical requests like financial compensation but also a curriculum that would teach about the Burge tortures in Chicago Public Schools and free enrollment in the city's public college program.

The ordinance, in the spirit of the longtime organizing efforts, laid the bulk of responsibility at the city's feet. "The chain of command in City Hall never stopped to investigate and redress the torture," said Mogul.

It's fitting, then, that what helped spur activists to introduce the ordinance was the mayor's attempt to close the book on police torture. In October 2013, the city's finance committee had just settled a $12.3 million suit with police torture victims Ronald Kitchens and Marvin Reeves. A journalist with the *Chicago Sun-Times* asked Mayor Rahm Emanuel if the police torture deserved an apology. In response Emanuel apologized — before he deflected, saying, "Let us all now move on."

The comment outraged activists who had been devising a proposal for justice. "We can't move on, there has been nothing done to meet the material needs of torture survivors," Mogul recalled thinking.

The group found a City Council member friendly with the mayor — Alderman Joe Moreno — to introduce the ordinance in October of 2013. The ordinance would then be stuck in committee until a burst of growth in the movement pushed it out.

A coalition began taking shape in early 2014 — Amnesty International brought its national platform to the project in April 2014. By the end of 2015, a local coalition called We Charge Genocide would bring the burgeoning power of the Black Lives Matter movement to the fight for reparations. Janae Bonsu, a member of Black Youth Project 100, organized with the fight for reparations. "If anyone is deserving of reparations, it's them," said Bonsu of the families receiving a portion of recompense.

The group upped their efforts, holding a bitterly cold Valentine's Day rally in 2015 and beseeching Rahm Emanuel, whose political future looked increasingly uncertain as he was heading into a mayoral run-off, to "have a heart."

Within a month of that February rally, the coalition met with the city three times to negotiate on the reparations package while continuing to hold public protests. A key demand was a hearing on the ordinance. "We wanted the public to have their say. We got a hearing date for April 14," said Mogul, but "on the eve of the hearing we ultimately reached and agreed on a reparations package."

The package eventually passed, offering cash payments, a formal apology, promise to teach the history of police torture in Chicago Public Schools, and funds for the creation of the community counseling center.

"No one believed it would pass, no one thought [Mayor Rahm] Emanuel would be OK with it and succumb to the pressure he ended up succumbing to. But you move your target and your people from what everybody expects, and you make the improbable possible," said Mariame Kaba, whose connection to both long-term Burge organizing efforts and the Black Lives Matter movement made her a key figure in the upswell of actions leading to the passage of the ordinance in 2015.

"We fought outside the legal box," said Mogul. "What we gained, what we won, was more expansive than any court could have provided."

On January 4, 2016, the checks to individual torture victims went into the mail. A needs assessment commenced among survivors and their families to figure out how the community center could best meet the needs of those affected by police torture. The city has agreed to provide three additional years of funding and in the meanwhile, planning for the curriculum and public memorial commenced.

However, the ordinance limits financial relief to people tortured during Burge's exact years on the force — between May 1,1972 to November 30, 1991 — despite evidence that it continued under his former subordinates. And, over twenty known Burge survivors remain incarcerated today, according to lawyers with the reparations committee.

For the CTJM team, the gains of reparations serve as a starting point and reminder of all there is to be done.

"The glass is only half-full because until we get those other brothers back to court and get fair and impartial hearings into their allegations of having been tortured," said Darryl Cannon, a survivor of Burge's police torture. "Then this fight must continue."

MOVING FORWARD

Aislinn Pulley, a co-founder of Black Lives Matter Chicago, considers the city's effort one of the most powerful examples of reparations. "Chicago…created new possibilities of what transformative justice, holistic justice, can look like and in addressing the modern problems of policing, helps us envision new demands and possibilities of justice," she said.

What's more, activists like Janae Bonsu, who worked on the reparations campaign, have taken their experience in Chicago and run with it. As a member of Black Youth Project 100, she has fought in recent months to keep open the historically black Chicago State University in Illinois and to partially "de-fund the police" in municipal budgets nationwide, advocating for the funding of programs benefitting Black communities in need of services instead.

Bonsu sees clear next steps for where the fight for reparations needs to move. "I think the conversation of reparations should be expanded to thinking about the War on Drugs, in thinking about [housing] redline policies — in all the ways systemic racism can be proved," says Bonsu.

The story of Chicago's ordinance suggests that local campaigns have the potential to broaden reparations in each of these ways. But in the absence of a national policy, how much harm can be mitigated by local laws? If hundreds of Chicago-style ordinances were replicated in every town or state where demonstrable systemic harm can be proved, how far would they go in addressing centuries of wrong meted out by the state against African Americans and other vulnerable communities?

Karl Kumodzi says that reparations are needed on multiple fronts — reparations for both specific harms, such as those wrought by Chicago's police torture ring, and oppressive systems as a whole. "What we think is really needed is an analysis of reparations, not just for very specific cases where you have to prove it," he says, but also for the intergenerational, community-wide, and lasting impacts of systems like slavery and policing. "They also have the same consequences, the same needs of their families — the same lasting traumatic effects."

However, under a Trump presidency, Kumodzi says, priorities in organizing will shift because conditions have shifted. "Fights that we could take on and things that we could try to win a month ago are things that just won't happen in the next four years at the federal level," he acknowledges. But Kumodzi also sees organizing at the state and city levels as a powerful means for keeping the larger dream of national reparations alive.

"Our vision for the world that we want to live in, our demands, our understanding of the policies that are going to get us towards that vision, that's not going to change, that's gonna stay the same for the long haul — whether it's four years, two years, ten years," he said. "There's been a lot of harms. Reparations have to be done to address those harms."

ORIGINALLY PUBLISHED IN THE SPRING 2017 ISSUE OF *YES! MAGAZINE*.

WYL VILLACRES

A cop car passed us, siren and lights going, and I stopped talking long enough for the sound to pass. Charlotte and I were walking to the Lincoln Restaurant on Irving Park, talking about my ex-girlfriend Jane that I was still hopelessly in love with. Or I was talking and Charlotte was listening. Or at least pretending to.

I was trying to figure out what I had done wrong.

"She said that she didn't want to be the one that made me miserable, that that's why we could never try again," I said, fighting back tears and tapping the ash off my cigarette with my index finger, getting too close to the cherry and burning myself.

"But you're always miserable," Charlotte said, looking at her reflection in a storefront. She was tired of hearing me complain about my girlfriends. But as my best female friend, I thought the job was hers. She tried to let me know otherwise. We became friends in college. She was the only other Latina in my classes one semester, so we just sort of bonded. Brown kids with white people names. Not the best basis for friendship, but sometimes you gotta do what you gotta do.

"I know." I flicked the unsmoked half of my cigarette into the street. Charlotte opened her pack — empty. She dropped it and kicked it under a parked car, the white and gold spinning like some koi fish in a pond or some jewelry or something else that rich people have.

We crossed Damen and headed in the back entrance of the Lincoln like we did every time. It was a long, dark, and empty tunnel that ends in the back of the old smoking section — all wood paneling, video poker machines, a bar that hasn't been used since 1970. It was a relic. It reminded me of my grandparents' basement. Inside, Jeff would greet us in his brown apron, all six-and-some-change feet of him wrapped with excitement.

Jeff had played hockey in college. He was a shit shot, but he was a strong skater and an even stronger hitter. I watched dude shatter the glass by shoving an opponent through it. Jeff's collegiate hockey career ended when he fought the entire UWM team and their coach.

And the ref. "Fought" might not be right. "Beat the ever-loving shit out of" might be better.

But Jeff wasn't a bad guy. He was sort of goofy, always grinning. Always friendly off the ice. We called him "The Streakin' Puerto Rican" because (1) He was Puerto Rican like me, and (2) Dude took his clothes off as a joke all the time. Jeff oozed Puerto Ricanness. Big, kinky hair that sort of stuck out in an early 1900s presidential way with the perfect, deep, perpetual tan I always wanted. His skin didn't smell like coconuts or salt water, but I wouldn't have been surprised if it had.

Jeff didn't speak Spanish, though. None of us did. But that didn't stop people from asking.

Our booth — the only booth we'd sit in — was in back by the kitchen door so that he could drop off untouched sides of toast or overcooked eggs as we sat there in our under-the-poverty-line, afternoon bliss. We'd pay for free-refill coffee and eat all day. The table was always empty, the noise from the kitchen making it less than desirable.

But then, Jeff was sitting in our booth, laying facedown across the table like he had been shot.

"Sup, dummy," Charlotte said, knocking on the table. They'd been friends since they were kids.

Jeff looked up, his eyes red and puffy. They reminded me of Jane when she told me she didn't love me anymore and then again when she moved all of her stuff out. I swallowed, my esophagus stretching through the floor, my stomach somewhere near Hell.

"Whoa, what's wrong?" Charlotte asked, squatting down to eye level.

Jeff took a couple shallow breaths. "Dude. Last night," Jeff bit at his lip. It was weird seeing someone so big cry. A mountain cracked by the first snowfall, a skyscraper collapsing under a bluebird's weight. "Last night, my cousin Derek was out burn cruising with his friends. They got pulled over by the cops and tried to cover the weed smell with cigarettes, but..." Jeff put his head back on the table. We had met Derek once. Derek was cool. Spoke fluent Spanish. Had great weed and bad tattoos. Always wore a flat brimmed Yankees hat, and even though he'd never been to New York, called himself a Nuyorican, and tried to rap. "The cops freaked out at him for smoking while they pulled him over. Dragged Derek from the car and," Jeff sobbed once, a couple tears rolling down his face. "And kicked the shit out of him! His friend in the back recorded it on his phone before they all got cuffed. Derek is in the hospital. He's in bad shape. Fuck!" Jeff pounded the table. Charlotte squeezed in beside him and threw an arm over his shoulders. She said those things that people say, the Sorrys and the Are You Alrights and the That's Fucked Ups. I didn't say anything, just offered a sad smile and thought about how Jane was really good at situations like this, would quote Chavez or something. I thought about missing her.

"Jeff!" came a voice from behind us. It was his fat, bald, white manager Bill, arms akimbo, his no-lip face scrunched in on itself. "Can I talk to you?" I thought I saw a glimmer of empathy in Bill's eyes, but he was hard to read. Bill was always sweating. He knew our game, but let us hang out anyway, however begrudgingly. But lately he had been shorter in his temperament.

Jeff stood up to go, Charlotte whispering, "We'll catch you later at your place, OK bud? We love you."

"Yeah, dude," I said. He lived in the same neighborhood Jane did, so we might run into her. My heart beat in two directions.

After a fifteen-minute walk north where we were weirdly quiet, we ended up at a bookstore. Charlotte wanted to grab *The Autobiography of Malcom X* so we popped in. I looked for this book that had recently been made into a movie because it was Jane's favorite and if I liked it, then maybe I could understand her more and we could reconnect, and if I didn't like it, then maybe I could start to move on, knowing our tastes were different.

In line, Charlotte said "We should do something for Jeff."

"Like what? Get him a card?"

"Yeah? Or Flowers? Booze? I don't know anyone that got beat by the cops before."

"Sorta weird, right?"

"Huh?" Charlotte stepped up to pay, our conversation growing louder.

"Like, cops don't particularly like brown folk. But neither of us know anyone, until now, that were beat. And you almost never see the Latinos who were beat or killed in the news." I flipped through a couple pages in the book, letting the text melt and swirl into quick pictures of Jane.

"Huh. Yeah. You think they'll put Derek on the news or something?"

The cashier, all blonde hair and baby powder skin, spoke up. "Someone was beaten by the cops?" She sounded confused, like that never happened.

Charlotte took her change. "Yeah, our buddy's cousin."

The cashier looked at Charlotte, then over to me, then back to Charlotte. "Well, what did he do?"

"What?" I asked.

"I mean, if he was beaten by the police, they must have had a good reason."

Charlotte turned to me, eyes wide, then narrow. "Can you grab that some other time?" she said, her jaw twitching at the end of the sentence.

The air in my throat slid down the wrong tube and I coughed. I wanted to say something to the cashier. And if I was in a different place in life, at a point where I was less in control, I would have gone off. But I looked down at the book, thought about Jane's impassioned pleas for me to read it at the beginning of our relationship, about how she looked so similar to this cashier, and took a step up to the counter, a twenty already laid across the book. "No," I said. "It'll only take a second."

We walked down to the Jewel because they'd have flowers and cards and something to eat that we could buy with my food stamps since we didn't get lunch from Jeff. The flowers were all wilted and the cards were all shitty.

"Fuck this," Charlotte said, holding up a sympathy card with gold script on it.

"What about a cake?" I said, my stomach rumbling.

Charlotte thought about it for a second before tossing the card on the floor and saying "Yeah," and we walked over to the bakery section and started looking for a cake.

It was bright in the store, like it always is, but I think I was sensitive to it more because I was buying a cake for my friend because his cousin had been beaten by the cops. It was uncharted territory. Jane would have just baked one from scratch. She was amazing. Charlotte and I looked down at the sheet cakes with the blank space to write things and flowers and stuff on the sides. None of them were right for Jeff. Jeff was a gasoline fume in a windowless garage. The cakes were all framed Georgia O'Keefe posters hung in working-class dining rooms.

"These cakes suck," Charlotte said, lifting up one with balloons on it.

"Yeah, but what else are we going to do?" I said, moving one with pink piping on the edges. "Go somewhere else?"

"We could decorate it better. Like, scrape off the flowers and put something he liked."

"But he liked skulls and snakes and shit," I said.

We looked down at the cakes and on the bottom was a totally undecorated one. Plain, white icing on top of white cake. Charlotte looked at me and smiled.

"We can't put a skull on a sympathy cake," I said. "Plus, I mean, dude is in the hospital. He might die."

"Jeff wouldn't want a sympathy cake. He'd want a 'Be Less Sad' cake," Charlotte said, picking up the cake and grabbing gel icing from the display above — black and red.

We sat down on the bench past the checkout lanes in Jewel and Charlotte popped the lid off and went at the cake, drawing skulls and knives and a bomb with a burning fuse. She was really into it. Violent morbidity can be cathartic, I guess. In the middle, in big capital letters, she wrote "SORRY SHIT SUCKS." One of the baggers kept eyeing us and I waved at them and they went back to putting too many boxes of pasta into a plastic bag.

"Done," Charlotte said.

"I don't know," I said.

"Doesn't matter. Time to make a delivery."

As we rode the bus, I started to feel jealous of Jeff. Like, he got all of this attention for feeling down about a cousin he didn't really see *that* often, but I was there, torn up about the love of my life saying she didn't even want to talk to me again, and *I* didn't get any cake. We headed up into Rogers Park, me scanning the sidewalks for any signs of Jane, and by the time we got off the bus, I was feeling worse than I had in a while.

Charlotte had been texting Jeff, saying, *Make sure you're ready. We've got something for you*, and Jeff saying that he just wanted some time alone.

At his door, the garden unit of an old two flat, Charlotte knocked with her foot, holding the cake out like a Publishers Clearing House check. Like the way Jane had held out tickets to see the Blackhawks on my birthday. Jeff opened the door and looked down.

"Sorry shit sucks," he read out loud.

I looked at Jeff, expecting him to be grateful, expecting him to be happy. Like I had with the hockey tickets. And color slid across his face, like light up letters scrolling on an LED sign. Like "Coming Soon." Like "Going Out of Business." Like "I Can't Go On." And then Jeff looked like he was going to explode with emotion, Charlotte smiling nervously across from him, and me just there. Just standing there, outside of the moment. Or at least that's how it felt. Like things were stopping or moving even faster.

Jeff made a sound, a rat's squeak, a rusty hinge's cry, and pushed past Charlotte, knocking the cake out of her hands. It fell forever before finally hitting the ground right-side up, the lid popping off and the cake bursting open, the text reading:

SO RY

S HI

UC K S

And we stood looking down at the cake. Frosting dotted his porch like a galaxy, and for a second I wanted to wish on one of the sugar "stars," to wish for things to be like they had been weeks before. Before Jeff's cousin was in the hospital. Before Jane had said she didn't want to be the one to make me miserable. Charlotte, who was quicker thinking than I am, first bent down to pick up the cake, calling "Jeff!" before thinking better of it, then thinking better of thinking better, then finally deciding that Jeff was more important than the cake. She turned, made it about ten steps before realizing that I hadn't moved, came back and grabbed me, and we chased Jeff as he turned the corner on to Howard.

Jeff, who was taller, more athletic, and more emotional than us walked much faster. By the time we made it on to Howard, he was about a block and a half ahead of us. His shoulders hunched, and as he moved toward the train, a squad car pulled up alongside him. Jeff, an upset, six -foot, Latino male, twenty-four to thirty-five, was a perfect candidate to be stopped and frisked. And I think Charlotte saw it all first — saw the scope and breadth of the situation where I only saw an annoyance that we've all learned to just put up with. Charlotte started running, yelling something I couldn't hear. But Jeff didn't want to stop, so he took off down a side street. How are you supposed to behave with the police after some of the fraternal order had beat the shit out of your family? I started running towards the mess, but I'm slow, and even if I was faster, what would I have done? What, jumped in front of the cops and said "He's just sad!" or sat everyone down to have a chat about community policing? I didn't have a chance. Didn't have the speed or knowledge or magical fucking superpowers to do whatever it was I needed to do. I turned the corner onto the side street saying something, screaming something, I don't remember what, and I guess it doesn't matter — the squad car, still on Howard, threw blue light in streaks across the little side street, the night hot, the Chicago summer sticky and oppressive. The cops' footsteps, the heavy footfall, sounded like a drum beat on the pavement, slap slap slap slap, the train rumbling by, car horns and dogs barking and kids playing late in the park a block away and rats and mice, the cacophonous noise of the city crushing down, out of time, one two three four one two one three one four four one.

Two shots sounded first.

Then three more.

Then two more.

When I got closer, slowing to a trot, then a stunned walk, I ran into Charlotte. I didn't see her on her knees, mouth open, silent tears running. I looked into the street where Jeff laid, one cop walking towards his body with his gun still on him, the other cop walking towards us, barking something, gun pointed towards the ground but arms still locked into a shooting position. Jeff didn't move.

One day, I'll be better. One day, I'll make sense of it. But for now, I just try to keep breathing when I see blue flashing lights race up my street.

The next night, after Charlotte and I had talked and talked and talked to cops and reporters and our families, I called Jane. She answered after the first ring, saying, "Oh my god, I saw the news. Are you OK?"

I thought about an answer for a long time. I could hear her breathing on the other end. I wanted to just say "No," to ask to come over, to ask her to hold me, to hide me from the world, to be the one person that I knew personally who acted like they understood. But she wouldn't understand. How could she?

After about a minute, her being patient and kind, saying "I'm still here," I said "You're not the one who makes me miserable."

"You don't —"

"I just wanted you to know that. I'm going to stop calling you. I don't want to try again," I said and ended the call. I thought about the book I bought, the one that was recently made into a movie. I had it in my hand when we went to Jeff's. I had it while I was running. I must have dropped it when I saw him. I thought about the book, splayed open on the sidewalk, the spine broken. I picked up the phone again and called Charlotte.

"Hey," she said, her voice a thousand years away.

"Hey," I said.

"You know," she said, like she had been the one who called me, "the last thing we said to Jeff was that we loved him."

"I know," I said, thinking back to the Lincoln.

"That's good," Charlotte said.

"Yeah," I said.

"I love you," Charlotte said.

"I love you too," I said.

"I hate that we have to say that, just in case."

"Sorry shit sucks," I said.

And she made a sound like a laugh. And we hung up. I sat staring up at my ceiling, looking at the swirls and cracks in the paint job and thought about being miserable. I thought about the funerals I had been to, how I thought I was becoming an expert in death, about how long it always took me to really feel like the people I lost were gone.

And suddenly, things felt different. Suddenly, with the cops and the lights and the exhaustion and everything everything everything, I felt like I was drowning. I thought about the cashier at the book store. And I cried. I cried because the cops killed my friend. I cried because someone would ask *well, what did he do?*

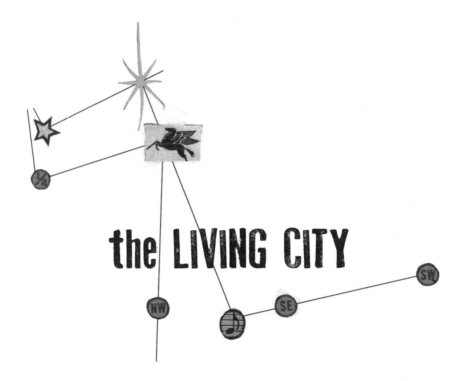

the LIVING CITY

For Girls Who Straddle Seasons

OLA FALETI

winter

When I say Chicago girls are tough, I don't mean Evanston or Dalton girls. I mean the girls that don't look long before crossing Milwaukee and Damen and North. Girls that step over yellow snow in Bronzeville. Girls that get their hair done by Seventy-ninth. I mean girls that fall asleep on the train before the Howard terminal in a train car smelling like urine.

Girls who walk fast in four-layers-of-cold January while their eyelashes freeze. It's 9° F and we wear our sheerest tights on Saturdays anyway because shit, we have flasks of Malort inside our bras. Bundles of stamina there, too. We sword dance with corner catcallers on the daily. Did you know there are sixty-seven different ways to say "fuck off" with your eyes? We will top that and give you seventy. We know Seasonal Affective Disorder is real because everyone's eyes deaden on the subway, post-Christmas. Silver linings: (a) it's cold enough to keep the street lords off their corners, and (b) we still know we're tougher than cracked heels coated in Vick's. That doesn't mean the chill won't make our hearts ice blocks. In the winter we try to be our own furnace. We try to burn.

spring

If we're lucky, by mid-May flowers begin to bloom. We follow suit by busting out floral prints at the first rosebud sighting, and bearing sun-poor shoulders to turn heads. We double-dutch on elementary concrete and hopscotch the path home. And then we forget to renew our Pablo Neruda poems from the Harold Washington. There's nothing like a city opening its eyes slow with the sun peeking through them. We will take an hour lost if it means getting to kiss the daylight a little longer, or playing in a millennium's worth of parks.

But don't be fooled. We're still tough. Still breakneck speed walkers at 2:00 a.m., when keys become knuckle wedge and we wish a motherfucker would. Still alley stumbling girls, peeing between dumpsters and keeping our feet far enough to not splash our toes. Still delicate, uncoiling flesh as our winter hunchbacks retreat.

summer

When summer bobs its fire head, it should feel like victory. We should relish the air's sweat scent, and sweet success from living through another winter. But when there's no sleep for the wicked, angels stay sluggish. That's what it feels like when sidewalks reek blood metal. Garfield Park becomes living graveyard and we, we are still coconuts. Still sweet meat under hard shell. But some of us are ghosts, and some of us have calves that glint in the sun with every pedal push, every stride, and every sweep of sundress. Too many of us spend summer inside with grandmothers and stale AC for company, dreaming of a heat that doesn't lull gangbangers to kill.

Chicago girls stay nocturnal. Warm nights cradle us while we nurse bottles of 312 and grip slipping August hands, incoming thunder rumbling over our heads, musk sticking to our thighs. Summer is still for all of us because we earned it. Summer is for all of us because we take our heat in many forms, from crisp to downright smothering.

fall

Come fall Chicago girls breathe cider and dead leaves. How easy it is for things to die. Our trees, our neighbors' pretty lawns, our faith in mayors. We tuck away one-pieces and lawn chairs. We think about tall boots. We sip all the pumpkin flavored drinks we can handle. We marvel in the streets at all the seeping orange. Summer deaths are ugly but Mother Nature is a dimepiece in September.

We girls go back to school with an extra twitch in our hips, and private relief for the school year that curbs those summer Bs: brazen boys, bared bellies, and blood. Blood that filled whole mouths. Blood that mothers swam in. Blood that washed away what we could have been, if given the chance.

THE urban rural

LINDA GARCIA MERCHANT

When I have written about Roseland, it is usually about tragedy and trauma as the result of generations of neglect. When I tell white people where I live, their response always begins with a recollection, "I remember growing up there and then moving away to (fill in the blank suburb)," leaving out the part of the story that includes why they moved, as if (as a person of color and native Chicagoan) I don't have to ask because I already know how the story ends, which I do. I know that the Roseland story ends with a riot on South Michigan Avenue as the result of the assassination of Martin Luther King, that scared the life out of every Irish, Bohemian, and Polish person still living in the beautiful Tudors, bungalows, and greystone two-flats close enough to Lake Calumet to get a decently cool evening breeze during our very hot summers.

I know the story because I too lived it, but not in Roseland. My story was a West Side experience — West Garfield Park, being burned down by people angry about the death of the same black man. I saw the Italians and Polish people fleeing to the suburbs of Melrose Park, Westchester, and Oakbrook, leaving our redbricks, two-flats, and greystones to Black neighbors. White people that had been our friends, neighbors, and classmates the day before April 6 but not the day after.

April 7, 1968 is the day the Urban Rural began in many of the neighborhoods that would be destroyed by rioting, then decimated by the diaspora to the suburbs. I remember growing up in a neighborhood where decline was the natural order; quality schools, community centers, the library, retail shopping, and small manufacturing followed our white neighbors — developers building malls and industrial centers convenient to these new communities.

What was left in our neighborhoods was the slow death and decay that comes from generations of neglect. Houses and office buildings were abandoned and eventually torn down, leaving absence, loss, and despair in their place. It was then that nature began its reclamation process, returning these concrete footprints, empty of structure, with eroding foundations naked to the elements, seeding these spaces with trees, grasses, and flowers. What I remembered of abandonment became distant in the face of concrete plains and shocks of daffodils peeking up from a set of worn, basement stairs.

I moved to Roseland because I grew up knowing that in the middle of this forgotten land, there is also beauty. The beauty of nature overcoming the rampant crime and poverty of this world. The beauty of spirit in the young people, their goals and dreams and lives, inhabiting this world with me.

Where I live, time stands still. Grown men drink at dawn, sharing their brown-bag bottle. They will sit on broken plastic chairs in front of momma's house, blank stares on sixty-year-old faces compressed into thirty-year-old bodies. We say hello each morning as we are familiar, but make no eye contact as we are both natives of the realm.

We understand the primary rule of survival: coexistence depends on a combination of deference and awareness. All eyes are focused on the realm and its movements, glances are reserved for decision, eye contact is reserved for action.

There are no retail conveniences in this urban rural. Commerce sailed away long ago when the colonizers stubbornly held on to their right to choose not to live amongst us peacefully. We have always come in peace no matter how challenged, pushed, bullied, or manipulated we have been in the conversation. When enough was beyond too much, we dropped our hands and raised our fists. The colonizers cried "foul," turned tail, and ran to make new spaces conclaved in the illusion of safety. "We cannot live in fear," they cried. "We cannot work with anger," they said.

Those colonizers left homes, some abandoned, worn down then torn down, that made way for groves of trees, weeds, and wildflowers. Stunning oases where nature reclaimed itself. The rats came, but so did the cats, the rabbits, opossums, raccoons, stray dogs, and birds of every kind. The homes that remain intact are places where natives continue to paint, sweep, cut grass, and tend gardens of vegetables — sustenance against the food desert. We maintain those homes, those proud, if faded, beauties. There is wealth here. Wealth in spirit, perserverance, and determination.

For a few weeks I rode the bus with a young college student and Roseland native. We talked about life, politics, current events, and books. Those daily conversations were moments where the rule of the realm did not apply, where eye contact and direct conversation resulted in an exchange of knowledge and friendship. It was heartwarming to hear the thoughts that live in a young mind that has some interest in helping her fellow man, or at least those younger and related to her.

We who return to communities like Roseland are not pioneers; there is no destiny unfolding or manifesting itself in colonization. We were here first, whether as native human, as tribal member, as indigenous transplant, and/or as thousandth generational victim of the diaspora(s). We are members of the realm, subject to the larger colony's rules, regulations, and expectations, no matter how different and unrelated our world is.

We are members of the "rural urban," where gardens are not hobbies, where caution and concern are written as the hard and flat notes of our life melodies. Where violence and death, life and living, daily work, and the stillness that comes from "nothing as everything" are not elements of a single character. They are each one a character, real and vocal in the daily conversation. Where commerce, or the lack of it, breeds ingenuity and cultivates the creative spirit.

Where children live and teaching has currency. On those bus-riding days, I would run into a group of children playing on a front porch of a house near the bus stop. They first spoke in an attempt to get my attention with shouts of "hola" in the curious and fearless way children will attempt to determine or confirm something — in this case, my cultural background. I finally stopped one day and said "it's not 'hola,' it's 'buenos tardes,' that means good afternoon." From that point on, they would greet me with "buenos tardes." I taught them several more words and explained, more than once, why I wouldn't teach them how to swear. That feels good.

Thorndale in February

JACQUI ZENG

Chicago wears stilettos,
pins us under the dark night of her heel,
squeezes hacking breaths out of us
even as the heat lamp melts snow
from our hair, sends rivers down our necks
sends the train, coming for us like a hunger.
We sit side-by-side and the el rocks us
back and forth, doe-eyed and woozy,
your head knocking my shoulder.
My sweater catches your brown curls
and we are caught in the hour when *being* takes effort —
too late to speak, too early to move.
You tack a silence to the window,
stretch it out like fresh gum.
I am glad that you can leave the air empty,
thankful for this reprieve you've given me,
and sorry for whispering *next stop's ours,*
for making the silence snap.

Slow Burn: Water, Oil, and Volcanoes in Indiana's Rust Belt

AVA TOMASULA Y GARCIA

We have driven past them more often than I can remember and more often than I can forget: ten-foot-high flames burning off gas from BP's oil refinery in Whiting, Indiana. My sister called them "volcanoes" when she was six and the name has stuck; now we drive through a ring of fire that has become as natural as it is pretty. My parents have memories of a sky that was perpetually orange; my tongue has a memory of the air that is thick enough to taste. A process of invisibilization: you look at something for so long that it disappears. This is how landscapes are made. People too.

The volcanoes cluster a dozen thick in what the newspapers call the Calumet region's Rust Belt: an area that spans the Indiana towns of East Chicago, Hammond, Gary, and Whiting as well as the outskirts of industrial South Chicago. They look brightest at night against a black sky but you can always see them, no matter the density of fog or smog or familiarity or whatever it might be that day that veils the eyes. You read about them in the paper, even, with the increasingly common flare-ups.

Rosa Estrada can see the volcanoes from her front door. "It seems like an imminent threat," she says. "One of their towers had a huge flame rising out of it with black smoke. It went 200 to 300 feet in the air. It was just enormous." 1,100 refinery workers have been on strike since February 2016. The people brought in to "replace" them are not well-trained, and flare-ups have, consequently, become a regular occurrence.

∘∘∘

I've lived along this 100-mile stretch of highway for all of my life. My family has spent years together in our car traversing it, if you add the hours up. This is where we are closest to one another: a metal tin hurtling down the road at eighty miles an hour, four of us inside. The drive generates new ways of measuring time and space. My knees are more and more smashed against the back of the driver's seat the older I get. All distances are defined by miles per hour. An hour away. Two hours. An hour and a half in good traffic. Next to me, my sister rolls down the window to try to escape the perpetual carsick motion of a body going faster than it's meant to, and gets a mouthful of heavy metals. This is the smog-filled panorama that people on their way in and out of Chicago from the Skyway know well — or rather, that they know from behind their windshields.

When I was younger, I looked at the long drive through the region to visit family on either side of it as wasted time spent going through a wasted place. This is a passenger's view of the world: outside is nothing in itself; the eyes glide over it. Different companies that have their offices in Chicago but keep their dirty operations just past the city's limits have eaten each other over the years through corporate mergers, assembly lines have been automated or shipped overseas for even cheaper labor and fewer protections. I ask my dad what the name of the factory he worked in was and we find out at the same time that it doesn't exist anymore. Forget because of proximity, not in spite of it.

Today we are driving to Wolf Lake, an 804-acre body of water on the Indiana/Illinois border divided in half by a floating I-90 highway and half again by the Harbor Belt Railroad causeway. We count volcanoes as we go.

$1 Burgers. Work-Related Injuries. 1 Volcano. Gentleman's Club. Next Exit. Next Right. Left. Cancer Lawsuits. ArcelorMittal Plant No. 1. Clark & Clark Attorneys. Exit 32. 1 ½ Miles Right. 2 Volcanoes. 3 Volcanoes. Best BLT in Town. Domestic Abuse. How did your Congressman Vote? Diabetes Clinic. 4 Volcanoes. Children's Hospital. Industrial Strip Club. Number One Cancer Treatment in the Country. Showgirls. Family First. Join Today, Pay Tomorrow. 5. South Shore Slag Co. Lions' Den Adult Superstore. Fridays at Ten. Unilever. Here. BP Oil. Standing with American Farmers. Cancer Lawsuits. 6. 7. 8. Horseshoe Casino, Next Exit. Cash for Gold.

Billboards and other testaments to desire give way to a narrow strip of grass, and a sudden cut to the left. If you turn to the west, you can see the volcanoes, blurring red heat into grey smoke on the horizon. If you turn east, you see geese, reeds, sand — water.

"Mayor Thomas M. McDermott, Jr. Welcomes You to Wolf Lake Memorial Park — Open Water, with a Real Lake Bottom!" The guidepost is your first introduction to the lake, The water is nestled between two ArcelorMittal and a U.S. Steel works, a BP oil refinery, AmeriStar and Horseshoe casinos, Exxon Mobil and Marathon Petroleum Bulk operations, and a Unilever chemical plant. On upwind days, my parents had picnics here growing up, accompanied by the roar of passing cars.

Most lakes in the area — including a large portion of Lake Michigan and the wetlands surrounding Wolf Lake — were man-made for mill usage, or were filled with excess slag during the region's steel heyday. In fact, until we saw the welcome sign, my family had assumed for decades that Wolf Lake was another fake. A Real Lake Bottom: Wolf Lake is sold as the more natural nature; it's presented as a glimmer of real in an expanse of postindustrial fiction. If you wanted, you could put on your rose-colored glasses and call this scenery an example of Rust Belt magical realism. But to do so would be to miss how very everyday this is.

Timothy Morton writes in *Ecology Without Nature* that the very idea of "nature" is far from natural itself. In fact, it seems to hover supernaturally above things, like a ghost. That is, the "natural" slides noiselessly over a list of stuff that it metonymically stands for but is not reducible to: "Fish, grass, mountain air, chimpanzees, love, soda water, freedom of choice, heterosexuality, free markets…Nature." It is a concept that is at once full of meaning, and oddly empty. At Wolf Lake, "nature" can stand for steel, slag, and pollution as much as it can stand for cool breezes and sandy soil. It can stand for the market's prerogative to destroy as many people and as much land as is "necessary" — to borrow one of capitalism's favorite words. It can stand for the slow burn of unspoken consent that you slip yourself into, that this is the way things are.

o o o

Those who visit the lake regularly say that you only have to block out the towering power lines, the 400,000-gallon oil tanks, lines and lines of billowing smokestacks, and distant red flames, and you can find yourself truly in nature. Transported to another time. You stand on the marshy edge of the water and sink back millennia: glaciers pant across the ground, melting in stop-motion time into a shallow lake twice as large as it is now. You can walk across the entire span, the water reaching between two and four feet deep.

Now speed up time as human histories of genocide and segregation spill into the nineteenth century. Illinois, Miami, and Potawatomi peoples are "removed." Immigrant Slovak, Polish, and Serbian workers first arriving in Chicago's settlement houses lay down tracks for nine different railroad corporations, making the area North America's largest center for freight shipping. Standard Oil's Rockefeller and other robber barons build debt-backed cartoon towns for their company men to live in — or better, to die in.

Fly backward into the 1950s, 40s, 30s, 20s, 10s. Black and Mexican workers fill jobs in the steel mills as they expand. Racial formations shift to make Slovaks and Serbs white, at the expense of the new arrivals. East Chicago becomes a perpetually growing landfill for its namesake city next door. Uranium clouds the sky as the city's coal furnaces heat up; liquid waste and manure from the stockyards lick at sandy beach shores. The lake shrinks in expanse as its edges are filled with steel slag dumped by at least ten different industries. Redlining cuts through Chicago as whiteness is, yet again, reaffirmed as a synonym for ownership. Wolf Lake is divided again and again, by dikes in the water and high-tension lines in the air.

Partitioned into ever-smaller areas, suddenly the water grows deeper, its Real Lake Bottom sinking further down as Wolf Lake is dredged in 1956 to build I-90 directly overhead. Most features of this landscape are products of profitability: a few miles over, Lake Calumet, originally six feet deep, was made to be thirty feet so as to be within the minimum depth of navigable waters for international trade. 1970: the steel corporations eagerly eat and are eaten by ever-larger multinationals. Some transmute into aluminum and plastic behemoths, but most wither. In only five years from 1992-97, employment in the United States grows by 13 percent — yet, according to the City of Chicago Department of Planning and the Calumet Area Industrial Commission's Land Use Plan for the area, this region loses more than 2,000 jobs. The multipronged, unspoken programs of disinvestment, deindustrialization, and labor informalization that spell globalization hit hard. Mills close and cause a rippling effect of poverty and slow rage which has not ceased.

o o o

Walking up to the lake, it is not hard to see this history. Or maybe it is the hardest thing about the area to see. It is like no place I've been before: nature put on display in the midst of one of the dirtiest places in the country. As we walk, we spot minnows in the water. We find the legs of blue crabs, dismembered by birds. Yet, the air is tinged with a metallic flavor. You can watch the white plumes from smokestacks like you watch the clouds, trying to pick out shapes. We are both amazed by the tenacity of nature to survive, and the tenacity of nature's opposite in turning such a landscape into money. How did this happen?

Wolf Lake and environs have been the focus of myriad revitalization projects bent on bringing into existence, in the words of one pamphlet, "Music and fishing and kayaks, oh my!" Each plan shows little effort to incorporate the area's heavy-metal past into the redevelopment project. But this is probably because there is too much present still around: the BP refinery whose volcanoes border Wolf Lake is the sixth-largest in the country and has been the site of a bitter, months-long strike, a poorly-covered-up oil spill into Lake Michigan, and massive lay-offs even as the company's CEO was given a $3.3 million raise. More than nine million shipping containers pass through the region every year — twice the amount of anywhere else in the country; third globally to Hong Kong and Singapore as of a 2001 report. ArcelorMittal still runs steel and tries to crush its workers' union at every turn. One abuse opens the gates for others. In the late 1980s, Donald Trump engaged in a decades-long scheme to open a casino in Gary that would, in his words, "empty the pockets of people in Chicago." As Jeff Nichols wrote for the *Chicago Reader*, Trump Hotels and Casino Resorts mismanaged the Gary operation into the ground — and walked away with millions.

o o o

There are two other families at the lake today, and a small cluster of high schoolers flipping skateboards. Like us, they have all driven here. The families walk the concrete path circling the water. A runner we saw battling traffic and gulping smog from our car windows half an hour ago, finally catches up with us and continues his exercise. My dad tells me he had always hated coming here — "A puddle in the middle of a parking lot." My mom remembers differently: catching tadpoles in ankle-deep water, "hiding in the reeds from the adults." We marvel at the difference in their memories and leave it at that.

A group of Canadian geese nervously pad back and forth, trying to cross the constant stream of cars to a patch of grass opposite the lake. A dead bird lies on the side of the road, hit long ago. The geese walk around it.

If it weren't so real, it could be an ugly metaphor: as Melissa Harris reports, during United Steelworkers' nationwide strike in early 2015, two of the eleven refineries and chemical plants striking were the sites of fatal accidents. In other recent news, seven died at a Washington Tesoro refinery in 2010 when a heat exchanger failed. Fifteen died and 170 were injured in a 2005 BP explosion in Texas, after which a U.S. Chemical Safety and Hazard Investigation Board found, as the *New York Times* wrote, "organizational and safety deficiencies at all levels of the BP Corporation. Warning signs of a possible disaster were present for several years, but company officials did not intervene effectively to prevent it." In addition, workplace fatigue was listed as a possible cause for the explosion. As the *New Republic* found, all operators that day had worked twelve-hour shifts for at least twenty-nine days straight after a staffing downsize from twenty-eight to eight.

In Hammond, United Steelworkers Local 7-1's ninety-three-day-long strike — the longest in the history of the 126-year-old refinery — demanded better safety conditions. In response, BP's corporate board courteously walked around the dead. People on their way into Chicago honk in support of the strikers as they zoom past. Still a passenger's luxury: drive by, drop in, leave. Even repetition does not make it permanent.

o o o

In 2000, a series of "Wolf Lake Bi-State Gatherings" were organized by the Association for the Wolf Lake Initiative and the National Park Service to "Imagine...a family-friendly outdoor destination of clean air, water and thriving wetlands...a natural paradise against the backdrop of the industrial and cultural heritage of the Calumet Region."

The 130 "stakeholders" — federal, state, and local agencies; community and environmental groups; local business and industry — decided on the principles by which Wolf Lake's redevelopment should abide. And so members of the Indiana EPA, the Eastwisch Girl Scouts, and the Illinois Audubon Society sat at the same table as BP Amoco Oil and Unilever Corporation representatives to decide the future of the lake. The guidelines' vague language of possibility verges on the depoliticized: Identify pollution sources. Identify cost-effective restoration and remediation processes. Establish a Wolf Lake program at environmental education centers.

One of the few designs to actually come to fruition is from 2002. In that year, the City of Chicago Department of Planning and Development implemented a Calumet Area Land Use Plan whose reach includes Wolf Lake. Embracing almost 200 years of heavy industry and a horizonless future of more, Chicago's then-mayor Richard Daley writes in the plan's introduction:

> Today the era of decline is ending and it's possible to see what a new era will look like. New industries will spring up in the Lake Calumet area, bringing new jobs and tax revenue. With careful planning and management, we can bring back Calumet's natural beauty and industrial strength.

The plan elaborates: Calumet contains 1,000 acres of land currently open for industrial development. Even with the last few decades' 40 percent reduction in the amount of steel produced, northwest Indiana remains the nation's largest steel processing region.

"Natural beauty and industrial strength." I wonder at the celebration of what could be called a contradiction. The plan imagines an abstract future of its own choosing. In language reminiscent of that used by the billionaire-funded Marcellus Shale Coalition to persuade their way into fracking, Daley conjures up a moment in time in which heavy industry and environment exist in harmony. Like all the redevelopment attempts and visions before it, the Calumet Plan proposes that the oil refineries and mills dotting the landscape play a central role in the area — now and forever.

o o o

And so: standing at the edge of Wolf Lake, you feel like you are choosing whether or not to take and put on the blindfold held out in front of you.

You can look at the water itself, the beautiful birds, the snail shells, the crabs. All of this is here. The lake has become a nesting site for endangered species like the crowned night heron, the little blue heron, and the yellow-headed blackbird. Three different species of swans have made their home here, and make an eerie sight when spotted from the highway. My parents are shocked by the changes of the past ten years: when they were my age, they say, you would have never seen a squirrel, even.

You can look for all these things, and you will find them. And yet: lift your eyes a little higher, and you'll find a roaring highway. Turn around, and you'll see four volcanoes burning bright. Dig a little deeper under the soft silt of the Real Lake Bottom, and you'll release a small plume of toxins. Sift through the blood of any of the lake's local visitors, and you'll find PCBs. Heavy metals. Lupus. Alzheimer's. Cancers. The choking feeling of never being able to *prove* the cause of any of it. The sinking realization that a trip to the lake might count as yet another "exposure."

Ghosts come in many different forms: chemical traces that bend you like invisible hands, a sense of timelessness that nevertheless passes too quickly. At the doctor, I watch my own blood as it is slowly drawn into transparent tubes. Compartmentalized. They want the black-red liquid in these bottles. My breath in these. I label the tube "Sample 1" and write my name on the glass as if I am identifying a body, which, after all, I am. Ask my father if he thinks working in the mills killed his parents. *Of course.* It is so obvious that it is background. This is where we live and this is us.

o o o

After our trip to the lake, my parents and I make a short drive to sit at the kitchen table of my mother's parents' house. They have lived here in Hammond since the 1950s. My grandmother was born in the Indiana Harbor; my grandfather was one of the Mexican immigrants paid in single dollar bills to lay railroad tracks that made Chicago boom. Each of them worked in the mills in different capacities. Today, my grandmother has Alzheimer's, which is "aggravated," to put it in the words of a medical journal, by her industrial surroundings. Her parents all died of pollution-induced diseases, as did my father's parents.

Visiting this morning are Ernestina and Juan, who live a short distance away. Ernestina is telling us about her three jobs: part-time cafeteria work at a grade school, part-time cleaning office buildings in Chicago, and then as a housekeeper in the area, to make ends meet. Juan drives two hours every day to his job at a sugar plant near Chicago.

Neither have health insurance, and the adults are all discussing home remedies for Ernestina's slipped disc.

Ernestina and Juan's employment situation is typical for the area. The median income in East Chicago is $26,538 — still more than Trump's Gary casino paid its employees (an average of $24,931, including tips and benefits). Few people living in Hammond, Whiting, or East Chicago know anyone who actually works at the ArcelorMittal mill, nor the BP refinery, although they are all familiar with the pollution from each. Instead, workers commute from more affluent towns and suburbs of Chicago, Michigan, and Indiana.

The kind of economic system that has created BP Oil, has created Wolf Lake, has created Ernestina's three jobs, has created the special texture of the air hanging over Hammond. As Trish Kahle writes, "neither neoliberalism nor austerity is only a social or political project — they are ecological projects, remaking our relationships with our (built) environments."

All the remediation plans that have taken place at Wolf Lake have been focused on what is visible at close range: making Wolf Lake a nicer park, a cleaner environment. This is, of course, extremely important. Yet this has also had the effect of creating Wolf Lake as a small island of relative ecological health in the middle of a toxic sacrifice zone — a "puddle in the middle of a parking lot." Plans for Wolf Lake and the greater Calumet region envision a future brightened forever by the light of the volcanoes — just, somehow, "greener." But those plans are brimming with contradiction, promising both "new industries…constructed in ways that don't harm the environment" and "new power generating facilities," imagined very much along the same lines as those that currently exist.

In *This Changes Everything*, Naomi Klein says that "we are left with a stark choice: allow climate disruption to change everything about our world, or change pretty much everything about our economy to avoid that fate." That is: BP Oil is a different kind of stakeholder than the Eastwisch Girl Scouts. What would a redevelopment plan for Wolf Lake look like that chooses not to wear the blinders? The answer is so clear that it becomes counterintuitive: to *really* redevelop Wolf Lake, you must look beyond Wolf Lake.

Any attempt to remake the area can't solely be concerned with incremental changes to the status quo — an added AquaPark, a refurbished music pavilion. Deep change means imagining a future in which attempts to rebuild the world are not neatly bounded into the space of a park. It means imagining Wolf Lake as part of a larger world that includes the view from its shores and the lives of the people that come to it. Deeply redeveloping Wolf Lake would mean extinguishing the volcanoes. It would mean replacing fossil fuel and other ecologically destructive industries with sustainable ones, while building a democratic and equitable economy that is rooted not only in divestment from disaster capitalism, but also reinvestment in the communities most exploited by extractive industries, and excluded from the wealth that they generate. It's a hefty task, and one that presents itself as totalizing in the same way that the extractive capitalism that dominates the Calumet is imagined as totalizing. It is hard to imagine the view from Wolf Lake without the constant flares.

Drawing up a list of what would need to happen to achieve a different view from Wolf Lake becomes an exercise in imagination, where you can more or less arbitrarily choose if what you're writing down is feasible or completely off the wall. Workers' co-ops. Wind farms. Community gardens. A strengthened EPA. An end to corporate lobbying.

And so you end up in the same position as those other redevelopment plans: proposing small changes that, you hope, will lead to larger ones down the line. There is a difference here, however: the end goal is not to merely "identify sources of pollution," nor to replicate the present. It is not merely to build a concert venue on the water and keep the highway that cuts through it. The future you imagine is nothing less than the end of the present. It is a view from Wolf Lake.

Prairie Water, Lake Sky

GRETCHEN LIDA

Lake Michigan flickers between skyscrapers on a northbound train. Did I see water rippling, or was it just a light spot in the sky? The tracks lead me further inland a block or two, a mile or two, a Chicago skyscraper or two. Get further north, go farther east and I know it is it, a singular it — Lake Michigan, the secondhand sunrise.

Lake Michigan is the child of glaciers, a parent of backwards streams, a sibling to other great lakes and conjoined twins with Lake Huron. The water and prairie blend in places. When it freezes over, I forget where the grasses and sand end. Where will I fall through the ice? Where will its burping, tinkering, ice sheets collide as it transitions from one season to the next? One eon to the next?

The lake is a dumping ground, playground, and foreground. Its mood shifts with the light, it is personified. It is the invader and the invaded. It feels more alive than "it." It is more alive than pronouns; too moody to be confined to small things like he or she or them. It is a friend to sit beside, a dance partner that's just a bit better then me, a jealous lover who bites at fingertips when I forget to visit and it pulls at the fragments of the sacred like light through stained glass.

Lighthouses surround its fresh water. The oceans, its cousins, surround their lighthouses. Lake sand is silt, old, sticky paint. Lake Michigan sometimes pretends it is an ocean when the wind comes to dance; the two spin together, the water churning in petticoats of froth. Seiches reach through, pulling at the body of the lake. Seiches are weather waves that move from shore to shore, mimicking true tides. Lake Michigan's own lunar pull is small, inconsequential to scientists.

Come fall, there is a moment of cold surf, enough for men in black-peeled skin to ride on flint-colored waves. The lake isn't a sea imposter, an ocean poser, a bayside wanna-be; it is itself, something else entirely. No, you can't see across it. Its currents kill sailors. Its beauty saves youth.

It is a lake of color. Some nights it is as black as a farm girl's skirt. On bright winter mornings it is as starched white as her blouse. Other days it is the same grey color of the L train cars pulling her to work, while in spring it can glisten green like the corn fields she came from. It can bring a solace of purple wind like the moors of her parents' European home, or drive in yellow bursts of heat if her family came north with the Great Migration. Sliver glints of prosperity catch the daylight. Brown bubbles of broken dreams surface like stockyard waste down Bubbly Creek on Chicago's South Side.

As my train moves, the corset strings of city give way to suburbs, the cotton suburb shift comes off, giving way to farmland. No matter the trappings, the barges, the naval bases, jetties, piers, and the invasive zebra mussels, the lake is the lake. Or maybe Lake Michigan is just water, just sky.

Chicago Water Taxi: Romancing the River

DINA ELENBOGEN

I am floating in the underbelly of the city, the way the summer my son was an infant, walking along the lake with him strapped to my body at dawn, I'd feel as if I were moving through the underbelly of the day. On this boat I take to work, floating under bridges and taking in new angles and facades of buildings, this city feels unfamiliar. It is like looking into a face you've known for a long time and seeing an entirely new quality of beauty.

I used to envy friends who were able to walk only steps from the train to their buildings, but now I realize that I am the lucky one. After a thirty-minute train ride on which I review for the writing class I'll teach later in the morning, I arrive in the city, walk a few steps, and my boat is usually waiting for me. I step off the pier at Wacker and down a few steps into the yellow boat. I usually sit uncovered on a bench in the back. Some mornings I'll commune with the red steel bridges that we pass between Madison (1919), and the Michigan Avenue Street Bridge (1920).

Other times it will be the glass facades of the newer buildings next to the old stone and turrets of Crain's Chicago Business and the Wrigley Building. If the boat didn't hit the cement at Michigan to disembark, I'd probably drift away with my thoughts all morning.

I have always lived within walking (or running) distance from Lake Michigan, have come to know her moods and vicissitudes, to acknowledge the seasons through her shades of blue, green, or grey. But the river and I have been casual acquaintances — until I started teaching at the University of Chicago's Gleacher Center, along the main bank between Michigan and Columbus. I've admired the way the sun glistens on the ripples of waves, but I haven't seen or thought about what lives beneath the river's surface — until today.

Beyond the surface there are fish, and an undercurrent that moves water back toward the lake. Once the Chicago River flowed into Lake Michigan. But as "the stinky river" got more and more polluted, the water was redirected toward the Mississippi. In 1887 the Sanitary District reversed the flow into the Chicago Sanitary and Ship Canal to avoid polluting the lake with river waste.

The river is by no means clean, but especially on the North Channel, people continue to catch warm water fish. There are smallmouth and largemouth bass, bluegill, catfish, and carp. There is no fishing on the south branch, once the sewer for the stockyards, and where barges still travel.

The jury is still out on just how toxic the river continues to be. Scientists at the University of Illinois at Chicago and the Chicago Water Reclamation District are in the middle of a large study to help determine this. We know the water is dirty, but the study will determine if activities like kayaking or catching a random splash of water is detrimental to our health. The EPA would like the water to be clean enough to swim in, but the Sanitary District, which maintains the water's standards, says it would cost billions of dollars to do so. And that has never been the purpose of the river.

The river moves people and barges and was built to keep waste out of Lake Michigan, where we can still swim.

Still the river has come a long way from those days, from "the sluggish brown stream" the poet Edward Hirsch describes in his poem "Family Stories," where the river is a central character in his saga of Chicago history, the river that still flowed into the lake.

Water service was born in 1962 as the RiverBus when the Wendella Tourist company started a rush-hour commuter service between Michigan Avenue and the Northwestern Railroad Station. Since then, the RiverBus has safely carried an estimated four million rail commuters. In 2006, the Water Taxi documented more than 19,000 departures.

The Chicago Water Taxi operates on a closed loop route, shuttling passengers between Madison Street on the south branch; La Salle Street and Michigan Avenue on the main branch; and River East on the main branch in Ogden Slip. During the summer and early fall, the boats depart and arrive from seven in the morning until seven at night. Usually the boats stop in October with the first chill of autumn; this year they'll run through December.

MONDAY OCTOBER 12

The river can be just as moody as the lake. The temperature outside plunged to the middle forties, hats covering the heads of children off of school for Columbus Day, the water seems darker and full of movement from the first winds of autumn. As I wait on the riverbank bench between Michigan and Wabash, I absorb, as if for the first time, modern office buildings with tinted glass windows, the old stone of Chicago's golden domes, the filigree of iron on the Chicago Avenue Bridge.

I sit inside on the way to class and notice the loafers of a gentleman who's been on the same taxi as me the last two trips. I remember when one of his buddies, who'd been complaining about the discomfort of his own new shoes, had commented to his friend about how much more comfortable his shoes looked. These are the Monday-morning boat buddies — nine o'clock shift.

On the way back I brave the elements and sit outside, although the wind stings my fingers. Kids climb all over, expressing the enthusiasm that I still feel about this ride but that I think my fellow passengers either lack or conceal.

Sailing to and from class makes me feel like a traveler in a foreign country. My brown backpack filled with books at my side, my eye alert to the passing terrain, I am on the outside, watching the city I once thought I knew, as it becomes unexplored territory.

When I've spoken to married women who find they have crushes on other men, the most common explanation is the desire to return to the thrill of discovering someone for the first time, to open a new book and begin with the first sentence — and to be looked at that closely as well. Is the river discovering me as I newly discover it?

OCTOBER 19

I can't help but notice the fumes, the sludge, the smell of sewer. My father, a biochemical engineer for the Sanitary District, spent part of his career in water reclamation, trying to clean this up. It is still a glorious day, the river glistening with autumn light, green waters, blue skies.

Especially on the water, there is still a chill in the air, mostly under bridges, shielded from the sun. Other times we are between buildings protected from everything but wind and water.

The woman who opens and closes the gate to the Water Taxi has a nametag that says Michelle. I want to know what she sees as she looks out at the water all day from the bridge at Madison to the bridge over Michigan — but to speak would make me conspicuous when all I want to do is blend in to the water and observe.

Today I am struck by the façade of the Civic Opera House, and how one sees a city differently from the angle of water. I sat inside that building, listening to opera with my husband when I was pregnant with our daughter, and I admired the grandeur of the chandeliers, red carpets, nineteenth-century opulence. But the Latin letters engraved on the outside speak of a more profound history.

As I study the Opera House from the vantage point of the river, I remember how, floating along the Seine, I understood Paris better by seeing her contained by water. Inside the Louvre I felt lost, looking first for Mona Lisa's smile, but from the outside I saw it all, the sprawling expanse, and I understood in a more concrete way, how central it is to the city and the world. But by seeing Chicago from the river, it is neither more or less. It is simply different, older, unpeopled.

OCTOBER 26

Thus far the Water Taxi has shown its devotion by always being there when I step off the 8:18 a.m. train from Evanston. Today I thought I'd test the waters by taking the 8:40 a.m. Metra from Main Street, arriving in Chicago twenty minutes later than usual. I wonder if on this shift I'll discover any familiar faces on the train ride down, someone to complain to about the damp day, my virus, my husband away at a conference and having to drive the 7:00 a.m. carpool shift. I find no friend, but gaze idly out the window, having planned my class in advance. I am greeted not by sludge at the river, but by debris I'd never noticed before, just below the Madison Street Bridge: beer cans, paper, cups left over from the weekend's festivities. When the Water Taxi arrives after a short wait, I realize it is the friend I had craved. Dressed in orange lights, a carved pumpkin is on the inside door seat where I sit today to avoid the wet from an early morning drizzle.

This little crush I have on the Water Taxi has the potential to sail into a full-blown love affair. But of course he is married to the river and I to my dear husband of thirteen years.

But I miss him on days that I drive and I'm already trying to figure out how to extend our relationship beyond the term's end or the river's end. My mandatory morning commutes will end by late November, but the Water Taxi keeps running through December. Suddenly I want to know everything about it, to see him through all seasons, with Christmas trimmings and even what happens when the water begins to freeze.

In writing class, when we try to find a nice way to describe what isn't working in someone's essay, I say I feel like I am floating from paragraph to paragraph but not getting anywhere. The boat and river remain with me while I teach. The longing I feel on the train or when walking alone through the city fades. I am swept up in the words of my students, the workshop process, and the larger contexts we need to tap into to make our writing better. Their essays are small windows into their lives. I begin to see them more and more as individuals. Yet the way they suffer is universal. We are buoyed by the way words connect us to each other's lives.

Things are getting serious. Instead of stopping for my usual salad bar after class at the River Walk Café, I go straight out to the water. Of course I'm not as hungry because of my virus, but part of me just wants to keep floating. Not to stay put.

On the way back to Madison Avenue I return to the inside cabin, next to the pumpkin. They turned the heat on so it is cozy and warm. I can't see the water, only the tops of bridges, the upper halves of buildings: Chicago Sun Times, glass, steel, and stone.

NOVEMBER 2

I'm part of the early morning rush hour, waiting for the Metra. It is normal commuting time for most, including two acquaintances who are distressed by an apparent delay. We are waiting for the 7:50 a.m. train that the announcer says will be fifteen minutes late. One gentleman says now we'll have to ride with the 8:00 a.m. riffraff. When I confess I'm usually an 8:22 a.m. commuter he says, only half joking, that I am really riffraff. One woman is concerned she'll be late for her 8:30 a.m. meeting.

I, on the other hand am calm, knowing the taxi will be there whenever I arrive.

This throng of people is both unpleasant and unfamiliar to me. It makes me feel lonelier.

The delay they keep referring to is because of the weather, but the weather is light rain. This same light rain caused me to get on the early train instead of walking to the local café to prepare class.

I thought that maybe the thing I'm really looking for could be found on an earlier train that leaves at the right hour.

What I find when I get downtown is the rush hour Water Taxi. It is a larger boat with a long bench in the center covered with clear plastic.

The rain is just petering off and yet the water is still choppy. At first I sit uncovered, hoping to commune with the river, but the bench is wet so I move inside and gaze into the bridge at Lake Street, realizing there is a track on top of it as a train passes by: the double-decker bridge.

There is no one to talk to in the morning. This makes me lonelier than when I am by myself in a large house. In the world, the thing I'm looking for may be there but isn't.

At home I already know that all I have, sometimes, is myself. The thing I'm looking for is something to remind me that I'm alive. The thing I've dressed for, that can look back at me with admiring eyes, notice the turquoise of my new blouse, the way it brings out my eyes, the color my family looks past as they rush out the door — uncharacteristically without me. (My husband does Monday morning carpool — both shifts.)

As we float toward Michigan Avenue, the sky begins to clear but the boat driver points out the darker clouds on the horizon. I realize today, traveling among the rush hour crowd of commuters, that the Water Taxi is not just for those with the luxury to drift to work unhurried or for shoppers or tourists, but is for everyone.

The boat driver who I thought understood something more about the sky than I do, was wrong. The dark clouds of morning have passed and during my much less populated trip back, a taxi is waiting and three of us head back toward Madison under sunny skies. I sit outside, notice the autumn leaves in the water and the sign that says "Do Not Anchor Under Bridge."

When I get off the boat, too early for the train, yet not enough time to really get anywhere, I realize that I am unhinged.

poetry

Late Storm on Lake Michigan
LAURA PASSIN

I dreamed a funnel cloud,
     its black finger pointing
to a shipwrecked past.

My head's not built
     to stand this pressure.
This city's a mistake

of human planning; concrete
     swells the sky to nothing –
flat streets ooze,

no horizon — wind rakes the high-rise
     glass cathedrals till they almost learn
to shatter, toys of natures,

battered and grateful for their scars.
     My parents met here.
We've seen how that worked out.

You can't love this city
     for long: you must allow
the great, flat machine

to mold you in its image.
     It won't condone
the hills and depths

of marriage. Not Chicago

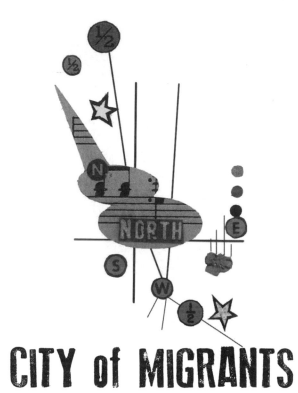

CITY of MIGRANTS

Illiana: Life on a Rust Belt Border

GRETCHEN KALWINSKI

I locked eyes with four, mangy-coated creatures across a chain-link fence. To the east, highway traffic hummed while towers pumped blue sulfurous smoke and freight trains rattled. I realized they were deer — urban ones, alert and eager, lean and scrappy. They scampered back to dilapidated buildings that had once been a steel mill.

It was dusk, and I was with my father at a park in my northwest Indiana hometown. We were on the Indiana/Illinois border, on a gravelly side street separating the mill from a residential street.

I'd never seen deer there before. But when I was young, the mills hadn't yet laid off 80,000 people. The deer reminded me of the pre-industrial landscape — marshes and wolves and prairie grass.

Hammond is in the Calumet industrial complex, between Chicago and Gary. It exists alongside Lake Michigan, the Grand Cal River, three sets of railroad tracks, two steel mills, and an oil-tank farm. The mills, along with Keil Chemical, Amaizo, and Lever Brothers, make pollution levels severe. As kids, we knew which times to stay indoors, to avoid putrid odors. At night, steel furnaces light up the skies in blue and orange.

ooo

That night, I had a dream set in that same alley: white horses exploded from a portal in the ground, into the neighborhood. The alley divided the street where my Polish paternal grandparents lived and the mill where my grandfather worked. Nazi Germany refugees, they moved to Illiana, aka "the Region" for the Eastern European community. It was blocks from our home and that of my Slovak-Hungarian maternal grandparents'.

As a quiet reader, I didn't mesh with Hammond life. My parents encouraged me to read — but other than one bookish, artistic girlfriend, I was lonely. Frivolity is frowned on there, an attitude that trickles down from the scenery. With grandiose infrastructure (twenty-story oil tanks, smoke towers, freight trains), I always had a depressive sense of insignificance. Factory workers are taught obedience, not culture and creativity.

When I watched *My Dinner with Andre* with my father, I instantly knew what I wanted from life. I didn't know how to get it, but knew I wasn't going to find these artistic peers to talk to in Hammond. So I delved into the worlds of Anne Shirley, Laura Ingalls Wilder, Nancy Drew, the brothers Grimm, Judy Blume, and Madeline L'Engle, sitting in my bedroom, leaving my body for other, more alluring, locations.

o o o

I shouldn't have felt so isolated: because the area is right on the border, Illiana is on Central time, not Eastern. Regionites visit the city frequently. They consider themselves suburban Chicagoans. They listen to Chicago radio and cheer for its teams. My second-generation family made city trips for rye bread, *sekacz, krakowska*, and *pachzki*.

It also helped that my father got his MSW at the University of Chicago. During those years, I latched on to images from when we visited a Hyde Park pizzeria, heard jazz, saw well-dressed people have interesting conversations.

My classmates were white, Polish, Slovak, Black, Latino, Serbian, and Italian. We ate homemade *pierogi* and tamales and legit deep-dish and duck's blood soup and grits and *kolachy*. It was a city lifestyle, even if we were thirty minutes from Indiana cornfields.

Still, my experience of Chicago was as a tourist. Public transit was confusing, and I couldn't afford the plays, stores, and restaurants. I was extra self-conscious after radio DJs created a song called "Indiana Hair," mocking Indianans' poofy hairstyles. I felt feral; Chicago was yards from home but a world away.

o o o

Loans took me to college down south, and when a frat boy called me a "Region-Rat," I knew Hammond was considered scummy. There, I discovered the power of language. If I talked about *My Dinner with Andre*, I'd find people who'd seen it and they'd introduce me to more things that sparked my interest. As I discovered Stein, Barnes, Woolf, Kubrick, Linklater, Kieślowski, and Campion, I started to feel more alive.

Using language to draw outside worlds closer to me reminded me of the Roman Catholic incantations of my youth, which used repetitive language for conjuring. I began considering words as spells.

o o o

Post-graduation, I moved to Chicago and frequented nineties outposts — Café Voltaire, Urbis Orbis, Leo's Lunchroom, Bite, Earwax, the Empty Bottle, and the Hideout. I read Gwendolyn Brooks and Stuart Dybek. I hung out with people who made zines, art, and music. Because I finally possessed the passwords to culture, I began feeling like a part of something.

I love Chicago for de-rubeing me. Geographically, Chicago's in the Rust Belt; it has factories and a deep love of meat. But unlike the Rust Belt of my youth, it values culture, ideas, and art.

But Chicago's racial and class divisions are deep, its sales tax is the nation's highest, its winters are brutal, and it leads the nation in population loss. The impenetrability I felt years ago is still present. Consider Upper Wacker Drive, which floats above Michigan Avenue's high-end shops and restaurants. Below is Lower Wacker, where homeless people live and drivers access service entrances, unseen by the privileged. If you've got a reason to access a skyscraper, you'll get a picturesque view, but many never do, never even visit the city's beaches.

o o o

I married a man from Elkhart County, Indiana. Last Christmas, while visiting in-laws I was looking out at the woods behind their property and started hearing incessant gunshots from the nearby gun club. It's normally quiet in Elkhart, where RV factories no longer thrive but Amish communities do. For me, the quiet is eerie; I feel safer in populated areas than in nature. Plus, it's Trump country. (Unlike the rest of Indiana, the Region votes Democrat.)

Being elsewhere in Indiana makes me appreciate Hammond and I was eager to depart for my family's *Wigilia* (Christmas Eve dinner). For all its faults, the activism and pride in the Region, (once described as a "barnacle hanging off Chicago's south side" by author Jean Shepherd), instilled in me a sense of social justice; that no one is more important than anyone else; that pretension is bad and compassion is good.

o o o

My husband and I work in creative fields. My parents don't understand why we insist on paying so much to live in Chicago. I've retorted that we can't live without art and bookstores. But now that we're older and spend a lot more time home, painting and writing, we've been asking ourselves if the higher rent is worth it.

Many say that Chicago is a great place to get your start, but you have to know when to leave. We're at that point, and if there's one thing I've learned, it's that place matters.

My kind, worried father used to say my Chicago life was a fantasy. He reminded me that in Hammond they understood what *real* life was about: jobs and mortgages and death. The older I get, the more this resonates. But it only tells half the story and the other half is delight: the love inherent in making art or engaging in culture. And for me, Hammond will never contain those things — I'm not moving back to Indiana.

For years, I've straddled two worlds. I look like a Chicago professional, but on the inside, I'm a feral Indianan with big hair, angry about being left out. As I consider leaving two places that have only partially felt like home, I feel myself nowhere and several places at once. I am only myself. I am Illiana.

NOT FROM AROUND HERE

GINA WATTERS

The bar was full of them: cops. Even out of uniform they were unmistakable: the postures, the voices, the haircuts. Drawn in by the promise of dollar beers, I passed through the thin blue line and took a seat at the bar. No sooner had I ordered my Budweiser than one of Chicago's finest split from the herd and sauntered toward me.

This particular officer was clearly several PBRs into his evening. He pulled out a stool and plopped down. The cop introduced himself, and although I have long since forgotten his name, I do remember that he told me at least three times that he was born and raised on the West Side of Chicago. He directed his eyes just south of my collarbones and gave me a knowing smile. With all the grace and skill you'd expect from a man with his cell phone clipped to his belt, he laid some of his best lines on me. But I wasn't biting.

As someone not remotely interested in hooking up with a cop, but rather absurdly obsessed with safety, I decided to make the best of this intrusion on my evening and press the officer for some professional advice. As a newcomer to the city, I told him about the canister of pepper spray I always had with me, to which he scoffed. "Yeah, pepper spray." He laughed as if I had just told him I carry a box of Triscuits around with me for protection. "I hate to break it to you, but that isn't going to do anything."

He took another swig of his beer. "Seriously, let me see it." I shrugged, opened my purse, and pulled out my pepper spray. It wasn't one of those cute, little, pink deals designed to look like a tube of lipstick or a pen. This was a black canister with a big red trigger, and written along one side, in the most no-nonsense of fonts, it said "AMERICAN DEFENDER."

"This?" he asked. "I'd spray this shit on my pizza."

At my blank look, he sighed. "Where are you from?"

"Michigan."

He shook his head. "Of course you are."

This was a reaction I had grown accustomed to since arriving in Chicago. It was 2003 and I had just graduated from college. I'd packed up my stuff and, along with a friend and fellow graduate, headed to the Windy City to — well, I hadn't figured that part out yet.

I'd arrived in Chicago with hopes high, but I came down hard and fast when I realized I was nothing but a cliché. Plenty of native Chicagoans made it very clear that their town was overrun with the likes of me. Be from Texas, Georgia, New York, but for the love of Richard M. Daley, no more Michigan State grads and their U-Hauls shall invade their fair city.

When people from Chicago looked at me, they saw Big Ten Barbie: She comes complete with everything you see here — a suitcase full of yoga pants, a jug of fake tanner, and a venti Starbucks latte! Degree in Communications sold separately!

Well, the last part was true, and I had to admit that as I walked the streets of my new city, I saw that I was clearly one of many. There I was at a bar on Lincoln Avenue! There I was living in a condo in the South Loop (courtesy of Mom and Dad)! There I was riding the Brown Line to my marketing job in River North! There I was blithely stomping around town in my Ugg boots, leaving a trail of gentrification everywhere I went. I didn't see myself that way, but it was painful to realize that others did. It hurt that I wasn't part of the city I already loved. In fact, I was a cancer on it.

It didn't help that I found my first apartment in Lincoln Park. It seemed an innocuous decision at the time, but in short order I learned that my neighborhood, like my home state, was a personal detail I was expected to be ashamed of when talking to "real" Chicagoans. Whenever I told some guy from Bridgeport where I lived, I had to pretend I didn't notice the "of course you do" hovering silently on the tip of his tongue.

But, in defense of myself and other newcomers to the city, it's difficult to venture out when you don't know what's there. While my roommate and I were apartment hunting, smartphones were still but a glimmer in Steve Jobs's eye, so the paper map we had to rely on actually cut off to the north at Lawrence Avenue.

"What happens after Lawrence?" my roommate asked. I shrugged, "Wisconsin?"

Other transplants, every bit as clueless as we were, warned us that it was dangerous to live too far north, west, or south; that Wicker Park was solely for hipsters and those pretending to be; that River North was expensive and full of assholes; and that Lakeview was a frat boy nightmare stuffed with a gooey, drunk-Cubs-fan filling. With so many warnings (and the least helpful map every printed), Lincoln Park seemed like a safe and logical choice.

And we might have been living in the land of Porsche SUVs, $1,500 strollers, and Lululemon clothes for everyone, but I'm pretty sure it was the worst apartment in the entire neighborhood. For one, it was directly over a bar. A bar that seemed to only serve some kind of spicy sausage and cater exclusively to very loud patrons. Lying in bed each night with a meat-scented pillow over my head, I tried in vain to block out the sloppy revelry vibrating up though my bedroom floor.

The place had all the classic features of a terrible first apartment: a leaky shower, wildly inconsistent temperatures, small dark rooms, and tiny closets. We owned no furniture except our beds and one broken recliner, which we fought over constantly. The loser was forced to sit on a nest of blankets on the floor in order to watch our tiny rabbit-eared TV.

Unsurprisingly, I tried to spend as little time as possible in that apartment, so I explored the city as much as I could, my circle growing wider with every outing. I wandered the streets, trying to somehow cram a lifetime's worth of experiences and understanding into my brain in one go. I was determined to connect with the heart and soul of this place that I so desperately wanted to call home.

I was trying hard, but my shortcomings were still a fresh wound when Officer West Side made a mockery of my pepper spray, and by extension, my attempts to feel safe in a new city. I watched him as he turned the canister over and over in his hands. I assumed that since this man was trained to use assault rifles, he knew how to handle himself around a weapon one could pick up at any 7-11. I should have assumed otherwise. Before I could stop him, the cop slid the trigger into position, aimed the nozzle into his mouth and shot pepper spray down his throat.

I set my beer down and watched his face for a reaction. At first, he shrugged as if to say, "See? No big deal." For a moment he was quiet as his eyes began tearing up. He coughed, put his hand to his mouth and stared straight ahead. Slowly, he rose from his barstool, turned, and walked calmly to the restroom. A moment later, the men's room door flew open and a cop-shaped blur whizzed past us, out the front door of the bar, into the street, and (I can only assume) on to the nearest hospital.

I returned to my beer.

The moment felt significant. Not a magical transformation of course, but something definitely shifted. Perhaps I'd never be a real Chicagoan, but maybe that didn't matter. In the following years, the Chicago Police Department would earn a reputation far worse than any my fellow transplants and I ever could. And from that moment on, any time someone treated me like an unwelcome guest in my own city, I could take comfort in the fact that although I am just a clueless girl from Michigan, even I wouldn't pepper spray my own face.

BENEATH THE WILLOW TREE:
THE EARLY DEATH AND IMMORTAL LIFE
OF LINDA PARKER

BY MARK GUARINO

Dead in 1935, Linda Parker left behind few recordings. Few people knew her, but thousands traveled miles to attend her funeral. Today, her headstone in tiny Pine Lake Cemetery in LaPorte, Indiana, is nearly impossible to locate. Maybe because Linda Parker, "The Little Sunbonnet Girl," didn't exist at all.

She was a character in the early years of the "hillbilly" record market, the agreed-upon name for 78-RPM records targeting rural whites. Those years were fertile ones for the recording industry: the "Barn Dance" radio format was sweeping the U.S., presenting singing cowboys, minstrels, novelty acts, string bands, and crooners dressed in overalls in a variety show format to listeners who then bought records, songbooks, toy guitars, and tickets to appearances at state fairs, local music halls, and theaters. The promotion machine was primitive to what we recognize today but the blueprint was the same: new faces were hyped through repeated exposure on the radio, which helped record and ticket sales.

Chicago's *Barn Dance* program, Saturday nights on WLS beginning in 1924, was not the first, but it was the biggest and most influential. Preceding the *Grand Ole Opry* by a year, but in popularity for twenty years, the broadcast made Chicago the nation's commercial heart of country music.

The *Barn Dance* was an incubator for stars like Gene Autry and Red Foley, who developed their craft before moving on to greener pastures elsewhere, most notably Hollywood and Nashville. During those first twenty years, the *Barn Dance* helped usher country music off the mountain and into the city, where mountain ballads and old folk songs, played in living rooms, front porches, and town dances, transformed into sophisticated entertainments. Bradley Kincaid, Patsy Montana, Lulu Belle and Scotty, and Karl and Harty, among others, not only kept these songs alive in circulation, they contributed to the songbook, their works covered over the decades by everyone from Hank Williams to Norah Jones.

Linda Parker didn't have that chance. She was only twenty-three when she died. Living fast and dying young didn't begin with Janis Joplin, Kurt Cobain, or Tupac. Nor did the commodification of mourning that, by now, we recognize through the T-shirts, the boxed sets, the tribute specials, and more recently, the hologram effigies. The culture of postmortem obsession originated with Parker, whose audience was clearly not prepared for her sudden death, especially of a performer WLS marketed as the angelic embodiment of youth. Thousands mourned, a phenomenon the station happened to stoke for profitable gain. The grief spread across the U.S. because Parker was more than an entertainer, she was a symbol. WLS called her "The Little Sunbonnet Girl." For listeners toiling under the weight of the Great Depression, the sweetness touched them, likely because there was so little of it around.

She was the first female country music singer to launch a successful solo career from outside a group, a simple gesture at the time, but the one that cracked open the door for her gender. Until then, the identity of women in the so-called hillbilly market was hitched to a male partner or existed within a vocal group. Women were side players, ornaments. Parker may have started as the centerpiece of a group of all men, but her singing voice, a sweet, crooning alto, gave her prominence. As soon as she joined, the Cumberland Ridge Runners, an established group of all men, turned into accompanists.

Parker was a high school delinquent from Hammond, Indiana, who even as a teenager knew who she was and what she wanted to become. She was born in Covington, Indiana, on January 18, 1912, as Genevieve Elizabeth Muenich, the daughter of Edward Muenich and Hazel Vyse, local laborers who had a shotgun marriage after Vise got pregnant at age seventeen. In high school Parker was a truant who was indifferent to learning; most of her classes she failed. After a suspension from Hammond High in 1927, she transferred to Hammond Tech, a vocational school for problem students. This time, she dropped out. She was sixteen.

Now with plenty of free time on her hands, she won an audition for a new Sunday afternoon variety show on WWAE, the same radio station Bill and Charlie Monroe would play music between shifts at the Sinclair Oil refinery, located next door in Whiting. Parker also plied her trade around town, singing at roadhouses and outdoor fairs. By September 8, 1929, the date of her WWAE debut, she already blazed a stage name: "Jeanne Munich, Radio's Red-Headed Rascal."

She sang blues songs due to the coaching of studio director Hank Richards, who eventually left Hammond to work at different Chicago stations, including WIBO located on the far North Side. She followed, and under his direction, switched to more sentimental fare. Suddenly Parker was "Jeanne Munich, The Red-Headed Bluebird." Weeks after joining WAAF, a station broadcasting from the Chicago Stockyards, a following started to grow. A talent scout at WLS named John Lair took notice and signed her to a contract in April 1932. He became her business manager and booking agent, pocketing 20 percent. The contract was airtight, dictating that Lair "shall write, produce, assemble or otherwise procure and furnish all songs, music, routines, spoken lines or sketches" and would control all bookings "in the entertaining, radio, sound motion pictures, phonographic, or theatrical field." Upon signing, Parker entered Lair's stable. In the contract, he laid out the same template for every aspiring singer or musician or minstrel who found their way to Chicago from the sticks, hoping for a stake in big time radio.

In 1930, Lair convinced WLS on the idea of creating a group consisting of musicians from back home. Besides mandolin player Karl Davis and Hartford Taylor, otherwise known as Karl and Harty, Lair hired banjoist Howard "Doc" Hopkins, a barber in Mount Vernon, and Gene Ruppe on fiddle, banjo, and harmonica. The group's appearance and sound emanated from Lair's imagination. He dressed them in plaid shirts, suspenders, boots, neck scarves, and felt hats, had them pose for photos in front of animated rural settings, and wrote scripts for them thick with mountain dialect. Two years later, he would rotate in other musicians based on their visual alchemy. Among them: Homer Edgar "Slim" Miller, a lanky comedian and fiddler from Indiana with crooked teeth who often was pictured barefooted. "Folks sometimes say that the Ridge Runners are like a chapter out of the past, suggesting the days of the long rifles and coonskin caps of pioneer Kentucky," the station's publicity copy read in 1935. "Many of their songs have come straight out of the hills where they were passed along from memory until these boys put them on paper."

The Cumberland Ridge Runners' recording output was slim, amounting to two recording sessions in 1933. But they represented a flagship for WLS, used weekly on different shows and also live appearances where they performed instrumentals, old-time sentimental songs, or novelty numbers. Onstage they would perform together and separately — Parker was usually given a solo spot of three songs in the middle.

With Parker, Lair's first priority was to distance her from WAAF. He rechristened Muenich as Linda Parker. As her contract stipulated, Muenich had no choice but to portray this fictional character who was not from industrial Indiana, but from Lair's idealized version of a Kentucky mountain home. In public and in pictures, she wore gingham dresses and a sunbonnet with pearls and high heels. The meshing of rural and contemporary styles added to the fantasy of "The Little Sunbonnet Girl." In photos she clutched a banjo and dulcimer but there was no evidence she knew how to play either. When she married Arthur Janes, a baritone singer in the *Barn Dance* comedy quartet the Maple City Four, the station kept it secret even though they kept their home nearby, at 104 North Pulaski Road. WLS wanted Parker's audience to only know her as a dreamy, virginal sweetheart who served as a calming presence amid the turmoil and insecurity of the Great Depression. "Have you been hearing 'Lindy' Parker, singing old mountain songs with the Cumberland Ridge Runners?" the station asked in her first year:

> If so, you cannot soon forget the wistful tone of her voice as she sings of the loves and sorrows and hopes of the mountain folk. Linda was born at Covington, Kentucky, so she sings of places and scenes that are familiar to her. She's a slender, quiet girl of nineteen, serious faced, often getting a sort of far-away look in her eyes as if she were day-dreaming of that beloved mountain country which she sings about.

As Parker, her recorded output amounted to just four sides released by the Sears label Conqueror in 1933 and 1934. Lair found old Southern ballads for her to sing, mostly sentimental fare like "I'll Be All Smiles Tonight," a waltz that predates the Carter Family's version by a year, and "My Ozark Mountain Home," a mournful-sounding ballad that sets her voice against Davis's trembling mandolin.

"Linda Parker sang beautifully," Karl Davis recalled in 1974. "She sang practically all beautiful sweet songs like 'I'll Be All Smiles Tonight.' That was, I would say, her feature song. She had a very low voice, a contralto voice, and her songs were absolutely beautiful."

Lair supplied her with original songs like "Mother's Old Sunbonnet," with lyrics that reinforced her nurturing image. Lair also reworked "Single Girl, Married Girl," an old folk song made famous by the Carter Family and sung from the perspective of a mother yearning for a different life. The new version, just titled "Single Girl," is less gloomy and instead idealizes the carefree life of youth: "Single girl, single girl, lives a life of ease / Married girl, married girl, has a boss to please."

Her popularity, therefore, was groomed by tours the Ridge Runners did across the Midwest, and the Saturday night broadcasts. But she also appeared throughout the week on WLS, playing Parker on *Mountain Memories*, *Play Party Frolic*, the *Hamlin Wizard Hour*, and the *Coon Creek Social*. Lair had created the Parker character as a kind of earthbound angel who transported listeners back to simpler times, with a fictionalized biography that met their expectations and taste. To WLS, singing "artlessly" was a promise of authenticity:

> When Linda Parker was a little girl around the old home at Covington, Kentucky, she learned many of the old ballads of the hills. Probably when her mother put a little sunbonnet on her head and sent her out to pull weeds in the garden, she little dreamed that some day this little girl would be captioned as "The Sunbonnet Girl," singing those same old songs for millions of people. You have doubtless detected her in singing that occasional plaintive note, so typical of the mountain music. She sings just as her mother and grandmother sang, artlessly, but from the heart.

No one in Elkhart, Indiana, knew on August 1, 1935, they were watching her final appearance. But there was one sign. Parker performed in pain, likely while holding her stomach. "Linda had courage," the WLS publicity machine later recounted. "She bravely continued with the performance." Two days later she was rushed to St. Joseph's Hospital in nearby Mishawaka. There she underwent two blood transfusions. A little over a week after that, at high noon on a Monday, she died of peritonitis, the result of a burst appendix. The Ridge Runners and Maple City Four both served as pallbearers. The amount of flowers WLS sent was described in the local paper as "an entire truckload." More than 3,000 people attended the funeral on August 14, which even garnered a mention in the *New York Times*. "As a singing guitarist, Miss Parker had a wide following, particularly among rural listeners," they noted.

The Ridge Runners never regrouped. "It was a big loss for us, and it was a big loss for the WLS audience, because she'd just reached the height of her popularity," Davis said.

Parker's death allowed WLS a final marketing opportunity, and in a way, it was in perfect alignment to her otherworldly image. "Linda sleeps beneath the largest weeping willow in the cemetery," the station reported in their obituary, a fictitious detail meant to emphasize "Bury Me Beneath the Willows," the Carter Family song she reportedly sang in

Elkhart just before being rushed to the hospital. Lair later confirmed the story in his column, recounting to readers of "that dreary pain-racked afternoon." By December, Parker's smiling image floated above a transcription of the song in *100 WLS Barn Dance Favorites*, a songbook Lair rushed out. "Her sweet voice first brought you many of the songs which you will find in this book," he wrote in his dedication. He added that the boost in price was worth it. "It's a dandy. There's a nice big picture of Little Linda Parker to whose memory the book is dedicated."

In January, Karl Davis wrote "We Buried Her Beneath the Willow," a song that contributed to the official legend. The Cumberland Ridge Runners recorded the song and profits were set aside to support Parker's mother.

The song is a simple but maudlin waltz that imagines the reasons why God chose Parker at such an early age. "A soft song fell within his hearing / he picked our girl / her soul, her voice," they sang. "Today our partner sings in heaven / God praised the angel for his choice." In 1959, Kitty Wells added a church organ, giving it a permanent home in the country gospel canon.

A year later, in January 1936, Parker was resurrected one final time on WLS. It was a special memorial on her birthday. Lair arranged all of the remaining female stars, such as Patsy Montana and Girls of the Golden West, to sing her songs. "Remember our Little Sunbonnet Girl, when she was young and eager for life…instead of thinking of her racked with the pain and torture of those last despairin' days before she left us," Lair implored his audience. Then he announced her mother's address. Hundreds of cards, letters, and poems showed up on her doorstep within a week.

With no film and little recorded evidence, there remains little evidence of Parker's talent. What we do have are publicity photos — one after another of her positioned in the center of the group, wearing a white or checkered dress, holding a dulcimer or banjo. In one photo she stares straight into the camera, the wide bow of the sunbonnet fastened below her chin. Another, she is atop a stool, legs crossed, towering over her accompanists. One more, an ad for Hamlins Wizard Oil of all things, shows her topping the stack of the group, a black fedora on her head, both arms clutching Harty Taylor's shoulders. There are also the stock glamor shots of a movie starlet. "Here's wishing all the luck in the world to my favorite guitar player!" she writes on one, to Taylor. The photo shows her with clutched hands below her chin, cloaked in a dress of sparkles and satin.

But then there is the banjo photo. The Ridge Runners surrounding Parker all strike action poses, cocked toward one another, holding instruments high, smiles all around. But Parker has only the hint of a smile. Her hands could be those of a mannequin; nothing about how they touch the banjo strings tell us how or if she can play.

No matter now. Her focus is away from the camera, to her left, toward something only she can see.

PORTIONS OF THIS ESSAY APPEAR IN A BOOK BY MARK GUARINO ON THE HISTORY OF COUNTRY AND FOLK MUSIC IN CHICAGO, FORTHCOMING FROM THE UNIVERSITY OF CHICAGO PRESS.

Last Call: El Trebol and the Cantinas of Pilsen

KARI LYDERSEN

August 2014: Pete Rodriguez sauntered into El Trebol dressed nicely in a tweed coat and fedora. "Mr. Peeeete," said Marcos Raya with a reptilian grin, sidling up to him. Marcos had sawdust in his hair — the type strewn on the bar's floor to sop up mud and spilled beer. His glasses were broken and askew. He smelled like he'd been sleeping in a burned out building. He hadn't eaten in three days.

What happened to you, asked Pete. Last week you were wearing a silk shirt and sharp hat and looking fine. Now look at you. Pete bought him cheap Chinese food. They went to a nearby building where Marcos was staying with a girlfriend and ate by candlelight. A soft glow illuminated the men, one burly, one wiry, who'd been walking these streets for decades, below the smokestack of the century-old, coal-fired power plant, the hulking brick factories topped by twisting metal pipes.

Both would be back in El Trebol soon enough. Pete had been going there since he was a little kid. He and his brother Art were shoeshine boys, a tradition brought from Mexico. They charged fifty cents for shoes, a dollar for boots. And they'd often get a full fifty cents or dollar tip, especially from the white men who still frequented El Trebol in those days — the remnants of the Polish and Czech population who'd settled the neighborhood in the 1800s.

A *trebol* is a lucky shamrock, a club on playing cards, and a spot in the Mexican border city of Monterrey frequented by prostitutes.

There used to be several bars like El Trebol on every block in Pilsen. It's always been a port of entry neighborhood, a place where immigrants land with virtually nothing but the shirt on their back, and their wits and determination to make a living in a new land. From the mid-1800s on, such immigrants came to Pilsen, filling the boarding houses with slanting hallways and sagging stairways, streaming out each morning to work in the surrounding slaughterhouses, steel mills, factories, and foundries.

The immigrant worker's life is a hard one, grueling and lonely. Such men need to drink.

Or at least find a place where they can disappear from the outside world, from the boss and all their troubles. To share camaraderie, drown their sorrows, and assert their manhood, whether through a brawl or flirtations with the women behind the bar. There have also been women immigrant workers in Pilsen, from the European Jews who started the famous garment workers' strikes of the early 1900s to the Mexican women who later populated Pilsen, laboring long hours making tortillas, dog collars, electronics.

But the bars — the old bars like El Trebol — were places for men. Or rather the customers were all men. Women had an important role, as bartenders and waitresses, far more of them on staff than needed to take orders and pour drinks. Their main job was to chat and dance with the men, make them feel desired and important, after long days or nights at tiring and dirty jobs where they had little power. And to keep the hard-earned money flowing, as the men bought the waitresses drinks — slender, over-priced Coronitas in clear bottles, lime juice dripping down the side.

"These men will see a pretty woman and blow half a paycheck," says Pete. "These big girls behind the bar with little tops on, it reminds them of the love they miss. White people can afford a shrink, Mexicans come here to have a few drinks and forget their problems. Their parents are buried, they can't go back. Tequila is their escape."

Some of the women would head outside the bars with the men too. But the men could buy sex any number of places. Only in these bars could they feel back at home.

The bars had names like El Jardin, where the owner would hang his flashy silk shirts in dry-cleaning bags behind the bar, presumably as a show of wealth. The 1040 Club, located at 1040 West Eighteenth Street. Los Tres Diaz. Doña Queta's. El Quijote. La Macarena. The Donkey. Club Intimo. Tito's Hacienda. My Mistake, a rowdy tavern across from the old police station, where cops danced to oldies and mingled with the same gangbangers they were handcuffing during their shifts.

MARCOS

Marcos Raya came to Chicago at age sixteen and settled with his mother Angela on Taylor Street just north of Pilsen, a strip owned by the Italians. Marcos's parents divorced when he was young and Angela came to Chicago while Marcos was raised in Guanajuato, Mexico, by his musician father. Angela was actually born in Springfield, Illinois, to Mexican immigrant parents. When she was eight the family was sent back to Mexico, among the million or so "repatriados": Mexicans and Mexican Americans including legal residents and citizens "deported" in a wave of public hysteria and xenophobia during the Great Depression.

Marcos is proud he never worked a "real job" in his life. He quit an early post washing dishes in a matter of days, and ever since he's made a living — or at least survived, sometimes barely — through his ingenuity and his art.

He has long been a well-known character in Pilsen, called Chinito for his Asian features, dressing like Jimi Hendrix and driven by his own passions and demons. He lived in Casa

Aztlan, the mural-covered building home to the Brown Berets and various artists and activists. He was the "artist in residence."

He's obsessed with clowns and robots, nurses and advanced medical technology. Fantastical scenes of surgery, prosthetics, and bandages, perhaps to heal his own fevered mind, his alcohol-soaked body or the whole suffering world. His alter-ego, celebrated in countless Technicolor portraits, is a short-haired dog slouching in an alley, wearing sunglasses and a potbelly, looking desperately cool, a wine bottle and crumpled beer cans nearby.

During his "dog days" Marcos would disappear into the netherworld for days or weeks at a time, prowling the alleys, eventually emerging battered and sick, clinging to life in hospital beds more than once. "I should have died a thousand times."

"Trebol was my home. Not because it was romantic, just because it was affordable."

Eventually Marcos broke the hold alcohol had on him. He knew he had already used up more than his share of second chances. His art had been there through even his darkest days. As he struggled toward sobriety, it was his anchor, his lifeline.

Marcos complained as the new people moved into Pilsen. But not too loudly, since they liked his work. He made stickers saying "Gringos No, Gringas Si." He didn't care for white men, but white women were alright, especially since so many of them were willing to pose for him nude.

PETE

Pete Rodriguez was born right in Pilsen, to a Mexican American family. Pete was a free spirit from a young age, with a sense of wanderlust and restlessness that took him around the world, but deep roots that kept bringing him back to Pilsen.

He went to high school at De La Salle, the private school where young mayor-to-be Richard M. Daley was educated. Pete joined the Marines, then went to New Mexico State University, but soon ended up back in Pilsen. In 1983 he got an apartment above a barbershop that later became the Jumping Bean Café — Pete calls it the Yuppie Bean. On summer days he'd set up a throw rug and arm chair on the sidewalk, an oil painting tacked to the brick wall: holding court as the Mayor of Eighteenth Street. His apartment was a folk museum of counterculture and Pilsen culture, walls and ceiling blanketed with thousands of photographs, fliers, paintings, and posters of musicians, artists, local characters, and beautiful women.

A skilled and prolific photographer and an astute observer of people and politics, Pete never presented himself as anything other than a regular guy who wanted to have a drink and shoot the breeze, equally at ease with homeless drunks and famous musicians or writers who came through town. He made a living at carpentry, painting, and other odd jobs. When he got a little extra money in his pocket, he took off for New Orleans or wherever else the Greyhound would carry him.

Whiling away the hours on the sidewalk or in the bars, he'd spin tales of his travels for anyone who would listen. The food, the music, the women. The drunks in El Trebol might never see New Orleans, New Mexico, or New York, but Pete's stories brought them there.

RAMON

In 1967 Ramon Verdin was living happily in Redding, California: "picking fruit, pruning, every kind of farm work" in the Central Valley which bloomed at the hands of many thousands of Mexican migrant workers.

But Ramon's uncle in Chicago was not doing well. He had run El Trebol since 1960, having taken over from the original owner. The uncle was Ramon's father's brother; they were both from the small town of Encarnación de Díaz in Jalisco state on Mexico's Pacific coast. There were only a few bars in the whole town of Encarnación, no women allowed.

Ramon's uncle was a serious drinker. He couldn't keep Trebol going, and he pleaded with Ramon for help. So Ramon headed to Chicago, intending a temporary stay to salvage the bar while his uncle got back on his feet. "I didn't want to go, but I had compassion," remembers Ramon, with the shrug and enigmatic smile that accompany most of his statements about the past.

Forty-five years later, pushing eighty, Ramon is still behind the bar at El Trebol. The business was struggling when he arrived in Chicago, and he decided to turn things around.

After three or four years, he actually began to like the place. In 1974 his uncle died of a heart attack. Marcos Raya was in the bar when he keeled over right next to him. Marcos liked the man, who often gave him free drinks to help him nurse a hangover.

Ramon realized he was there for good. "Everybody was working" back in those days, he remembers. A sprawling machine shop called Tool & Engineering was just down Eighteenth Street, and the union steelworkers would come in every night, joining clusters of men from other workplaces.

El Trebol today looks very much like it has for ages. The battered, grey, metal cylindrical cooler is filled with Mexican beers, Bud Light, and Heineken. There's a grungy sticker of an American flag, and a bumper sticker that says "I (heart) Nopales." Dusty gold Christmas-tree garlands adorn the faux wooden awning. "It's always Christmas in Mexican bars," notes Franky Piña, a writer and editor from Mexico City who became a regular at Pilsen bars after moving here in the 1980s.

LUIS

Like many Trebol customers, Luis Sanchez has been coming here for decades, from the time he was a kid. His father Refugio was once a regular—a stern steelworker from Mexico near the border of Jalisco and Guanajuato. So too his uncle, a rubber worker. Back then, Pilsen was "real nice, peaceful. There were a lot of Polish people. Then the Mexicans came, and we took over."

Luis dropped out of Benito Juárez, the nearby high school which was built after protests by neighborhood activists. "I was getting into bats and chains," Luis remembers. Gangs filled the neighborhood, and he was an active member.

Gang fights would often break out in El Trebol, which was near the dividing line between the Latin Counts and the Ambrose. In those days someone might rip a gold necklace right off your neck, or forcibly take your cash right inside the bar, Luis remembers. But he wasn't afraid, he was stubborn and tough. Ramon's brother-in-law Sammy had the morning shift; he would often kick Luis out. One time Luis was told not to come back, and he stayed away several months. But he begged forgiveness, and Ramon let him return.

Luis eventually got married and moved to the southwest suburb of Cicero. Then he got divorced and moved back to Pilsen. He left Pilsen again with his current fiancée; she had had enough of Pilsen. But Luis's parents still live across the street from El Trebol, so he still comes to Pilsen — and the bar — almost every day. His mother Epifania taught him how to make homemade hot sauce and other dishes; now he cooks, cleans, and irons for her. "I'll always be a Mama's boy."

Luis never did get his high school degree, but he learned how to hustle. He worked at a gas station and as a tow truck driver. Then in the 1980s he "hooked up with politics" and became a guard at the Cook County jail, the sprawling institution which houses more than 9,000 people a few miles southwest of Pilsen. Luis loved it. Guys from his gang days would call out to him, but he'd ignore them. After eighteen years at the jail, an early retirement with a nice pension was just around the corner. But it all "went down the drain" one day as Luis was drinking at the 1040 Club. A friend kept buying him drinks, then said, "let's go for a ride."

It turned out the friend had a trunk full of marijuana, Luis says. The officer who discovered this was not impressed when Luis tried to show off his county sheriff's badge. Luis was locked up himself in Cook County jail. He remembers waking up in a "puddle of blood," after a beating from inmates who recognized him as a guard. Luis spent a lot of money on a lawyer and almost a year in jail. He lost his job and his pension.

It was a painful slide. But Luis turned to God, to the faith instilled in him as a boy going to mass at St. Procopius across the street from El Trebol. He pulled his life back together and got a Teamsters union job driving a forklift, making more money than he had at the jail.

The 1040 Club is now closed, and the only Pilsen bar Luis frequents is El Trebol.

"Don Ramon treats me like a son. He remembers when I was bad, and he sees how I've changed."

Today, at age fifty, Luis is a calming force in the bar. He'll see people from his old gang days, and sometimes they try to start something, but he never takes the bait. He often intervenes to avert fights. Luis's fiancée sometimes gets jealous about him spending time in Pilsen; he could run into women from his past. But she doesn't mind El Trebol, since she knows there are no women there.

"I appreciate life now," Luis says. "Seeing my son grow up, my five lovely granddaughters. As an ex-gangbanger, I thought I would never see that."

CHANGING GUARD

Into the 1990s and early 2000s, many bars like El Trebol still existed in Pilsen. Even as hipsters, students, and white artists moved into the neighborhood in droves, these cantinas hung on, a symbol of the two parallel worlds that exist in a gentrifying neighborhood. Some newcomers ventured into the bars, intrigued by the atmosphere, like they had crossed the border by crossing the street. But mostly the bars remained the domain of Mexican men, even as the steel mills, stockyards, and factories closed up and they were more likely to work in a restaurant or warehouse, if at all.

By 2014, most of the old cantinas are gone. Some of the signs still remain, twisted neon tubes, faded plastic, and peeling paint. But the storefronts are boarded and locked up tight. They've lost their liquor licenses. Been busted for drugs. Lost their leases as property values rose. Seen their clientele fade away, their owners pass away or go back to Mexico to live out their golden years.

Today there is no shortage of places to get a drink in Pilsen. Lots of new bars have opened up.

But the atmosphere in these joints could hardly be more different. The new bars offer elaborate cocktails and a wide selection of imported beers, along with goodies like bacon-wrapped dates and quinoa.

On a summer night in 2014, there's no one in Tres Diaz. A bartender languidly watches TV, below the portrait of proprietor Maximiliano in his younger days, a majestic pompadour rising above his chiseled face. Maximiliano's throne is empty — the plastic chair on a raised platform on the wall across from the bar, cordoned off with a plastic chain and a "Reserved" sign.

While Tres Diaz is silent except for the television, across the street, Dusek's is hopping. That's the new bar and restaurant opened in Thalia Hall, the ornate Prague Opera House replica which had stood vacant and deteriorating for years, pigeons and homeless people moving in. Now it serves gourmet food and elaborate cocktails with ingredients like lager-tea syrup and Letherbee Malort.

A few of the old-time bars have changed with the times, becoming hot destinations for a multicultural crowd of beautiful youngsters, including twenty-something children of immigrants who came to Pilsen to create a better life for their kids, and succeeded.

Harbees and Caminos de Michoacan, for example, were once rough, gritty Mexican cantinas. They had makeovers, the dusty piles of knick-knacks replaced with sleek modern lights.

"Before those were places for all working people," notes Franky Piña. "It was their life, their church — especially if they didn't believe in God. They'd talk about the factory, their problems, football. Now it's something cool, something cute, a playground for intellectuals."

MOVING ON

El Trebol has helped Ramon and his wife take numerous vacations to the Caribbean, Hawaii, and South America. They sent their kids on to college and white collar jobs — one is a doctor. Other than the vacations, Ramon has spent virtually every day at El Trebol, 5:00 p.m. to 1:00 a.m., between the dim back room bar and the slightly brighter liquor store in front.

Does he ever plan to retire?

"I have to stay busy doing something. If I stay at home I don't feel too good. To come here, to me it's not a job."

Will El Trebol go the way of Tito's Hacienda, the 1040 Club, El Jardin, and the countless other bars that are now just a fading memory? Ramon doesn't seem too concerned. He's noticed all the white people in the neighborhood and the new bars selling fancier drinks. But inside El Trebol with its musty decorations and wood-paneled walls, time stands still.

On many nights it still fills up, especially on Fridays — pay day. Men crowd around the jukebox.

Someone will invariably plant his hands stolidly on it, lift his face to the ceiling, and offer up a grito — the loud passionate whoop that embodies all the pain and glory of being Mexican.

"This is the Last of the Mohicans!" Pete Rodriguez announces as he drinks a $3.50 Squirt and tequila. His hands and trousers are encrusted with paint from a mural he's helping paint outside an Eighteenth Street café.

Marcos Raya lives across the street from El Trebol with a woman he calls his nurse. But he doesn't hang out at the bar much anymore — just now and then if he wants a beer before bed. Trebol depresses him, giving him flashbacks of the old days. He thinks Ramon should fix the place up. "Some people think things should never change. I don't agree."

On a sunny, crisp morning, Marcos parks his convertible, red BMW with comfortably battered brown leather seats on Eighteenth Street. His clothes match the car: a red silky shirt with a jaunty hat and brown leather bag, artsy glasses with striped round rims. He looks healthy. He's been in London twice, Spain and Germany recently for shows.

"All those old buildings in Europe — when I was younger I would have thought they were romantic. Today I just think they're boring. I'm thinking ahead. Forget the past. I'm looking to the future."

Chicago Notebook

RYAN SCHNURR

After Joan Didion

A sharp wind is blowing in Chicago this afternoon, sweeping in off the lake and wrapping itself roughly around buildings and cars and pedestrians, turning up collars and beating flags against themselves, disrupting any semblance of order or stillness. Chicago's wind is a defining feature of the city, like the lake, or the Great Fire, or nineteenth-century steel mills. Living here, feeling this wind, I have become intensely aware of my proximity to the most powerful elements of the natural world. Air; water; fire; earth — this is a city shaped by forces that cannot be described or explained so much as they must be experienced. The wind blowing recklessly in off the lake is a reminder that Chicago itself is profoundly elemental. It, too, is transformative. It, too, can only be felt.

o o o

My wife, Anna, and I moved to the city from Indiana, like so many of our generation, in order to learn what life was like beyond the scope of our hometowns, and so that I could attend graduate school. Two years and a master's degree later, the main thing I've learned is how little I actually understand.

o o o

"Chicago is an October sort of city even in spring," Nelson Algren wrote, and after a few years here I am beginning to appreciate what he was trying to say. Chicago is a city in constant transition. Interstates 90 and 290 — which I learned early on to refer to not by their numbers but by their namesakes, the Dan Ryan and the Eisenhower, respectively — have been under construction since the day I moved here, and new buildings seem to all but jump out of the earth. Chicago is also among the largest transportation hubs in the country — rail lines begin and end here, and you can catch a flight to places all over the world. Perhaps as a result, there is a great unsettledness to the whole city. To live in Chicago is to accept, consciously or not, the law of perpetual movement.

o o o

A friend of mine told me about a spot downtown, out near the lakefront, where, if you stand right, you can look across the river and see an arresting juxtaposition. Above ground, there are high-rise condos with expensive balconies on the lake. And underneath these, below surface-level, you can see into the side of an underground road where tents and shopping carts mark the presence of another group of citizens, whose homes are less glamorous and less permanent. Isn't that how it goes? Divisions are built into our infrastructure. Here are people living mutually invisible lives, right alongside one another, separated arbitrarily and unevenly — and both of them with the same view.

o o o

I am slow to do most things. So my glacial movement when adapting to Chicago was not unexpected. I have, in the years since, come to be grateful for this city, to believe myself a part of it. But I have not yet become comfortable. My time here has shaken me deeply, and continues to do so — though with what result it's difficult to say.

o o o

This past winter, we took the L to meet some friends for drinks. The temperature had dropped twenty-three degrees below freezing, and the wind whipped between ice-covered buildings. People huddled together in warm, brightly-lit apartments and under weak heat lamps on elevated platforms. On the train, a guitar player with heavy eyeliner and battered jeans who called herself Kez Ban took requests from passengers. She claimed to have spent some time on *American Idol*, and that Nicki Minaj had once called her a "crazy psycho." Somebody asked if she knew "Where is My Mind" by the Pixies, and she said yes and began to play. I tried to count the lighted apartment windows that passed by outside, but lost track fairly quickly. Kez Ban sang the line "where is my mind" over and over, and I realized how warm it was in the train car. As if winter hadn't come. As if, for a moment, the wind had sat down to rest.

o o o

Two men on the train talk about overdosing on amphetamines. One man says, "I've almost died a bunch of times, but I always come back from the dead."

o o o

The construction signs read: "Building a New Chicago." But I wonder, where did the old one go?

o o o

We have decided to move away from Chicago, back to our home state of Indiana. I have found it difficult to write about this city during my time here, in the same way that it is difficult to make sense of any experience from the middle. Everything is blurry when held so close to your face.

I'd like to write about Chicago sometime. Maybe I'll be able to after we move. I don't know how long you have to wait before you can understand how a given experience has affected you — five years? Ten? Maybe you can never fully know. Or maybe it never stops.

o o o

Recently, Anna and I took the Blue Line from its western end around and up to the North Side of the city, to Myopic Books, a used bookstore on Milwaukee Avenue. Three years ago, we were engaged in front of the big bay window on the second floor while a late afternoon sun poured through, filling the room as if it was lit from within. But this time the whole place seemed more ordinary than I remembered. The room was slightly longer; the windows, older. The sky was overcast.

Anna browsed through the volumes on French cooking as I talked with a tall man about, I think, landscape photography. I looked around at the other people in the room, thinking about how none of them knew what had happened there, right by that table, near where a few of them were standing. I wanted to explain how important this place was — about the ring and the sunlight and the three years since. But I could not have done so even if they had asked. So I took a long last look at the shelf in front of me and gathered my things to go.

"Leaving?" the tall man asked as we headed for the door.

Leaving, I thought — what an impossible word.

The City Hasn't Killed Everything

SHARON DORNBERG-LEE

At Devon and Western Avenues,
above the signs for halal meat, Islamic books,

    a flock of pigeons
    unravaged by winter
    swoops and glides, to and fro,
    what we would call dancing.
    Shards of morning light catch
    the white undersides of wings.

Four blocks west in the Jewish section,
the old fishmonger, hand shaking, unlocks his door.

CHIASMUS:
A NARRATIVE OF ASCENT

RAYSHAUNA GRAY

It's 1986 and I'm born on the South Side of Chicago. My mother Sharon's a Chicagoan too — born in 1964...six years into her parents' northern life. My grandma Pearlie Mae is born in 1942 in a Mississippi Delta town founded by formerly enslaved people. My great-grandmother Wyona's the first of us to be born in the twentieth century and would be eleven when white women got the vote, forty-five when segregation fell on paper, and fifty-nine when Dr. King was shot. Her mother Trudy was born in 1887 just up the road in the town where W.C. Handy first heard the Blues. Her mother Lucinda was born in 1862, one year into a war that'd color the conscience and collective memory of a nation. Her mother Martha was born in 1820, part of the generation begging for that slouch toward justice, and would be forty-one years old when it began.

It's been said that Black Americans are wedded to narratives of ascent — "up from slavery," "up from the American South in the Great Migration," up from, up from, up from...

...but sitting with history forces me to dig in deep — deep into language too constrained to hold our humanity, deep into philosophies and theologies that sanction terror written into law...and deep into the stories of how that became our cultural inheritance.

Well, it's 2016 and I live in Cambridge now, with a great chunk of country between where I am and where I'm from. I'm in a part of the country where (let them tell the story) History was invented, where the lore of revolutionaries looms large, and the hooves of Paul Revere's horse are louder in national memory than Crispus Attucks's death rattle. What's Black memory in comparison? What's there to say about the tin-like ping of Blues theology in the ear of a heaven that gave the pen to the other side? Who am I, more than some modern person, more than just a descendant, than some grandchild of a Great Migration with Chicago in my step and Mississippi pooled in the corners of my mouth like warm milk?

(Sometimes, I feel so ungrateful.)

Sometimes I think that my ancestors were tricked, that weighing time had come and though they'd picked and ached, were found wanting. Sometimes, I think that they were insufficient in their push, lackluster in their grasp at some kind of justice, that they were naive to assert to an unjust nation that justice wasn't only its moral mandate but our human birthright.

...and I feel ashamed...of myself.

I run my hands along brick buildings and peer down at folks walking on the street from coffeeshops on Brattle Street. I pull back walls in historic buildings on Tory Row and see symbols from the Stamp Act era. I occupy space in what's known as the cradle of American history now and I'm reeling.

"Whose story is this? Whose books are these? Are these mine? Can't be — I'm one of forty-two million. I'm from that nation within a nation. A people isn't borders, it's shared circumstance."

Every day, I'm surrounded by the specter of New England's primacy reminding (always reminding) that they were first. I hear 1630 all the time in Harvard Square and I wonder where my people were, how we lived, how we felt. I wonder about the first of us here in the States — about what they desperately needed to hear and would pass away before knowing. I think about my dad's mother, the one like Lena Horne, and think about the men from other countries — the ones with eyes from France and last names from England. I think about overseers and their families in Ireland and their descendants navigating the same Boston streets. And I think to myself:

"How did I ever think I could inherit the gift of (historical) grace without the terrible burden of context?" || "How'd I ever think I could document our family history without being undone by it or highly sensitive to it?" || "How'd I ever think I could have unbridled language for Black humanity in a world so dedicated to binding us up?"

So, I remind myself of the little things...like being able to walk on the sidewalk. I silence the part in me who forgot she can drink out of any water fountain she chooses, the one that forgot she chose the high school she went to. You know, the one who forgot that people just like her fled the South — first in a trickle and then in droves, six million over sixty years, spurred by world wars and a yearning for the warmth of another sun. I think about my relatives and the ones who came before — the ones desperate for that space from Mister Charlie only to have them be met with race riots and immigrants finding their own America in Detroit and Chicago. I think about people that crammed their culture into hatboxes, ones who fingered the frayed edges of the promise of a kinder mistress as they traveled north (with Jazz, Blues, and Gospel in tow). I think about that six million, the six they left behind, and the grandchildren of both waves of that Great Migration wherever we all may be.

...and I think about living in a place that's chock full of History and devoid of memory. I think about how it's impossible for a nation to have a conscience if it doesn't have a memory.

As family historian, I go to my elders to collect their stories now and I ask 'em, I say:

"What made you leave Mississippi? Did you find what you were looking for? Are you disappointed in us? Does it matter that the Chicago you stepped into is the one eatin' us alive? Are you proud of us for fighting?"

And then I think: "What if what got us here was never meant to keep us?" I wonder if all that Southern sorrow and woe followed us up here. I wonder if we'll never be rid of it. If we'll be canaries in coal mines forever.

But the story can't end with despair, so I try to go with what I know and that's language. I plant my feet and I dig in deep and I say out loud, I say:

"The lie of our inhumane treatment is old, but the truth of our humanity and right to walk the earth and flourish is much older." // I say to my elders: "It was hard, forging a grave freedom in a nation that suckled at your breast and grew strong on sociop- athy — but you were right" // I say to us: "Thank you for holding a vicious nation to a standard of virtue inconceivable to anyone but us" // "Thank you for creating and passing down language for our humanity so we could stand living in a country whose tongue is decidedly stuck in a vise grip of hateful words."

I'll honor it because when the nation needs a reminder (and of course, it always will), we'll need people with cultural memory to tell the stories.

One of the most heinous lies Black America was ever told was that we were a people without history, that we don't come from anything, that coming to the States was our saving grace (how sweet but discordant that transatlantic sound). That's the lie people use to claim our cultural memory is the stuff of madmen's imaginations. But Black suffering is matched and surpassed by Black joy and the sight-beyond-sight that makes us relentless in our reach for something better...and our ability to render it into dance, reverie, and language. The spark that gets us from glory to glory is what got us from the hollows of ships to where we are today...and it hasn't dimmed because we're on the other side of the Migration.

We still have some ascending to do.

PREVIOUSLY PUBLISHED BY *THE IDEOLOGUE* AND SHARED BY *SOUTH SIDE WEEKLY.*

WHEREVER

NAOMI HUFFMAN

When I was young, my father said he was going to tell me how to get anywhere I wanted and never get lost. He opened his atlas of Indiana on the kitchen table, the site of prayer and ritual and nourishment for my family, and now, the site of finding yourself.

The world on the map did not look familiar: the land was orange, and threaded with white rivers and blue roads. I was only beginning to understand the implication of things. When my father pointed to our road and said, "This is where we live," his index finger covered up our whole county.

He explained that each road was numbered; we lived on County Road 500 West, which was five miles west of the center of the county. He pointed out the counties that surrounded ours, all more or less rectangular, unmarked, and therefore indistinguishable. The roads inside each county were plotted on the same grid. The secret to never getting lost, then, was in placing myself within these lines and boxes. I noticed, too, that there were four sides to everywhere. It seemed there was no way out. But there was; I found it, anyway.

It would take growing up and leaving home to know what my father was actually showing me on that map: that his entire life was contained within those lines, and he didn't expect me to go very far. (And why would he? My father had lived his entire life in the same place; I think he was simply unable to see any further.)

When I moved to Chicago after high school, I was glad to be navigating within a familiar system — a tessellating grid ruled by the cardinal directions, with street numbers that got larger as you traveled further from the center — especially since most of what I had known to be true actually wasn't. Sometimes the center is elsewhere. Knowing where you are doesn't mean you are not, also, lost.

○ ○ ○

When I came to Chicago, I became a person. By this I mean I began, a bit belatedly, the unremarkable task of asking what it means to be a person in the world — to not just ask what it means to be a woman, daughter, sister, friend. I mean the things you can only know about yourself when you ask them in a hard, certain light: How do I say a prayer to no gods? How do I say 'I love you' to man with a heart like that? How do I get myself out of bed when I can't get myself out of bed? What do I say to a friend who is losing pieces of her body to cancer? How many pillows does it take to turn my couch into a bed? What do I mean when I say "yes"? How do I write a poem? How do I care for my friend, a brand new widow? What do I tell my mother when she asks me if I am OK?

There are new questions every day. I feel lucky to ask them.

o o o

When he was in a good mood and the conditions were so, my father could be playful. He liked to sing silly songs, make up nonsense words. I liked him best this way, of course; he was otherwise given to violent tantrums that sometimes ended in one of my sisters or me getting hit. (My mother watched. I know now it was all she could do, she was afraid, too.)

In one of my father's favorite games, he pretended to be lost while we were in the car, heading home. He would ask my sisters and I, "Which way do we go?" Even though at first I could not read the street signs, I was very good at this game; I often volunteered to sit between my sisters in the backseat so I was afforded the entire view through the windshield.

Turn right on Nebo, after the bend with the red barn.

Pass the house with the barn we could only see I winter, when the trees were bare.

"Now what?" he would ask, our eyes meeting in the rearview.

Left at the highway.

Right at the white house on the corner.

Pass the tower and its red eyeball, pass the white church, its small park with the tall slide.

Then, two oak trees in the crabgrass: one small, one tall, like siblings. The swing hanging still on the slat porch. The blue '78 Impala, the color of a clear sky but parked for all of time at the end of the gravel drive. The house, low-slung, unembellished, shutterless windows staring like the flat eyes of a housewife. My father laid the bricks himself.

o o o

I'm not sure how to go home anymore, so I don't. It's been a couple years now.

I spent Christmas alone last year. I had high hopes for the day, but it didn't turn out to be all that great. I placed a large order at a nearby Chinese restaurant and when it was delivered, the food was cold; the vegetable egg foo young was clotted in its white carton like it was already leftovers. I ate a few bites, scraped at the other boxes and containers — all of it wormy, gluey goop. I threw it all away.

I thought a lot about my ex-boyfriend, whose absence made my collarbone ache, still, months after our break up.

I tried to write but it was all *nevermind* and *this is shit*.

I sent text messages to my friends to let them know I was enjoying the solitude.

I had agreed to feed a friend's cats while she was visiting her family. I'd planned to walk to her apartment building in Logan Square earlier in the day. From my apartment in Humboldt Park, the walk is about fifty minutes — about twenty-eight blocks, twelve west, sixteen north, but I walk fast. It's a walk I enjoy; there are shortcuts to be taken through both Humboldt Park proper and Palmer Square Park. Anyway, I'd put it off, and suddenly it was five o'clock. I headed out in the early winter dark thinking about the extent of friendship and favors and how long her cats could survive without food; they had always seemed skinny to me.

About ten minutes into my walk, as I entered the southwestern edge of Humboldt Park, it began to drizzle. I thought, *Right, this.* Fortunately, I had thought to grab my umbrella, of the spindly drugstore sort, but refused to lift it until I couldn't ignore that the drizzle had turned into a blowy and needly rain. In the center of the park, I stood beneath an oak or elm or maple, whatever, something big and generously branched, to shake out my umbrella and check my progress on the maps app on my iPhone. My teeth were chattering. I wasn't even halfway.

When I got back to my apartment ninety minutes later, everything I was wearing was wet, my stomach hurt, and I was crying. I was frustrated because I knew why I was crying but didn't want to acknowledge it, and I couldn't stop. There are miles between loneliness and solitude.

I turned out all the lights in my apartment. I yanked off my soggy boots and got in bed with my damp clothes on. I just wanted to sleep, I just wanted the day to be over.

Still, I wasn't lost. I'd taken myself somewhere and back, and I was glad to be home. Show me a map, I'll tell you where I am.

Reasons Why I Do Not Wish to Leave Chicago: An Incomplete, Random List

ALEKSANDAR HEMON

1. Driving west at sunset in the summer: blinded by the sun, you cannot see the cars ahead; the ugly warehouses and body shops are blazing orange. When the sun sets, everything becomes deeper: the brick facades acquire a bluish hue; there are charcoal smudges of darkness on the horizon; the sky and the city look endless.

2. The way people in the winter huddle together under the warming lights on El stops, much like young chickens under a light bulb. Human solidarity enforced by the cruelty of nature — the story of Chicago and of civilization.

3. The American vastness of the Wilson Street beach, gulls and kites coasting above it, dogs sprinting along the jagged waves, barking into the void, blind to the distant ships on their mysterious ways from Liverpool to Gary.

4. Early September anywhere in the city, when the sunlight angle has changed and everything and everyone appears kinder, all the edges softened; the torments of the hot summer are over, the cold torments of the winter have not begun, and people bask in the perishable possibility of a gentle city.

5. The basketball court at Foster Street beach, where I once watched an impressively sculpted guy play a whole game — dribbling, shooting, arguing, dunking — with a toothpick in his mouth: the hero of the Chicago cool.

6. The tall ice ranges along the shore when the winter is exceptionally cold and the lake frozen for a while, so ice pushes ice against the land. The process exactly replicates the way some mountain ranges were formed hundreds of millions years ago, tectonic plates pushing against each other. The primeval shapes are visible to every cranky driver plowing through the Lake Shore Drive mess, but most of them look ahead.

7. Looking directly west at night from any Edgewater or Rogers Park high-rise: like stunned fireflies, airplanes hover and glimmer above O'Hare.

8. The blessed scarcity of celebrities in Chicago (Oprah, one of the Friends, and a

couple of other people whose names I cannot recall). We like to ship them off to New York or Hollywood, where they can falsely claim their humble Chicago roots, while we can be proud of them without actually being responsible for the vacuity of their famous lives.

9. The Hyde Park parakeets, miraculously surviving brutal winters, a colorful example of life that adamantly refuses to perish, of the kind of instinct that has made Chicago harsh and great.

10. The downtown skyline at night as seen from the Adler Planetarium: lit windows within the dark building frames against the darker sky. It seems that stars have been squared and pasted on the thick wall of a Chicago night; the cold, inhuman beauty containing the enormity of life — each window a possible story.

11. The green-grey color of the barely foaming lake when the winds are northwesterly and the sky is chilly.

12. Humid summer days, when the streets seem waxed with sweat; the air is as thick and warm as honey-sweetened tea; the beaches are full of families: fathers barbecuing, mothers sunbathing, children approaching hypothermia in the lake's shallows. Then a wave of frigid air sweeps the parks, and a deluvial shower soaks every living creature. (Never trust a summer day in Chicago.)

13. Suburbanites in Hard Rock Café shirts patroling Michigan Avenue, oblivious to the city beyond the shopping and entertaining areas; the tourists on an architectural speedboat tour looking up at the steep buldings; the bridges' halves symmetrically erected; the street performer in front of the Wrigley building performing "Killing Me Softly" on the tuba.

14. The fact that every year in March, the Cubs fans start saying: "This year might be it" — the delusional hope usually betrayed by the time fall arrives. It is one of the early harbingers of the spring, bespeaking a beautifully naive belief that the world might right its wrongs simply because the trees are coming into leaf.

15. A warm day one February, when everyone present at Bornhofen's, my butcher shop, remembered the great snowstorm of 1967: cars abandoned and buried in snow on the Lake Shore Drive; people trudging home from work through the snow like refugees; the snow on your street up to the milk truck's mirrors. There are a lot of disasters in the city's memory, which results in a strange nostalgia somehow akin to Chicagoan's respect for and pride in "those four-mansion crooks who risk their lives in crimes of high visibility" (Bellow).

16. Pakistani and Indian families strolling solemnly up and down Devon on summer evenings; Russian-Jewish senior citizens clustering on Uptown benches, warbling gossip in soft consonants; Mexican families in Pilsen crowding Nuevo Leon for Sunday breakfast; African-American families gloriously dressed for church waiting for a table in the Hyde Park Dixie Kitchen; the enormous amount of lives in this city worthy of a story.

17. A river of red and a river of white flowing in opposite directions on Lake Shore Drive, as seen from Montrose Harbor at night.

18. The wind: the sailboats in the Grant Park Harbor bobbing on the water, the mast wires clucking; the Buckingham Fountain's upward stream turned into a water plume; the windows of downtown buildings shaking and thumping; people walking down Michigan Avenue with their heads retracted between their shoulders; my street completely deserted except for a bundled up mailman and a plastic bag fluttering like a torn flag in the barren tree-crown.

19. The stately Beverly mansions; the bleak Pullman row houses; the frigid buildings of the La Salle Street canyon; the garish beauty of old downtown hotels; the stern arrogance of the Sears Tower and the Hancock buildings; the quaint Edgewater houses; the sadness of the Cabrini Green high-rises; the decrepit grandeur of the Uptown theaters and hotels; the Northwest side warehouses and body shops; thousands of empty lots and vanished buildings that no one will ever remember — every building tells part of the story of the city. Only the city knows the whole story.

20. If Chicago has been good enough for Studs Terkel to spend a lifetime in it, it is good enough for me.

FIRST PUBLISHED BY 3 BOOK PUBLISHING © ALEKSANDAR HEMON, 2006; AND SUBSEQUENTLY IN *THE BOOK OF MY LIVES*, PUBLISHED BY FARRAR STRAUS AND GIROUX, ©2013 BY ALEKSANDAR HEMON.

RACHEL Z. ARNDT has written for *Popular Mechanics*, *Quartz*, the *Iowa Review*, and elsewhere. She received MFAs in nonfiction and poetry from the University of Iowa, where she was an Iowa Arts Fellow. She lives in Chicago.

JAKE AUSTEN is editor of *Roctober* magazine, author of several books, and has freelanced for publications including *Harper's*, *Vice*, the *Chicago Tribune*, and the *Chicago Reader*. *Playground* (Glitterati Incorporated, 3/14), his forthcoming collaboration with Paul Zone, is a coffeetable book of photographs and stories from New York's early seventies pre-punk scene.

MARTHA BAYNE (editor) is a freelance writer and editor, and a senior editor with Belt Publishing, producing independent books and journalism for the Rust Belt. Her features and essays have appeared in *Belt Magazine*, *Buzzfeed*, *Crain's Chicago Business*, the *Chicago Tribune*, the *Rumpus*, the *Baffler*, and *Latterly*, among other national and regional outlets. A member of the Theater Oobleck artistic ensemble, she is also founder of Chicago's long-running Soup & Bread community meal project and author of *Soup & Bread Cookbook: Building Community One Pot at a Time* (Agate, 2011). See marthabayne.com for more.

RAYMOND BERRY is the author of the poetry collection *Diagnosis*. He is published in the journals *Assaracus*, *Reverie*, and *Cactus Heart*, the anthologies *To Be Left With the Body*, *Spaces Between Us: Poetry, Prose and Art on HIV/AIDS*, and elsewhere. He is an English professor at the City Colleges of Chicago.

SHARON BLOYD-PESHKIN is an associate professor of journalism at Columbia College Chicago. The former editor of *Chicago Parent* magazine and senior editor of *Vegetarian Times* magazine, she is now a teacher, a freelance writer and editor, and the advisor to the award-winning student magazine, *Echo*.

ELAINE HEGWOOD BOWEN earned undergraduate and graduate journalism degrees from Roosevelt University and has been writing for the *Chicago Crusader* newspaper since 1994. She is a native southsider, and *Old School Adventures from Englewood — South Side of Chicago* is her first book. @englewoodelaine.

LOGAN BREITBART is a Chicago-based writer and theater artist. He's a member of the Runaways Theater Lab and a full-time GED instructor in Cook County Jail.

ANDREW CANTRELL is the author of *Stratigraphy* (2015). A Pushcart Prize nominee, his poems and performance texts have been published widely in journals and anthologies. He has taught literature and writing at the University of Illinois, and facilitated classes and workshops for union members across the Midwest. Originally from Atlanta, Georgia, he lives in Chicago where he organizes educational workers and serves as Secretary of the Chicago News Guild.

KEVIN COVAL is the author of *Schtick*, *L-vis Lives!: Racemusic Poems*, *Everyday People*, *Slingshots: A Hip-Hop Poetica*, the editor of *The BreakBeat Poets: New American Poetry in the Age of Hip-Hop*, and co-author of the play *This is Modern Art* with Idris Goodwin. Founder of Louder Than A Bomb: The Chicago Youth Poetry Festival and Artistic Director of Young Chicago Authors, Coval is a four-time HBO Def Poet. He teaches hip-hop aesthetics at The University of Illinois-Chicago. His *A People's History of Chicago* was published in the Spring of 2017 by Haymarket Books. Coval documents graffiti around the planet and in Chicago, and can be found on the gram @kevincoval #chgotsyle.

GARIN CYCHOLL's recent work includes *Country Musics 20/20* (Locofo Chaps, 2017) and *Circuito Interior*, a translation of poems by the late Efrain Huerta. His essay, "A Contract with Distance," on Sterling Plumpp and the Black Arts Movement in Chicago, will appear in the upcoming *Chicago Review*. He lives in Homewood, Illinois.

PAUL DAILING is a Chicago-based writer, magazine editor, and tour guide. He is the creator of *1,001 Chicago Afternoons*, a twenty-first-century version of Ben Hecht's famed 1920s *Chicago Daily News* column. The project won a Peter Lisagor Award for Exemplary Journalism in 2013 and is currently featured as part of the Chicago History Museum's "Chicago Authored" exhibit. He is also the creator of the Chicago Corruption Walking Tour, has lectured on election fraud for *Atlas Obscura*, once found a triceratops femur, and co-organizes the Welcome to the Neighborhood illustrated reading series. Originally from Rockford, Illinois, he's constantly astounded by the number of Chicagoans who have opinions about whether you can put ketchup on a hot dog. It's not only just a hot dog, it's my hot dog. You don't get a vote here.

ROBERT DEAN is a writer, journalist, and cynic. His most recent novel, *The Red Seven*, is in stores. He is from the South Side of Chicago. Currently, he's working on his newest novel, *Tragedy Wish Me Luck*. He also likes ice cream and koalas. He currently lives in Austin.

SHARON DORNBERG-LEE's poetry has appeared in *Sow's Ear Poetry Review*, the anthology *Mamas and Papas, Literary Momma*, and *Earth's Daughters*. Her essay "Cold Turkey on Big Bird" was featured on the Chicago Public Radio program *848*. Recently, she was featured on WBEZ's *Dynamic Range* ("Sharon Dornberg-Lee: A poet who bears witness"), which "showcases hidden gems unearthed from Chicago Amplified's vast archive of public events." A geriatric social worker, Sharon is a clinical supervisor at CJE SeniorLife and has been an adjunct instructor at the University of Chicago School of Social Service Administration (SSA). She currently teaches in SSA's Professional Development Program. She lives in Chicago with her husband and seventeen-year-old daughter, Sophie.

PAUL DURICA is a teacher, writer, and public historian. From 2008-2015 he produced a series of free and interactive public history programs under the name "Pocket Guide to Hell." These talks, walks, and reenactments used costumes, props, music, and audience participation to make the past feel present. Paul's writing on Chicago history and culture has appeared in *Poetry*, the *Chicagoan, Mash Tun, Lumpen*, and elsewhere, and, with Bill Savage, he is the editor of *Chicago By Day and Night: The Pleasure Seeker's Guide to the Paris of America* (Northwestern University Press, 2013). He is currently the Director of Programs for Illinois Humanities.

DINA ELENBOGEN, a widely published and award-winning poet and prose writer, is author of the memoir *Drawn from Water* (BkMk Press, University of Missouri) and the poetry collection *Apples of the Earth* (Spuyten Duyvil, New York). Her work has appeared in anthologies including *City of the Big Shoulders* (University of Iowa Press), *Beyond Lament* (Northwestern University Press), *Where We Find Ourselves* (SUNY Press) and magazines and journals including *Lit Hub, december magazine, Prairie Schooner, Poet Lore, Bellevue Literary Review, Tikkun, Paterson Literary Review, New City Chicago*, and the *Chicago Reader*. She has received fellowships in poetry and prose from the Illinois Arts Council and the Ragdale Foundation. She has a poetry MFA from the Iowa Writer's Workshop and teaches creative writing at the University of Chicago Graham School. She has just completed a second poetry manuscript entitled *Most of What is Beautiful* and is working on an essay collection called *Losing Our Sages*. You can visit her at www.dinaelenbogen.com.

OLA FALETI is a native northsider with a penchant for all things sweet. Her writing has appeared in *Moonsick Magazine* and the *James Franco Review*, among other places.

EILEEN FAVORITE's novel, *The Heroines* (Scribner, 2008), has been translated into seven languages. Her essays, poems, and stories have appeared in many publications, including, *Triquarterly*, the *Rumpus*, the *Toast, Chicago Reader, Diagram*, and others. She's received fellowships from the Illinois Arts Council for poetry and for prose. She teaches at the School of the Art Institute of Chicago and The Graham School of Continuing Liberal Studies at the University of Chicago. She's a founder of the Chicago women writers' business group Her Chapter.

TONY FITZPATRICK (cover artist) was born in Chicago in 1958. He is still there.

CAROL GLOOR has been writing for many years, mostly poetry. Her work has been published in many print and online journals, most recently in *Picaroon Poetry, Electric Wire Pen*, and *Helen Presents*. She has upcoming work in the journal *DuPage Valley Review*. Her poetry chapbook, *Assisted Living*, was published in 2013 by Finishing Line Press.

RAYSHAUNA GRAY is a storyteller, coordinator with Harvard Business School's gender initiative, and historical researcher at Tufts University's Center for the Study of Race and Democracy. After years of serving as her family's genealogist, she began drawing on cultural memory to inform her writing. "Chiasmus" is the result of woe, Malbec, and a very welcoming writer's workshop at Yale. She currently lives in Cambridge, Massachusetts but her heart is always back at home in Chicago. She's a Roseland girl.

MARK GUARINO writes for the *Washington Post*, the *Guardian, Crain's*, and *Politico*, among many other outlets. For six years he was the Midwest bureau chief for the *Christian Science Monitor*. His book, a history of country and folk music in Chicago, is forthcoming from the University of Chicago Press. Visit mark-guarino.com.

ALEKSANDAR HEMON is the author of *The Question of Bruno, Nowhere Man, The Lazarus Project*, and his latest short story collection, *Love and Obstacles*, was published in May 2009. His collection of autobiographical essays, *The Book of My Lives*, was published by Farrar, Straus, and Giroux in March 2013. His latest novel, *The Making of Zombie Wars*, was published by Farrar, Straus, and Giroux in 2015 and he is working on his next novel, tentatively titled *The World and All That It Holds*. He was awarded a Guggenheim Fellowship in 2003 and a "genius grant" from the MacArthur Foundation in 2004. From 2010 to 2013 he served as editor of *Best European Fiction* anthologies (Dalkey Archives). He is currently the Distinguished Writer in Residence at Columbia College Chicago. He lives in Chicago with his wife and daughters.

ANDREW HERTZBERG is a writer living in Chicago. His work has most recently appeared in *Cheat River Review, Moonglasses Magazine, Third Coast Review* and other various corners of the Internet. He tweets at @and_hertz.

KELLY HOGAN is a musician — a solo artist, a member of her current band The Flat Five, and an in-demand stage and studio singer for Neko Case, Mavis Staples, The Decemberists, Jakob Dylan, and many other heavy hitters. She loves dogs, thrift stores, dogs, Bill Hicks, dogs, Lynda Barry, dogs, and Chicago — especially the alleys.

SONYA HUBER is the author of three books of creative nonfiction, including the new essay collection on chronic pain, *Pain Woman Takes Your Keys,* as well as *Opa Nobody* and *Cover Me: A Health Insurance Memoir,* and a textbook, the *Backwards Research Guide for Writers.* She teaches at Fairfield University, where she directs the low-residency MFA program. She lives in Connecticut, but her heart is a far eastern island of Chicagoland. More info at www.sonyahuber.com

NAOMI HUFFMAN is a writer and editor. Her work has appeared in the *Chicago Tribune,* the *Rumpus, Newcity, Bookslut,* and elsewhere. She is at work on a book.

DAVID ISAACSON has written about sports for *This American Life* and the *Paper Machete* podcast. He has written about Freud for Chicago's Theater Oobleck. And he wrote about *The Great Gatsby* for Ms. Long, his high school English teacher.

BRITT JULIOUS is a journalist, essayist, and storyteller. Her writing has appeared in *Esquire, ELLE, GQ,* the *Guardian, Rolling Stone, Vice, Pitchfork,* and many other outlets. She's a columnist for the *Chicago Tribune* and a regular contributor for Vice's *THUMP.* She also hosts *The Back Talk,* a podcast featuring original stories from women of color. She is working on a book of essays.

GRETCHEN KALWINSKI's work has appeared in the *Chicago Reader, Stop Smiling, Time Out Chicago, Make Literary Magazine,* and Featherproof Books. She has appeared as a panelist on WGN radio and *Chicago Tonight,* and was awarded a 2009 Ragdale artist residency. She holds an MFA in writing from Northwestern University.

YANA KUNICHOFF is an investigative journalist and producer based in Chicago who currently works with City Bureau and Scrappers Film Group. Her work focuses on policing, immigration, and education, and has appeared in the *Guardian, Al Jazeera America,* and *Pacific Standard,* among others. Yana was awarded a March 2016 Sidney Hillman award for her investigation into how Chicago's police union controls the narrative around police shootings.

QURAYSH ALI LANSANA is the author of eight poetry books, three textbooks, three children's books, editor of eight anthologies, and coauthor of a book of pedagogy. He is a faculty member of the Writing Program of the School of the Art Institute of Chicago and a former faculty member of the Drama Division of The Juilliard School. Lansana served as Director of the Gwendolyn Brooks Center for Black Literature and Creative Writing at Chicago State University from 2002-2011, where he was also Associate Professor of English/Creative Writing until 2014. *Our Difficult Sunlight: A Guide to Poetry, Literacy and Social Justice in Classroom and Community* (with Georgia A. Popoff) was published in March 2011 by Teachers and Writers Collaborative and was a 2012 NAACP Image Award nominee. His most recent books include *Revise the Psalm: Work Celebrating the Writings of Gwendolyn Brooks* with Sandra Jackson-Opoku (Curbside Splendor, 2017); *A Gift from Greensboro* (Penny Candy Books, 2016); *The BreakBeat Poets: New American Poetry in the Age of Hip Hop* with Kevin Coval and Nate Marshall (Haymarket Books, 2015), and *The Walmart Republic* with Christopher Stewart (Mongrel Empire Press, 2014). Forthcoming titles include: *The Whiskey of Our Discontent: Gwendolyn Brooks as Conscience and Change* Agent, with Georgia A. Popoff (Haymarket Books, 2017), and *Clara Luper: The Woman Who Rallied the Children* with Julie Dill (Oklahoma Hall of Fame Press, 2018).

GRETCHEN LIDA is a nonfiction writer, a Colorado native, a Great Lakes transplant, and an equestrian. She focuses on nature writing, and is always interested in the connection between horses, history, and humans. She received her MFA in nonfiction from Columbia College Chicago in 2017. Her work has appeared in *Brevity: A Journal of Concise Literary Nonfiction, New City Lit, The Horse Network* and others.

KARI LYDERSEN is a Chicago reporter, author, and journalism instructor at Northwestern University, where she is fellowship director of the Social Justice News Nexus. She was previously a staff writer for the *Washington Post* out of the Midwest bureau and her work has also appeared in the *New York Times,* the *Economist,* the *Guardian, People Magazine,* the *Chicago Reader, Discover,* and other publications. She currently is a staff writer at *Midwest Energy News.* Her books include *Mayor 1%: Rahm Emanuel and the Rise of Chicago's 99%* and *Closing the Cloud Factories: Lessons from the Fight to Shut Down Chicago's Coal Plants.* One of those coal plants is in the Pilsen neighborhood where Kari lives, and where she leads mural tours and sometimes frequents the remaining local bars; more at www.karilydersen.net.

SARAH MACARAEG is an award-winning investigative journalist with The CJ Project, a collaboration between the Asian American Journalists Association, the Associated Press, and Investigative Reporters and Editors, which produces stories on under-reported topics in criminal justice. Her work has appeared in *Chicago Reader,* the *Guardian,* and *VICE* and has been cited by *Al Jazeera, Democracy Now!,* and *Fusion* among other outlets. Macaraeg can be reached on Twitter @seramak.

SANDRA MARCHETTI is the author of *Confluence,* a full-length collection of poetry from Sundress Publications (2015). She is also the author of four chapbooks of poetry and lyric essays, including *Sight Lines* (Speaking of Marvels Press, 2016), *Heart Radicals* (ELJ Publications, 2016), *A Detail in the Landscape* (Eating Dog Press, 2014), and *The Canopy* (MWC Press, 2012). Sandra's poetry appears widely in *Subtropics, Ecotone, Poet Lore, Sugar House Review, Blackbird, Southwest Review,* and elsewhere. Her essays can be found at the *Rumpus, Words Without Borders, Mid-American Review, Whiskey Island,* and other venues. Sandy earned an MFA in Creative Writing — Poetry from George Mason University and is a Lecturer in Interdisciplinary Studies at Aurora University outside of Chicago.

DAVID MATHEWS earned his MA in Writing and Publishing at DePaul University. His work has appeared in *Eclectica Magazine, After Hours, CHEAP POP, One Sentence Poems, OMNI Reboot, Word Riot,* Silver Birch Press, and *Midwestern Gothic.* His poetry was nominated for The Best of The Net and received awards from the Illinois Women's Press and the National Federation of Press Women. He lives in his hometown of Chicago where he teaches and writes.

KELLY O'CONNOR MCNEES is the author of three historical novels. She lives in Rogers Park with her husband and daughter.

LINDA GARCIA MERCHANT, an award-winning Chicana filmmaker; a Digital Media Partner of the Chicana Por Mi Raza Digital Memory Collective (University of Michigan, University of Illinois Urbana Champaign), the Somos Latinas Oral History Project (University of Wisconsin Madison), and the Chicana Chicago/MABPW Collection Project (University of Illinois Chicago); and a board member of the Chicago Area Women's History Council, is a doctoral student at the University of Nebraska-Lincoln specializing in Chicana/Latina Literature Studies and Digital Humanities. Her work focuses on the restoration and reconstruction of the counter narrative as an aid in rehabilitating the historical discourse of resistance and social movement.

ROB MILLER is the co-founder/co-owner of Chicago-based Bloodshot Records. Since 1994, they've trafficked in overlooked roots-inflected music ranging from the traditional to the subversive. He was born in Detroit and moved to Chicago on Labor Day in 1991. He remains perplexed and dismayed that Alan Trammell has yet to be rightfully inducted to the Baseball Hall of Fame. If Detroiters are wondering, he prefers American to Lafayette. They'll know what he's talking about.

TONI NEALIE is the author of *The Miles Between Me,* an essay collection about borders, homeland, dispersal, heritage, and family, published by Curbside Splendor. Her essays have appeared in *Guernica, Hobart,* the *Offing,* the *Rumpus,* the *Prague Revue, Entropy, Midwestern Gothic, Essay Daily, Chicago Quarterly Review* and elsewhere. Her work has been nominated for a Pushcart Prize and shortlisted for a *Chicago Review of Books* nonfiction award. Originally from New Zealand, she teaches and writes in Chicago, and is Literary Editor of *Newcity.*

IRIS ORPI is a Filipina writer living in Chicago, Illinois. She is the author of the novel *The Espresso Effect* (2010) and two books of compiled poems, *Beautiful Fever* (2012) and *Cognac for the Soul* (2012). Her work has appeared in dozens of online and print publications around the U.S., the U.K., Canada, and several countries in Asia. She was an Honorable Mention for the Contemporary American Poetry Prize, given by Chicago Poetry Press, in 2014.

LAURA PASSIN is a writer, scholar, and feminist at large. Her writing has appeared in a wide range of publications, including *Prairie Schooner, Adrienne: A Poetry Journal of Queer Women,* the *Toast, Rolling Stone,* and *Best New Poets 2013.* Laura lives in Denver with too many cats.

CHRISTINE RICE is the author of *Swarm Theory,* which was recently included in *PANK'*s The Best 21 Books of 2016, named one of three finalists in the Chicago Writers Association Best Books of 2016, included in Powell's Books Midyear Roundup, the Best Books of 2016 So Far, and was called "a gripping work of Midwest Gothic" by Michigan Public Radio's Desiree Cooper. Other writing has appeared in the *Rumpus, McSweeney's Internet Tendency,* the *Millions,* the *Big Smoke, Chicago Tribune, Detroit's Metro Times,* the *Good Men Project, TheUrbaness.com, CellStories.net,* the *Literary Review, Rusted Radishes* (University of Beirut), *Bird's Thumb, F Magazine,* among others, and her radio essays have been produced by WBEZ Chicago. Chris is also the founder of Hypertextmag.com, *Hypertext Review,* and Hypertext Studio Writing Center. She also teaches in Columbia College Chicago's Department of Creative Writing.

KATHLEEN ROONEY is a founding editor of Rose Metal Press and a founding member of Poems While You Wait, as well as co-editor with Eric Plattner of *Rene Magritte: Selected Writings* (University of Minnesota Press, 2016). Her most recent book is the novel *Lillian Boxfish Takes a Walk* (St. Martin's Press, 2017) and her reviews appear regularly in the *Chicago Tribune*. She teaches at DePaul University and lives in Chicago with her husband, the writer Martin Seay.

SHEILA SACHS (book designer) is a graphic designer living in Chicago. She has designed hundreds of LPs, CDs, and posters for record labels (Thrill Jockey, Bloodshot, dBpm, Anti-, Overcoat, Pravda, Comedy Central Records, Delmark, and many others) and individual musicians/bands, as well as countless brochures, flyers, T-shirts, tote bags, stickers, invitations, envelopes, programs, business cards, catalogs, and a couple of cookbooks. Before going freelance she was for many years the art director at the *Chicago Reader*. For more see sheilasachs.net.

BILL SAVAGE teaches courses on crime fiction, baseball narratives, the Great American Novel, and Chicago literature, history, and culture at Northwestern University and the Newberry Library. His Chicago teaching and research focuses on the construction of American identities as shaped by the dynamic of public, semi-public, and private spaces and places throughout the grid of the cityscape. His most recent book publication is an annotated edition of George Ade's anti-Prohibition jeremiad *The Old-Time Saloon: Not Wet, Not Dry — Just History* (University of Chicago Press, 2016). He has published book reviews and essays in the *Chicago Tribune*, the *Chicago Reader*, *New City*, *Crain's Chicago Business*, and other places with "Chicago" on their masthead. He also performs in various live lit venues, including Paper Machete, the Frunchroom, Tuesday Funk, and 20x2. He is a lifelong resident of the Rogers Park neighborhood on the city's far North Side.

RYAN SCHNURR is a writer and photographer from northeast Indiana. *In the Watershed: A Journey Down the Maumee River*, his first book of nonfiction, is due from Belt Publishing in Fall 2017.

CHLOE TAFT is author of *From Steel to Slots: Casino Capitalism in the Postindustrial City* (Harvard University Press, 2016). She has a PhD in American Studies from Yale University and has taught urban studies at Yale and Lake Forest College. She lives in Lakeview.

CLAIRE TIGHE is a writer whose work has appeared in the *Village Voice*, *Ms.*, *Bitch*, *Belt Magazine*, and elsewhere.

AVA TOMASULA Y GARCIA was born in Chicago and grew up in Indiana. She is currently a student at Yale University, where she studies the "human" in human rights rhetoric as an ontological category under pressure from contemporary capitalism. She will continue working for environmental and economic justice — as well as for broader radical change — in the Midwest, where she lives, for as long as she lives.

MICHAEL A. VAN KERCKHOVE is a Detroit native with nearly twenty years of Chicago living under his belt. He is a 2013 graduate of DePaul University's Master of Arts in Writing and Publishing. His nonfiction, poetry, and interviews have appeared in *Off the Rocks*, *Midwestern Gothic*, *Consequence of Sound*, *How Long Will I Cry?: Voices of Youth Violence*, *Entropy*, *Belt Magazine*, *Silver Birch Press*, *TYA Today*, and other publications. He has told stories as part of many of Chicago's live lit events including Essay Fiesta, Flick Lit, Guts and Glory, Is This a Thing?, Mortified Chicago, Serving the Sentence, You're Being Ridiculous, and others. He recently moved to Nashville, Tennessee. Much more at MichaelVanKerckhove.com.

WYL VILLACRES is a bartender from Chicago. He is the author of *Bottom of the Ninth* (WhiskeyPaper, 2015) and his work has appeared in the *Rumpus*, *McSweeney's*, and the *Best of the Net* anthology, among others. Find him on twitter: @wyllinois.

GINA WATTERS is a writer living in Chicago. She has read her work around the city at shows such as Essay Fiesta, Miss Spoken, Story Club, That's All She Wrote, You're Being Ridiculous, and Write Club.

SCOTT WILSON is a recent graduate of Columbia College Chicago's MFA nonfiction program. He writes art and music reviews for *Quip Magazine*, assists with editing for *Hotel Amerika* literary journal, and co-hosts the Chicago monthly reading series Chimera. His work has been published by the Chicago Center for Literature and Photography and *Conquista Quarterly*. His thoughts on bikes, industry, and the city are catalogued on his website, bikeblogordie.com.

JACQUI ZENG is an MFA candidate at Southern Illinois University, Carbondale. Her work appears or is forthcoming in *Tinderbox*, *Natural Bridge*, and *Nightjar Review*. She was born and raised in Chicagoland and loves her city dearly.

ZOE ZOLBROD is the author of the memoir *The Telling* and the novel *Currency*. Her essays have appeared in places such as *Salon*, the *Guardian*, *Lit Hub*, the *Manifest Station*, and the *Rumpus*, where she served as the Sunday co-editor. Born in Western Pennsylvania, she now lives in Evanston, Illinois, with her husband and two children.

ACKNOWLEDGMENTS

I am grateful to Belt Publishing founder Anne Trubek for enlisting me to work with her in 2014 and for her support of this book through thick and thin, and to Nicole Boose, Bill Rickman, and everyone else at Belt. Thanks also to Ryan Schnurr, for invaluable editorial assistance and poetic insight, to my friend and brilliant book designer Sheila Sachs, and to Michael Jauchen for proofreading. And thank you to Tony Fitzpatrick, whose beautiful cover art surpasses imagination. Lastly, thanks to the writers, for your patience and your talent; I'm so happy you've let me harness just a little bit of it in these pages.

—*Martha Bayne*